THE DECEIVED GENERATION

SUSAN SEYMOUR

CREATION
HOUSE
A STRANG COMPANY

APOSTASY by Susan Seymour
Published by Creation House
A Strang Company
600 Rinehart Road
Lake Mary, Florida 32746
www.creationhouse.com

This book or parts thereof may not be reproduced in any form, stored in a retrieval system, or transmitted in any form by any means—electronic, mechanical, photocopy, recording, or otherwise—without prior written permission of the publisher, except as provided by United States of America copyright law.

Unless otherwise noted, all Scripture quotations are from the King James Version of the Bible.

Definition of *apostasy* is from *Webster's Dictionary* (New York, NY: Lexicon Publications, Inc., 1989).

Design Director: Bill Johnson
Cover designer: Judy McKittrick

Copyright © 2008 by Susan Seymour
All rights reserved

Library of Congress Control Number: 20008932497
International Standard Book Number: 978-1-59979-456-3

First Edition

08 09 10 11 12 — 987654321
Printed in the United States of America

I would like to dedicate this book to my parents, Jim and Jean Seymour. I have been blessed and privileged to be their daughter. They are consistent in love, discipline, and keeping God at the center of their lives. Their primary goal was to teach their children about the Lord and to put Him first. Their decisions were purposefully made to align with the Bible, and they modeled what it means to stand for truth no matter the cost. I am thankful to have been taught that obedience to God's Word is of utmost importance in life.

CONTENTS

a•pos•ta•sy |*eh'pästäsee*| *noun:*
the public abandoning of a religious faith,
esp. Christianity, for another

INTRODUCTION

WHEN I FIRST started teaching at a Christian school, I had expectations of teaching a classroom filled with students of above-average character. I expected children to have the basic desire to do right, although I knew it would not always be possible for them to act out of that desire. However, it did not take long for me to understand that my expectations had been too high. I realized quickly that there was little difference between the children of Christian parents and the children of the world.

George Barna, author and president of the Barna Research Group, Ltd., found that only 9 percent of today's Christian teens believe in moral absolutes.[1] As a teacher in a Christian school, I saw firsthand the lack of foundational biblical thinking among Christian youth. In my eleven years of teaching, I saw considerable compromise with the world and a steady drift from truth. Yet, the church seems to be asleep. The urgent danger is that Christians who believe their children are safe and going to heaven may one day face the reality that they are not.

The last eight years of my teaching experience were marked by extreme concern. There were many times when I had to seek refuge in a bathroom or in the back corner of a room to shed uncontrolled tears. Occasionally, tears flowed at inopportune times. I struggled to restrain my weeping as I taught a few of the Thursday morning chapel services.

During those times, I was overwhelmed by the urgency of the moment. I felt how critically important it was to instill truth in young people and how tragic it was to gloss it over with hype and fleshly appeal. The burden of the Lord would heavily press upon me as I prayed, like Joel, "Spare thy people, O LORD, and give not thine heritage to reproach, that the heathen should rule over them" (Joel 2:17).

The chapel services were usually disappointing. Most of the services were shallow, and many of the youth pastors who taught only tried to entertain and be amusing. The children were often haughty in their worship and then exhibited no evidence of being affected by the service as they went about their day swearing, mocking, and disobeying.

Each year, I saw less and less confrontation of this behavior. School administrators were passive and wanted to appease adamant parents who only wanted to protect their children from consequences. Persuasive parents and the doctrine of tolerance were soon dictating the actions of the school staff. The Holy Spirit was surely grieved.

I began to take notes on all that I had observed and heard from sermons and churches I came in contact with, as well as television ministries. Each year, I added new examples to my growing pile of evidence that apostasy is dominant in the character of today's churches.

The falling away from truth is obvious in the fact that numerous denominations are supporting same-sex unions, ordained gay ministers, and censorship of Israel. Certain other forms of apostasy that are defying God's holiness are continually going unnoticed by the average Christian.

Barna also found that more than two-thirds of all adults who have accepted Christ as their Savior made their decision before the age of eighteen.[2] It is, therefore, imperative that our young people are told the truth now, before their hearts have had time to harden. Converting souls at a young age is vital in these last days. Godlessness is increasing and Satan has his intentions set on this generation. Jesus said, "Suffer little children, and forbid them not, to come unto me: for of such is the kingdom of heaven" (Matt. 19:14). Children are hungry, and it matters if we give them candy or nourishment, error or truth.

Sadly, in spite of dangerous peril and hazardous spiritual storms, there is arrogance in our modern church mentality. The responsibility of the church is immense, yet the church is frustrating the kingdom of God. We are accepting the belief that there are no consequences for sin and that since grace abounds, we can continue in sin (Rom. 6:1). There is a complacency and passivity in our attitude toward sin that only causes our children to grow up to believe the same. The enemy has invaded our camp by bringing in worldly doctrines designed to sear the conscience. Improper behavior is being modeled for children, only influencing them to accept more and more ungodliness as they grow older. Hype and unreality dominate much of their time in the world and in the church.

I came to see the intense danger of raising children in this atmosphere. I realized this generation was walking on thin ice. By the end of my eleven years of teaching, the enemy had made it clear that he wanted the souls of the children who were supposedly being brought up as Christians. I saw that they were in a precarious position spiritually and that the risk was high. I observed a generation hanging in the balance in their vulnerable exposure to blatant error. I saw them as defenseless, while their churches held the answer but led them astray. Observation made it clearly evident to me that Satan was leading an all-out attack on this generation and that his main front was inside the church, not outside.

I felt it of utmost importance to write this book. A warning had to be sent to the churches of America. I could not be silent. Like Jeremiah, this message was "in mine heart as a burning fire shut up in my bones, and I was weary with forbearing, and I could not stay" (Jer. 20:9).

I knew God would hold me accountable if I did not warn of the danger I had seen. I knew I was accountable because of what God told Ezekiel.

> Son of man, speak to the children of thy people, and say unto them, When I bring the sword upon a land, if the people of the land take a man of their coasts, and set him for their watchman: If when he seeth the sword come upon the land, he blow the trumpet, and warn the people; Then whosoever heareth the sound of the trumpet, and taketh not warning; if the sword come, and take him away, his blood shall be upon his own head…But he that taketh warning shall deliver his soul. But if the watchman see the sword come, and blow not the trumpet, and the people be not warned; if the sword come, and take any person from among

them, he is taken away in his iniquity; but his blood will I require at the watchman's hand. So thou, O son of man, I have set thee a watchman unto the house of Israel; therefore thou shalt hear the word at my mouth, and warn them from me.

—Ezekiel 33:2–7

Satan's priority is to confuse this generation with mixed messages. Unclear lines cause Christianity to be indistinguishable from other, false religions. Even today's modern Christian church clouds truth to the point that it is very unclear and hard to stand for. The grayed lines make it almost impossible to know when one is crossed, so young people and countless adults do not realize when they are compromising. As a result, truth is being denied on a daily basis, and when given time, supposedly Christian teens succumb to worldliness.

Satan is satisfied when people, by an act of their will, deny truth by not rejecting error. Many are being sorely deceived as a result of Satan's clever tactics. Christians must return to a diligent search of Scripture in order to know unchangeable truth. Then, they must throw out all that conflicts with it and clearly define lines between truth and error.

False teachers are forerunners of the Antichrist. The greatest characteristic of the final days of the church before the Rapture is that of false teaching and half-truths. They are the mark of the great falling away called apostasy. In this time of abundant decline, we owe our loyalty to a God whose love was made evident by His Son, Jesus. God's love for this misled generation who has been lured by well-intentioned but deceived people is so strong that He will not be silent.

I am reminded of His great love in the hymn by F. M. Lehman:

> O love of God, how rich and pure!
> How measureless and strong!...
> Could we with ink the ocean fill
> And were the skies of parchment made;
> Were ev'ry stalk on earth a quill
> And every man a scribe by trade.
> To write the love of God above
> Would drain the ocean dry;
> Nor could the scroll contain the whole,
> Tho stretched from sky to sky.

Think of God's love being so immense that He would become a man and allow Himself to be killed by the very ones He came to save. God's love is uncaused and undeserved. Yet, He loves us with "an everlasting love" anyway (Jer. 31:3). But, there is nothing, absolutely no thing, in humans that could possibly attract the love of one as holy and just as God. (See Jeremiah 17:9; Isaiah 64:6–7; Matthew 19:17.) Self-esteem teachings in churches are teaching children that God loves them because they are worth it. At Easter, a young boy was quoted in a newspaper as saying, "I can't believe an almighty king like Jesus would decide to take all this sin and pain just so He could be with us in heaven."[3] Did Jesus die so He could be with us in heaven, or was it the exact opposite? I'm sure his parents were gloating at how he reflected Christ, but in reality, he was reflecting the influences of self-centeredness and the belief there is something in us worth having. It's called humanism.

Children today are not hearing of their need for a redeemer. Instead, they are being misled into thinking they have an inner beauty that resides somewhere deep and hidden under their hurts. Children today believe God is chasing them similar to a man madly in love with a lovely maiden, but God is not "attracted" to us. It is true He will "allure" us as His bride, but it's motivated by His great love, not His attraction to us (Hosea 2:14). Chasing is not the same as alluring. To the contrary, God is "of purer eyes than to behold evil" (Hab. 1:13). The love of God is being misrepresented when they are told that God's love is pursuing their beauty. We should have "no confidence" in our flesh (Phil. 3:3). Seeing our hopeless state will cause us to cry out to Jesus as our *only* hope.

Adam's sin instantly caused him to have a corruptible image. As a result of sin, our image is corruptible, too. God's image remains incorruptible. Yet, man is constantly trying to change the "glory of the incorruptible God into an image made like to corruptible man" (Rom. 1:23). Modern man is now "creating God" into his own image. Every man born since Adam has been depraved, causing there to be nothing of value in him that should initiate God's desire to have a relationship. Adam was shunned from the garden after he sinned. He was not worthy of it anymore.

Since the time Adam was banned from the garden, each person's destiny, or his predetermined lot, has been to go straight to hell. Modern churches are contradicting Scripture by saying we are really good by nature. They claim God desires us to become who we "really are." But, our true selves are corrupt, defiled, wicked, immoral, and rotten. It is our sin nature that dooms us. Man is in desperate need of a redeemer. God's love provided that Redeemer, who saves us from sin, and thus, from ourselves.

God Himself died and took our deserved sentence of hell. To say man is loved by God because of our hidden potential negates what Jesus suffered for us, because without Him, every man automatically goes to hell. Just as gravity affects a ball and causes it to fall back to earth every time it is tossed into the air, man is pressing toward hell. Christ said, "He that believeth not is condemned already" (John 3:18). Man's sin nature, or corruptible nature, sentences him to death. Psalm 119:155 tells us that "salvation is far from the wicked: for they seek not thy statutes." Gravity's downward pull is constant, and man's downward slide into the open mouth of hell is constant. It is only natural for man to go to hell. It is not natural for man to submit to his Redeemer and be saved. It is a major spiritual battle won every time a man is saved from himself. Man deserves to go to hell because of his betrayal of God's law. God has no compulsory obligation to keep us from hell. It's His own law that sends guilty men there.

Yet, God loved man anyway and provided a way into His presence. God's love is so great, it is not explainable. Only when Jesus' blood is applied to a life, is God appeased. Man is not born with that blood applied to his life. Man is not born with a favorable destiny. God gave man a will to choose the blood or reject it. By not saying yes to the blood, a person is saying no to it. God's love is available to everyone, but many refuse it. Nobody seems to be telling the children in our modern churches that they must choose Jesus. Instead, they are being told over and over that Jesus has chosen them. They are told they are the "chosen generation." Consequently, young people feel automatic security. What they are not told is that God requires in 1 Peter 2:9 that the chosen generation be called out of darkness.

Only he who believes that Jesus' sacrifice is the sole escape from hell can have everlasting life. Jesus' birth, death, and resurrection alone will save man from hell. He sealed and secured hope for us when we were without hope. Even if all the scientists were given a billion centuries, they could never come up with a formula to restore man's hopeless position of corruption. It defies natural laws to escape hell. If anyone ever doubts that there is only one way to heaven, tell him you're surprised there is even one way.

Humans tend to make a hierarchy of importance. We put God at the top, then man, then the animals, then insects. But God, who is not created, doesn't even fit into a hierarchy. Everything else is in the far distance below Him. God is so remotely distant from His creation that it makes all created things appear to be at the same level. Everything is so far below Him that it is impossible to reach Him.

In spite of the impossibility of closing the great gulf between us, He made a way for us to reach Him. That gap was a void so enormous that only God could close it. We cannot truly fathom with our feeble brains the concept of

His love. God's character included love before man was ever created. It was not man that caused His love. We try to compare His love with earthly love, but it does not compare. His love is far above carnal love. Catching a glimpse of His undeserved love should humble us. Our hearts should melt, our hands should tremble, our spirit should faint, and our knees should become as water.

The purpose in writing this book is to help this generation become Christians, not merely in name, but in truth. There are "multitudes, multitudes in the valley of decision: for the day of the LORD is near in the valley of decision" (Joel 3:14). We must return to the basics and teach children the simplicity of John 3:16:

> For God so loved the world, that he gave his only begotten Son, that whosoever believeth in him should not perish, but have everlasting life.

We cannot assume our children "already know that," because they don't. Biblical foundations have been attacked, and Satan is whetting his appetite for a huge gathering to his side. The days are short and the battle is here. I pray that it is not too late and that this book will shed light on the error that has crept into our churches. The church is in desperate need of a great awakening and reformation. We must again put as our priority the proclamation:

> That men may know that thou, whose name alone is JEHOVAH, art the most high over all the earth.
> —Psalm 83:18

Chapter 1

PASSIVITY OF LEADERSHIP

Woe be unto the pastors that destroy and scatter the sheep of my pasture! saith the Lord.

—Jeremiah 23:1

PASSIVITY OF PASTORS

THE MAJORITY OF pastors today are weak. They tickle the ears of their congregation and avoid confronting sin. They are worldly-minded, shallow, and influenced by the world rather than God's Word. They are big-crowd gatherers and people-pleasers, and they are leading the church headlong into apostasy.

Spiritual leaders are even more important than our national leaders. People naturally trust pastors and follow them, just as sheep follow a shepherd. Therefore, it is very important for pastors and preachers to seek God on a daily basis for assurance of staying in His will. They must pray that they will not lose heart or interest. They must not fail to see the gravity of leading people responsibly. They will be held to a higher standard, because to whom much is given much is required. (See Luke 12:48.)

A true leader does the right thing, no matter what the majority of the crowd thinks. He should lead the right way and do what God says regardless of popularity. Pastors need the wisdom to realize the fickleness of people's opinions and not follow what polls say. For a pastor to know what God is saying, he must seek God and stay on his face before Him. A pastor's job is not easy. Young men seeking to be pastors and preachers should be advised of its obligations rather than its fame.

Gradually, but steadily, pastors have drifted from God's will. They have not walked worthily of the vocation to which they were called. (See Ephesians 4:1.) They have not stressed the importance of God's Word and have resorted to preaching other topics of more interest to their flock. These topics usually include messages on blessings and destiny. Why has God's will suddenly become His "destiny" for our lives? We are passive in letting our language become that of the world.

Since people like to hear how they will benefit and what's in it for them, congregations continue to grow. Some preachers have even added unbalanced teaching and worldly mixture to their sermons and church activities in order to gain new members. These pastors do not want to mention consequences for sin, nor do they refer to God's judgment of sin. They fear that type of preaching will reduce numbers in their church's attendance. Altar calls for repentance are rarely seen among today's church services. This causes lack of accountability among church members and especially among new converts. The fear of the Lord is condemned as heresy because it doesn't fit the "God is only love" focus of modern-day churches.

Isaiah 9:16–17 denounces these leaders for causing their congregations to err in their refusal to teach the whole truth. It warns that those that have been led astray end up being "destroyed:"

> For the leaders of this people cause them to err; and they that are led of them are destroyed. Therefore the Lord shall have no joy in their young men, neither shall have mercy on their fatherless and widows: for every one is an hypocrite and an evildoer, and every mouth speaketh folly.

Today's church also contains "hypocrites and evildoers" and their "mouths speak folly." Does the world see Christians as role models? No, they see no difference.

I have heard a pastor say, "We all need entertainment." He then mentioned how he had attended R-rated movies and remarked that, "The Lord was right there with me." Since pastors have led their congregations astray from God's Word to other ear-tickling doctrines, some Christians have become weak in their stand for truth. As a result, they are proceeding from evil to evil (Jer. 9:3). Even more distressing is what is said a few verses later in Jeremiah 9: "Through deceit they refuse to know me, saith the LORD" (v. 6) We have a serious problem in the church if people are refusing to know the Lord. This refusal is coming from the top, but "woe be unto the pastors that destroy and scatter the sheep of my pasture! saith the LORD" (Jer. 23:1).

Truth and doctrine are vital. But lately, Scripture is being replaced with doctrines of man. Psychology, tolerance, clever spins on Scripture for personal gain, and even the use of mythology are common with many pastors. Fattening up a congregation on junk food is unhealthy. According to Acts 20:28, pastors are required to take heed to themselves and to their flock, over which the Holy Ghost has made them overseers. They have the obligation to "feed the church of God, which He hath purchased with his own blood" (Acts 20:28). If they continue to be like the world in their teachings, people will easily be led astray.

The misapplication of tolerance teachings in churches leaves out the truth: tolerance can be deadly when applied to sin in our lives. A message of love and nothing else misleads the hearer into thinking God never hates anything, but it is evident in Scripture that God hates sin. He hated sin so much, His Son died to rob it of its power.

The influence of psychology is causing Christians to focus on human feelings. It is producing self-centered, flesh-appeasing Christians. When pastors do not speak to warn the wicked from his way, that wicked man shall die in his iniquity; but the pastor will be held accountable for his blood (Ezek. 33:8).

Traditional meanings for scriptures are now being replaced with new meanings. This destruction of context enables leaders to appear to be using Scripture when they are really setting forth their own church-growth agendas through wrong interpretation. It is a big step downward when a pastor wants to apply false doctrine to serve his own purposes.

Other pastors are like passive parents who can't say no to a child who continually wants candy. Pastors must say no. They must not continue to give their "children" too much candy and disregard the consequences. The same is true of their biological children. The Bible clearly states that a "bishop" or overseer of God's flock must rule well his own house, having his children in subjection. Also, he must have good behavior, be patient, and not be covetous. He should be the husband of one wife. She should be grave and not a slanderer, faithful in all things. (See 1 Timothy 3:1–16.) It's shocking to see how many pastors fall woefully short of these biblical requirements.

I have heard a pastor say that to be the husband of one wife means "at one time." This was to justify his many assistant pastors, who had been married, divorced, and remarried. He willingly called polygamy a sin. But, that was a sin not actually occurring under his leadership. Some choose to call any act "sinful" when it is seemingly worse than what is actually occurring. What is actually occurring at the moment is justified in the name of it being "not as bad" as what he or she is doing. This allows the individual to avoid any feelings of condemnation.

Some Christian marriage counselors give the approval for divorce, but forbid dating for the period of one year. Wait a minute. It's the divorce that needs to be confronted; dating is a secondary problem. Where is counsel that advises against divorce, warning that those who remarry could be found guilty of adultery? Oh, it's in Luke. (See Luke 16:18.)

The Old Testament, the law, and tradition are thought irrelevant and are, therefore, not being taught in many churches. New and improved teachings, supposedly well-fitted to this generation, are being supplanted in place of the old, proven methods. Hebrews warns that "we ought to give the more earnest heed to the things which we have heard, lest at any time we should let them slip" (Heb. 2:1). Paul said that the things which were "written aforetime were written for our learning" (Rom. 15:4). When God's people forget Him and "burn incense to vanity" and pastors cause members to "stumble in their ways from the ancient paths, to walk...in a way not cast up," their land becomes "desolate" (Jer. 18:15–16). Jeremiah calls the old paths, the "good way" (Jer. 6:16). But, today we call it the out-dated way.

A shepherd's neglect in preaching God's Word is dangerous because the Word is our sword. When the sword of defense is passively let down, Satan jumps at the opportunity to come into our midst. We become vulnerable when the watchmen are blind and are like dumb dogs that do not bark when danger is near. They sleep and look out only for their own gain while promising abundance to their followers (Isa. 56:10–12).

As a tragic result, the American church is under siege. The enemy is coming into the camp while pastors sleep. We've all been asleep. The church has been dark and quiet with slumber and the saints have been dreaming dreams of destiny and self-fulfillment. We are imagining that if the shepherd has his dreams of success fulfilled, then so can we. After all, the wealth of the wicked is supposed to be ours, right? We have been told that we are even going to reap what we didn't sow.

God warns in Ezekiel 34:2–3, "Woe be to the shepherds of Israel that do feed themselves! Should not the shepherds feed the flocks? Ye eat the fat, and ye clothe you with the wool, ye kill them that are fed: but ye feed not the flock." Zechariah 11:17 speaks of the idol shepherds who are weak and deficient for an obvious reason—"they have set up themselves as objects of undue veneration."[1] Do you know of congregations that worship their pastor as a person would worship an idol? Sure, we do. It happens often. We're heard saying, "There he is!" or "He spoke to me!" Why don't we say that about the Lord?

Apathy for God's law has caused pastors to be negligent in dealing with sin. They would rather cover it up than clean it up. Habakkuk says that "the law is slacked, and judgment doth never go forth: for the wicked doth compass about the righteous" (Hab. 1:4). Do we see the wicked outnumbering the righteous today? Christians have allowed it. Edmund Burke said, "All that is necessary for the triumph of evil is for good men to do nothing."[2] The law speaks of judging sin, not tolerating it. Sin is very serious. It results in a separation between us and God. Yes, even Christians can experience separation from His presence because of sin in their lives. The Lord said, "Your iniquities have separated between you and your God, and your sins have hid his face from you, that he will not hear" (Isa. 59:2). Only Christians can call Him "our God." He is not the God of the wicked.

Sin must be dealt with, not ignored. Isaiah 59:4 says, "None calleth for justice, nor any pleaded for truth: they trust in vanity, and speak lies; they conceive mischief, and bring forth iniquity." To trust in vanity and to speak lies is to say that sin is harmless or as to say sin is a result of mistreatment. That belief brings forth iniquity. Evidence that churches are avoiding truth about sin is clearly seen in the downward turn our culture has taken. Children today have no fear of consequences for sin because they rarely see it.

Isaiah 61:8 says that God loves judgment. Imagine that. He loves something we consider to be hateful. At the same time, He can hate what we consider to be love. God hates our tolerance of sin and our love and acceptance of everyone's "differences." Judgment is important to God. For a pastor to judge the sin in his congregation is for him to love his congregation. Pastors have the responsibility to "judge righteous judgment" and call sin what it is (John 7:24). *Judgment* is placed with *righteousness* in several scriptures, so they must be complementary. Amos 5:24 tells us to "let judgment run down as waters, and righteousness as a mighty stream." (See also Jeremiah 22:3; 33:15; Psalm 33:5; 72:2; Proverbs 2:9; Hosea 2:19; and John 16:8.)

Some pastors and Christians are careless in judgment. Today, we fear "judging" others. Of course, we should never judge others according to our own standards, nor can we judge motives. We would then be in danger of judgment ourselves. But, we must use God's standard and be judges of right and wrong behavior in the earth. (See 1 Peter 4:6; Ephesians 5:11; and Romans 12:9.) When right judgment (whether discernment or correction) goes forth, righteousness results.

It may seem extreme, but Paul also wrote in 1 Corinthians for Christians not to keep company with fornicators, the covetous, extortioners, or idolaters. He said that God judges people outside the congregation, but we are to "put away from among ourselves the wicked person" (1 Cor. 5:13), that is to say, those who call themselves Christians who engage in those activities. Today, we call that intolerance. God calls it righteous judgment. We fear being too harsh, but we don't fear God enough to believe that He says what He means.

Several prophets said that we are to keep judgment. (See Isaiah 56:1; Ezekiel 20:19; 36:27; and Hosea 12:6.) Evidently, it is something that can be lost. Paul gave the church at Corinth an interesting reproof concerning judgment.

> Dare any of you, having a matter against another, go to law before the unjust, and not before the saints? Do ye not know that the saints shall judge the world? and if the world shall be judged by you,

are ye unworthy to judge the smallest matters? Know ye not that we shall judge angels? how much more things that pertain to this life? If then ye have judgments of things pertaining to this life, set them to judge who are least esteemed in the church. I speak to your shame. Is it so, that there is not a wise man among you? no, not one that shall be able to judge between his brethren?

—1 Corinthians 6:1–5

According to these verses, we should find judges for the church. It is a shame not to have wise men judging the congregation. It is possible to show mercy and compassion in judgment or the Lord would not have commanded it in Zechariah 7:9. It's not a bad thing to deal with sin. We need to take the time for altar calls after sermons. We need to preach on sin and repentance so that people can come and deal with the little foxes that spoil the vine. Church should be the place where people can get answers to their problems.

The humility required in repentance is avoided in sermons because people may not want to come back after they hear a sermon that does not encourage them. However, an understanding of God's Word enables us to see that repentance is encouraging. It puts courage in us as we trust God and not ourselves and it enables us to stand against Satan in our spiritual battles.

Pastors must wake up to the importance of sticking to Scripture. Warnings are sounding out to the shepherds of the flock. Jeremiah declares, "Howl, ye shepherds, and cry; and wallow yourselves in the ashes, ye principal of the flock:

for the days of your slaughter and of your dispersions are accomplished; and ye shall fall like a pleasant vessel" (Jer. 25:34). Also in Jeremiah, God warns that if a man makes the people "to trust in a lie," He will cast him "off the face of the earth" because he has "taught rebellion against the LORD" (Jer. 28:15–16). James also warns that there should not be many "masters" because they shall "receive the greater condemnation" (James 3:1). God says, "I will require my flock at their hand" (Ezek. 34:10). Pastors are accountable for what they teach and what they don't teach.

Pastors must seek the Lord and seek where He is. Jeremiah noticed the priests of his day didn't even ask, "Where is the Lord?" (Jer. 2:8; 10:21). Pastors must "feed the flock of God...taking the oversight thereof...not for filthy lucre [money], but of a ready mind" (1 Pet. 5:2). When there is no evidence of true conversions because change in behavior is not seen from one year to another, the pastor must adjust his sermons. Jonathan Edwards spoke of true results from proper preaching. He said, "Until they are affected, they will never be changed."[3]

Find a pastor who adheres to Scripture and preaches the simplicity of the gospel. God requires obedience to all Scripture and calls for repentance. We must be vigilant. Finally, we must all ask ourselves what David asked Israel: "Do ye indeed speak righteousness, O congregation? Do ye judge uprightly, O ye sons of men?" (Ps. 58:1).

Passivity of Youth Pastors and Teachers

> Come, ye children, hearken unto me: I will teach
> you the fear of the Lord.
>
> —Psalm 34:11

> By mercy and truth iniquity is purged: and by the
> fear of the Lord men depart from evil.
>
> —Proverbs 16:6

It is the duty and responsibility of every teacher to train children in the way that they should go. That way is clearly explained in the Bible. It is a way that includes teaching the fear of the Lord rather than giving in to the "no fear" mentality of society. It is vital for all children to receive spiritual training. We cannot disregard this charge.

> Whosoever shall offend one of these little ones
> that believe in me, it is better for him that a mill-
> stone were hanged about his neck, and he were
> cast into the sea.
>
> —Mark 9:42

The founding fathers of this country realized the significance of this task and were sure to place biblical doctrines as priority in the schooling of America's children. At the core of *The New England Primer*, which taught colonial children to read, was a Bible alphabet, Bible questions, and the Shorter catechism, whose first question (of 107 questions) asked, "What is the chief end of man?" The answer stated, "Man's chief end is to glorify God and enjoy Him forever."[4]

Today, we have shifted our priorities. The devil sees our passivity, but he is not passive in his methods. Lethargic youth pastors and teachers seem oblivious to this danger, as though they think we have time on our side, since children are so young. However, the situation is critical. We have no time to waste, because if we do not teach them the truth, the devil will destroy them.

While our churches are spending time entertaining children and telling them to dream big for worldly things, children are neglecting their salvation. Our job is to equip young people with the whole armor of God (truth, the sword of the spirit, the helmet of salvation, the breastplate of righteousness, the shield of faith, and continual prayer; see Ephesians 6:13–17). Only then will they be able to ward off the enemy. We must teach children to resist evil on a daily basis.

We should be militant against sin and Satan's underhanded craftiness. We should teach the children to be militant, too. If Satan is given an inch, he will take a mile. Many kids who have been in church all their life are growing up to be ignorant of truth. This should not happen. We have no excuse for our careless disregard.

Instead of continual Bible teaching, churched kids hear from their leaders, "Oh, I know you've heard that a hundred times." No, they haven't heard it. The body language that comes with their nonchalance when mentioning Scripture causes children to not even listen at all. Many leaders don't even require children to bring their Bibles with them. Most children realize they don't even need to bring their Bibles because they are never asked to open them.

We, as adults, should show God to this generation. (See Psalm 71:18.) One great fault in churches, according to Charles Spurgeon, the great English preacher of the 1800s, is that the responsibility of teaching the children is left to the young people, though it's the older members who have the wisdom to do it.[5] The blind are leading the blind. Novices should not be given responsibility over other novices.

Small children are very easily persuaded. They tend to believe what they hear. Therefore, we must be careful that they hear truth. Teenagers need truth to combat what they are hearing from the world. They are being indoctrinated with lies telling them to find their own truth because there is no absolute truth. It is a major battle to make truth penetrate young minds and neutralize the muddy deception from the world. I fear it may be more dangerous for teenagers than we realize.

Churches should never bribe or falsely entice children with candy, flattery, or false promises. We are neglecting our duty to teach God's Word and choosing, instead, to give our children sports, candy, money, and entertainment. The consequences will prove costly. The time spent with children at church competes with the time the world has them. We must focus on principles of morality, godliness, the evil of sin, repentance, a sensitive conscience, and the true joy of living in obedience to God's Word.

It seems to be a rare occasion in today's church for children to be led to repentance, humility, or acknowledgment of sin. Sins may be brought up, but they are usually referred to lightly and portrayed in a way that is easy to swallow. Doses of pacifism are implemented, saying sin is really just normal behavior and isn't that bad because everyone does it. Children, especially teens, are taught that all is well between them and God. If any guilt arises in their hearts, they are told that Satan is trying to condemn them.

Children continually hear the portion of scripture that says all things work together for good. But, they fail to hear the requirements of that verse: all things work together for good *for those who love God*. (See Romans 8:28.) They assume they love God, but are not taught that loving Him requires keeping His commandments.

Children are being taught that Christianity is all about fun. They think there should never be a time when life lets them down. They hear that they can have their dreams fulfilled in Christianity. Hearing this is no more promising or hopeful than what the world offers. In fact, the world is currently promising that very thing. Reality proves that most people's dreams don't come true. Real life is reflected in Job's words. He said, "For the thing which I greatly feared is come upon me, and that which I was afraid of is come unto me" (Job 3:25). No wonder some Christian kids are depressed. They've been misled away from the reality of life.

Sometimes the occasion arises to lead a child to repentance, but the devil is given the opportunity to snatch it away. Passive leaders are not alert, and the devil is so slippery. He veers the attention away from repentance ever so slightly, and the focus soon turns to the child's hurts or regrets or mistreatment by parents and friends. When leaders see tears, they think God is doing a work in the child's life. Isn't it disturbing to realize the devil is the one actually working and causing the child to think about how he's been hurt and not how he's hurt someone else? (I am not currently addressing the genuine problem of hurting children who have been neglected, abandoned, and even rejected. Christian compassion and caring for these needs should be taking place daily, and our observance of these issues should be heightened. The problem I'm referring to is at the altar and during the presentation of the gospel, which is about Him and not us.)

I heard a youth pastor say, "You've been beaten down and hemmed up by hard sermons." Those particular kids were not hearing hard sermons on my watch of several years. Pastors can get reactions and tears from vulnerable kids by using those lines. They can even get great results at altar calls, but we fail to realize that no true life-changing repentance is actually occurring.

When today's children hear, "Come and lay your burden on the altar," they interpret it to mean a hurt committed by someone else. They do not see their own sin as being the burden. They don't hear about sin being a burden. They hear that sin is normal human behavior. They hear it is easily and quickly forgiven without even repenting because God loves people so much. They hear that they can commit a sin over and over and Jesus will forgive them. But, true repentance changes our habits and turns us away from sin. Grace does not allow us to return to sin to repeat it over and over. God forbid.

I have seen the devil snatch away a key moment many times. Once, I witnessed a foot washing while on a mission trip with some teenagers. The genuinely tender-hearted leader started off by washing a student's feet and humbly asking his forgiveness. Afterward, the students washed each other's feet. Starting with the first teen, the mood changed. Afterward, each one, without exception, told how funny the person was or how much they liked him or how nice he was. Laughter soon filled the air. Direction was not given to guide them back to the true significance of the foot washing. Humility soon flew out the window along with reverence for a solemn practice. The Holy Spirit was quenched and not allowed to move. Later, I was saddened further when the kids talked about how "awesome" it was. They had never experienced the true awesomeness of God to know the difference.

Having worked in a Christian school as a teacher for eleven years, I have seen passivity in the area of dealing with sin. Humans find excuses for not confronting it. Of course, it is easier to ignore sin and excuse it, especially when it is someone else's child. However, we, as Christians, are still obligated to demonstrate to this generation the serious-ness of sin. This can usually be done through consequences and always done through our immediate reaction to bad behavior.

Today, if correction to a child is needed, it is often tempered with humor or at least a smile. Some leaders even laugh at misbehavior. This is to dismiss our duty and reinforce the child's sin. This is the easy way out and the cost is to the child. Certain children are not behavior problems as long as they get a laugh. But, when their mockery is confronted, the true rebel is revealed.

I have yet to figure out why youth leaders laugh at children's misbehavior. It is not cute to sin. It's as simple as that. Weak leaders fear the reaction of the child, especially from big, scary, hairy teenagers. So, they humor them with laughter. Sometimes leaders fear reactions from parents after confronting children, and the child is appeased as a result. Children need to see the blunt reality of sin's ugliness, and our reaction should demonstrate to them how serious it is. A solemn face versus a smiling one would benefit greatly.

I've also seen pastors use only laughter and humor while preaching. I don't know if they are doing this to be well liked or if they just see teaching God's Word as a light thing. Some think it will draw more children to their class or group, but God's Word does not need to be administered with a spoonful of sugar. Most will come only for the sugar-coating, then spit the medicine out. Observing some of these pastors will show that they do nothing but clown around. Their goal is for children to say, "That pastor is funny." Their goal is not for children to say, "That pastor knows God."

One youth pastor, who felt this was the best way to minister to young people, went so far as to make the kids laugh when he talked about Judas' betrayal kiss. He turned it into a "gay" moment of laughter. Inappropriate! How dare we mislead kids away from the solemn significance of Jesus' betrayal.

Another excuse for not dealing with sin in children has been to say, "Remember, foolishness is bound in the heart of a child" (Prov. 22:15). That scripture is not saying that foolishness is blameless just because it is there. Foolishness is the trait of a fool, and the fool says in his heart that there is no God. We are told that the rod drives this foolishness far from the child. We must not quote partial scripture to the detriment of our children and leave out the other sections which may be beneficial to their Christian walk.

Some Christians use the excuse that they must give grace and not be legalistic about enforcing rules. I've heard it is better to err on the side of grace. To err one way or another is not recommended. Jesus suggests that it is better not to err at all, as His life's example showed. (See Hebrews 4:15.) Remember, foolishness is bound in the heart of children, and it's not a good thing. Humans are born deceitful. They must be taught to turn from sin.

Micah 3:9 speaks to the heads of the house of Jacob, correcting them for abhorring judgment and perverting equity. People today pervert equity when they use "situation ethics" to determine if they will confront sin. The circumstances surrounding a situation should not make a violation less than it really is. Actions should be determined to be a violation against God according to the Bible, not according to individual circumstances.

When I was in high school, many of the girls on the basketball team drank alcohol one weekend. The coach found out and told all the girls involved that they could not play the following game. This game was with our main rival, and we were soundly defeated because many of the key players were benched. Some girls claimed to have only had one drink or just to have dipped their finger in to taste. Nonetheless, the coach benched them all. This was not situation ethics, but a lesson in abstaining from even the appearance of evil. This happened in a secular school.

Today, things are different. What was taught in the public school then, isn't even in the Christian schools now. I could write another book on the examples of situation ethics I have seen. One particular case involved a conflict over a rule that was constantly a battle for the teachers. It involved the dress code and required students to tuck in their shirts. It was a known rule at the school where I taught. After several weeks of seeing shirttails out because of passivity in the leadership, the principle announced in homeroom that shirts must be tucked in. Two high school girls arrived at school late that day and did not hear the announcement. That afternoon a teacher corrected them by telling them to tuck in their shirts, but they were given no consequences because they had not been at school that morning to hear the announcement. Their reprieve was in being tardy. They weren't held accountable since they had not heard the reminder, even though it was an established rule.

Does this not affirm the idea that if you do not hear instruction, you do not need to obey it? It encourages "deafness" in order to avoid accountability. Who doesn't notice the negligent listening skills in today's youth? They've learned it pays not to listen. It gets them off the hook. Isaiah 26:10 states that if we "let favor be shown to the wicked, yet will he not learn righteousness." If we think that doesn't apply to children, we must remember we are all "wicked" until we are saved. A child who has "foolishness" or "wickedness" in his heart must be taught righteousness. Proverbs says that "it is not good to have respect of persons in judgment" (Prov. 24:23). Proverbs 11:1 tells us that a "false balance is abomination to the Lord."

Judgment that is based on situation ethics delays leaders' actions for several weeks. Other situations addressed at school became complicated because each student had to be interviewed to determine his part in the current violation. In one case, the students' actions ranged from having one drink to two drinks, to being with a drunk friend and "unable to get out of the car," to being the one supplying the beer, to being the one who actually became legally drunk. Each action received a separate consequence. Some lied and denied and were dismissed for good behavior. Others confessed and were punished for whatever they admitted to. Others were given leniency for being honest. Ecclesiastes 8:11 states that "because sentence against an evil work is not executed speedily, therefore the heart of the sons of men is fully set in them to do evil." Shouldn't Christians have an easier time dealing with sin than the world? Shouldn't we apply rules without situation ethics?

Avoiding gray areas and determining an action to be either right or wrong is not being legalistic. Our children need to see clear lines between right and wrong, between danger and safety. The cloudiness of gray in Christians' standards for behavior is a disservice to our youth. We have avoided drawing clear lines for them. Conviction is being avoided in our churches, but conviction leads to confession which, in turn, leads to salvation.

As another example from my experience with a Christian school, memos were circulated for youth dances, such as homecoming games or end-of-the-year activities. The students were told to have all tattoos covered and any jewelry connected with "non-standard" body piercing was to be removed. As in the earlier illustration of how pastors define what is acceptable in church, school administrators bumped the margin of error to the next level, too. Evidently, having a tattoo or piercing is not wrong, but showing it is. The world advocates this same message by saying, "You can drink, but don't you dare drive." The clear message to the children is, go ahead and sin, just don't get caught by the repercussions. What a confusing mess of legalism. The very churches who condemn legalism are the ones neck-deep in it.

The best way to teach righteousness is to teach righteousness. Bankers can ascertain a counterfeit bill in their hands instantly. This skill comes from handling the real thing over and over. When a counterfeit touches their knowing hands, it doesn't match. It feels different. Also, their trained eye sees the difference. If bankers were sent to school to learn and feel all of the different counterfeits, they would be confused on the job. Their hands would have experienced several weights and textures, and it would be too difficult to remember the one true bill. Just like bankers who quickly sense a counterfeit bill in their hands, our children need to have the skills to define the clear difference between good and evil.

To teach the truth only makes our job as leaders easier than we think. Much time is wasted in today's churches sponsoring special classes on drugs, sex, alcohol, and other sins. News flash! Our kids already know about those things. Seminars on these subjects only talk about it and avoid the hundreds of scriptures that stress that we should think on things that are pure and holy. (See Philippians 4:8; 1 Timothy 5:22; and James 3:17. The word *pure* and its derivatives appear 154 times in Strong's Concordance. *Holy* and its derivatives have 647 listings.)[6] If we had classes on pure and holy subjects, many teen problems would take care of themselves. This sure goes 180 degrees against what we hear in the world, doesn't it? Good. I know a better way than the world's way. It's called God's way.

The focus of our Bible classes should be on Jesus and not on a child's concerns about daily life. Modern-day moms are delighted to know that their child is in a class that concentrates on "teenage" issues, but teenagers do not need to hear more about teen issues, even though they love hearing about themselves. Some may disagree, but the Bible does not promote humanism. It teaches Jesus-ism.

I have seen Christian teachers beam with pride that they are sharing Harry Potter, the Da Vinci Code, or even evolution with their students. Some misled Christians argue that the kids need to choose for themselves and they shouldn't be "forced" to be Christians. People who support this notion believe equal time should be given to all subjects. With this attitude, how can we build up from a foundation if we continue to camp out in the valley of indecision? Besides, kids who enroll in a Christian school are there to learn truth.

One teacher sadly commented that a student was "so protected from the world that he didn't know anything." She continued with the fact that "he freaked out when he saw another student light up a joint." This, my friends, is the wrong perspective for a Christian leader. How passive about sin can we be? First of all, no kid—not one—is as protected as they were in the 1700s and 1800s. We have television to thank for that. Secondly, a "freaking out" reaction from Christian children is the goal rather than a neutral non-reaction governed by a seared conscience.

Jesus never sinned once. Isaiah prophesied that Jesus would eat butter and honey so that He would know to discern between good and evil (Isa. 7:15). Butter and honey are good things. To say Jesus was too protected is to be totally deceived. Let's not ever be tricked by Satan into thinking we must teach our kids about sin in order for them to avoid it. We must go back to the Bible. It has made very clear that sin is to be shunned. The New Testament condemns even thoughts of sin. Also, God tells us that it is a shame even to talk about certain things (Eph. 5:12).

If we have to face persecution for believing this way, then so be it. We do not have to teach our children about sin to prepare them for the real world. They are more prepared knowing truth, instead. In fact, the more truth a person knows, the more he understands sin. When he encounters it at college, he will see the blatant difference. When he is faced with doctrine that is contrary to truth, he will be prepared. This is in opposition to popular opinion, but I have the Bible to back me up.

It is different when a person is a mature adult in the Lord. He may study the tactics of cultists, evolutionists, or other false doctrines. Also, older children can be introduced to older topics as they mature. Parents are responsible for this task. I do recognize the sad result of current culture in the world today where first graders are talking about things they shouldn't even know about. Christian parents have the serious dilemma of facing difficult questions from their young children. However, passivity in letting young children watch certain cartoons and other programs contribute heavily to this problem. It's a legitimate concern, but it should not sidetrack us in our teaching of the gospel and truth.

Our children must know that there is a marked difference between right and wrong. Ezekiel 22:26 warns us that

Jerusalem was judged for not putting a difference between the holy and the profane. Today's young Christians don't really see sin as being wrong. It's more normal than wrong. Little by little they have been taught by indifferent teachers that they have the "freedom" to do anything they want. We do have freedom to do what we want—when we want to do the right thing. Children have been taught that God is in all things and that He loves you no matter what. They aren't hearing the other side of the coin, that God hates sin. They aren't hearing how God was so mad at Aaron (one of God's people) that He wanted to destroy him (Deut. 9:20).

I have heard children say that Jesus died because they are worth it. How has this generation of Christians fallen so low? Don't we believe God's Word when it says, "There is none that doeth good, no not one" (Ps. 14:3). If any man at any time was worth it or had some redeemable good within him, somebody might have pulled off not breaking the law, but it was impossible because we are worthless, having no worth or redeeming quality in our natural state, without Christ. (See Mark 1:7; Luke 21:36; and Revelation 5:4.) The humanism in America has influenced our teachings to infer that man is basically good or at least he tries to be good. I had to deal with one of my classes for a whole year on the issue of man's depravity, and the wall had already been built by false teaching. They believed that all humans have strength, power, and goodness within them, apart from God.

Time is short and the Bible has so much to offer. A lifetime cannot plumb its depths. It behooves us to not waste time. The Old Testament is full of stories for children that teach character, discipline, and give answers to difficult questions. In these End Times, as evil men and seducers wax worse and worse (2 Tim. 3:13), we can expect persecution (not fulfilled dreams). A person doesn't get persecuted for following the world. He gets persecuted for righteousness' sake (1 Pet. 3:14; Matt 5:10), His name's sake (Luke 21:12), or for the Word's sake (Mark 4:17). The more we are like Jesus, the more we are persecuted. (See John 5:16; 15:20–21; and 2 Peter 2:2.)

As for our dreams, we are promised the desires of our heart *if* we delight ourselves in the Lord (Ps. 37:4). Also, unto us are given "exceeding great and precious promises" (2 Pet. 1:4). But, our dreams usually involve self-exaltation and visions of fame or merely fleshly comforts. God's will is to fulfill His desires, not ours. If we could rephrase "fulfilled dreams" into the "promises of God," the shift in focus would be toward God and not man. (See 2 Corinthians 1:20 and Hebrews 11:33.)

Children need to hear about the sacrifices made by Bible heroes. They need to spend time hearing about Esther's courage before the king, Daniel's bravery before the lions, and Elijah's boldness before the 450 prophets of Baal. Children, as well as adults, need to be nurtured in the doctrines that encourage standing up for truth, even to the point of death. We must be taught that the Bible is truth. A person will not stand up in defense of something if he is not convinced it is true, especially when something that sounds better comes along to tempt him.

It's a total waste of time when churches show movies, play games, sing dream-chaser songs, and eat candy and donuts. Kids should just stay home when church offers the same thing as the local mall. We could print bumper stickers saying, "Save gas. Don't go to church." Children today are full of treats and entertainment. More of it causes the flesh to cry out for even more. We must offer spiritual food and stop all the flesh-appealing extravagance. This may sound harsh, but we shouldn't even bother with a fish cracker snack. Arguing that Jesus fed the multitudes before he preached to them is hollow. Jesus met needs. That's not the same as meeting desires. If your church is located where hungry children live, then they should be fed, first. But, I am addressing the problem of mainstream snackaholic children.

We must not be passive any longer. We must press in offensively against our enemy. Defense is not enough. Both offensive and defensive strategies are needed in any spiritual battle. We must understand that the enemy is aggressive and vicious with tactics of keeping, yes keeping, our kids. They are bound for hell until we get them from him. We can't think we have a crop until we have fruit. When we have them, we still cannot let our guard down. Satan will still harass. We must be vigilant and resist him so that he will flee. Our purpose is to raise soldiers. They must wear God's armor in order to stay alive. Complacency, passivity, and ignorance are costly.

Sin stinks. This generation must smell it or face devastating results. The psalmist said, "My wounds stink and are corrupt because of my foolishness" (Ps. 38:5). According to William Penn, foolishness is in the category with blasphemy, pride, thefts, murders, adulteries, and wickedness.[7] He didn't see foolishness in the heart of a child as harmless, youthful behavior. We must be like the men of the past who viewed sin as the putrid filth it really is.

Passivity of Christian Parents

> And thou shalt teach them diligently unto thy children, and shalt talk of them when thou sittest in thine house, and when thou walkest by the way, and when thou liest down, and when thou risest up.
>
> —Deuteronomy 6:7

Parents have a duty to teach their children about God and His commandments so that "it may be well" with them, and that they may "increase mightily" (v. 3). It is made clear to us in this text that there is no time for off-duty. A continual teaching must occur.

I am thankful for parents who took these verses seriously. When any opportunity arose for my parents to teach a life lesson, they took advantage of it. They were constantly pointing us to God. I remember lessons while we were sitting at the supper table, walking in the mountains, or lying out on the trampoline at night looking up at the stars. There are numerous daily lessons that I don't remember in particular. It was just a part of my everyday life.

Parents should seek out opportunities to teach and not take lightly a missed opportunity to direct attention toward God. Parents today have to compete with television and movies and a variety of games that draw their children's attention away from things of value and substance. Parents should not neglect to teach their children about the Lord. They should themselves know His Word so that they will be able to instill its life into their children.

Life lessons do not just consist of instructions about being nice, sharing, or always saying thank you and please. There are multitudes of lessons to be taught. Some lessons cannot be learned until a child has learned the basic essentials. We should be instilling these essentials and start focusing on obedience, respect, dependability, self-control, honesty, attentiveness, and accepting correction. It is not wise to wait to build character in a child. There is no time to waste. Lessons about God's holiness, immutability, wisdom, faithfulness, goodness, justice, mercy, grace, and love should be filling our days. Time wasted day after day results in a child being fodder for the enemy.

A child's life can be cut short when he does not honor his parents (Exod. 20:12; Deut. 5:16). Many children do not even know this helpful hint, and parents who withhold this information from their children fail to fully ensure his or her well-being. Parents abdicate their duty by bringing up dishonoring children, advocating the idea that their child should have more freedom than they had growing up. These parents feel they were unfairly restrained by their parents and were robbed of a pleasant childhood as a result.

They are looking at child development from the wrong perspective. If their parents tried to instill honor into them, they were good parents who obeyed God's Word. If a parent refuses to instill honor, that parent has failed and been disobedient to God's Word. Many parents today are rebelling against their parents by vowing to "do it differently." If they were submissive to the instruction to honor their parents, they wouldn't have such hard feelings about honoring them. Their persistent hard feelings tend to indicate rebellion. Of course, this does not apply to every case in life, but it is generally true. I have a couple of friends who were sadly mistreated as children, yet they honor their parents anyway.

Other parents abdicate teaching their children godly essentials for the seemingly just cause of building self-esteem. They lay aside correction and carelessly ignore discipline so they will not hurt their child's feelings. They feel their child is the victim of unfair circumstances rather than viewing him as a human with a sin nature. These parents listen to the world's view and believe that human feelings are priority and that even selfishness is legitimate. They are neglecting a very important duty and, in ignorance, causing the problem to be even worse.

To nurture every feeling of the child as legitimate or rooted in a "hurt" and to view feelings as more important than a child's duty and responsibility is a disservice to that child. The parent will find himself facing more and more self-centeredness in the child and less and less obedience.

Eli, as priest of the Lord, overlooked his duty to impart the significance of his work to his sons. As a result, they were called sons of Belial in 1 Samuel 2:12. The Bible says that "they knew not the LORD." They made themselves "fat with the chiefest of all the offerings of Israel" and they "lay with the women that assembled at the door of the tabernacle" (1 Sam. 2:22, 29). As a result, their lives were cut short in battle. Sons of Belial are not sons of God. What a regretful shame for Eli to have the blood of his own sons, Hophni and Phinehas, on his hands for not teaching them the ways of the Lord.

Sometimes, passivity in parents is passed down from church leaders. One speaker soothed her audience with these words, "Don't worry, your kids will run into what God has for them. They will come into their destiny. They'll just run from your preaching if you preach to them." So, is it safe to assume that God will raise our kids for us and we don't have to bother with all those scriptures on training and building character? The sad but true part of her statement is that without training, a child will truly meet his or her "destiny." It's just not the same destiny many are preaching about.

Parents must not fail to see the solemnity of teaching their children. Parents must instruct their children to understand that they must "take fast hold of instruction" and not let it go, for it is "life." Parents must warn that it is dangerous to "enter into the path of the wicked." Children should be told not to go the "way of evil men" and to "avoid" them always. They need to understand that the "way of the wicked is as darkness." Parents must teach their children by example to "put perverse words far" from their mouths. Finally, they must "not turn to the right hand nor to the left" in compromise, but remove their feet from evil (Prov. 4:13–27).

Righteous authority protects the home. Parents must watch for the souls of their children because they will one day give an account to God (Heb. 13:17). If they are like Eli and neglect to establish the importance of every action and every heart motive, results will be heartbreaking. We must set limits and give responsibilities to our children and expect obedience. God set limits on us because He loves us and knows that beyond those boundaries is danger and even death. Children are able to learn what is right, but not without teaching and modeling of God-honoring character. Training, discipline, and daily prayer for help from the greatest teacher of all are pivotal in this day of great peril for our youth.

Today's parents remain indifferent about daily instruction for their children. They either assume the church will take care of it or, even better, a Christian school will appropriate the task. People say, but don't seem to believe, that the daily life at home has the most impact on a child. Children need a godly church and a godly school, but especially a godly home. They need continual teaching to combat the strong forces that are pulling them toward worldliness.

Christian parents must apply Scripture to daily events. Also, Scripture can be applied to TV programs constantly. If parents do not offset the lure of television's marketing that "it's OK to sin," the TV will win the tug-of-war and the child will go the way of the world. We must point out the true evil of sin, especially when it is portrayed to look like something good. Parents' passivity allows so many opportunities to go by, and these chances, once lost, cannot be regained.

It is a very serious duty to raise a child in the fear and admonition of the Lord, and it does not happen without a struggle. It is an uphill fight against the natural, corrupt tendencies of the flesh. Parents must pray for discernment to confront sin in their home. It seems we fear confrontation and searching things out. Confronting sin is not popular, but sin hides in dark places; it doesn't confess itself.

Some parents insist that they must "pick their battles." The regrettable truth about this claim is that a parent ends up dealing with the easy "battles" and abdicates the larger ones. They pick which battles to overlook, but do not pick battles to engage in. Sometimes, they decide a battle is unimportant because they are too tired to deal with it. What about the desire to overlook problem behavior when it's a special occasion or the child's birthday? Even then, parents should be grabbing the sword of the spirit for battle. Instead, we pass it off as one of those battles we'd better let slide so we won't always be "hounding" our child. Satan loves to accuse Christians of riding their children too hard.

If you look back on the record of a "pick my battles" parent, they generally haven't fought one important battle because the circumstances weren't ever quite right or they just didn't want to be too harsh. Are the circumstances ever right? No. A child always seems to need correction at inopportune times. Parents need to decide beforehand what they will allow and what they will not. Otherwise, unexpected behavior will slide in just when they aren't ready to deal with it.

Another area of neglect is when modern parents allow lying and deception from their children. We must show concern for our child by not allowing him to lie or hide his actions. This applies to all ages, not just teenagers. Have you seen how early a child can lie? The sin nature of a child automatically causes him to defend his own actions. If he doesn't defend his actions, he's quick and clever enough to say, "Oh, I misunderstood" or "I didn't hear you." Parents who believe this untrue defense are in favor of letting their child go through life untrained and undisciplined.

Sometimes children are innocent and need the freedom to explain their side, but this is not true most of the time. I am continually frustrated by parents who think their little Johnny is innocent and victimized by other kids. If a parent is called to meet with a teacher or principal more than once, then he should get a clue.

Parents must not let their child continually lie. He will just become a master at it. He will soon lie with no shame and no remorse. In fact, he will lie knowing by experience that it pays. Minimizing sin when it should be maximized is the fatal plan of our enemy, Satan.

Refusing to deal with sin in a child indicates rebellion in the parent. Justifying sin is a red flag. The sad symptom of ignorance in modern parents is gloating in pride that they are doing a much better job of raising kids than their parents and grandparents did. They are deceived.

Rebellion is sometimes quickly revealed in how parents of teenagers act. Passive mothers dress like their teenage girls and talk like them, using teen vocabulary and slang. They complacently let slide their duty of representing motherhood to their daughters. I have lost count of the times I have seen relief on a mother's face when she hears her teenager call her a cool mom. That mother smiles in glee while neglecting her duty to tell her daughter to get some clothes on because she is immodestly dressed. Fathers, too, love having the "cool" label. The sad reality is that teenagers really want a role model of maturity rather than a try-to-be dude. To act young and immature should not be the goal of any parent.

Television has drilled into our minds the idea that real parents are stupid. How sad that Christians fall for it and are not separate from the world. Do Christians really want to be cool? Think about what TV represents as cool. It's a haughty, worldly attitude that Jesus condemned.

It's a shameful scene in America to see how many teenagers rule the family. Parents are walking on eggshells to protect their child's weaknesses. Parents guard their own "uncool" reactions, fearing their child will reject them if they become preachy. Instead of confronting their child's behavior, parents opt for the reaction of laughing, which automatically signals that inappropriate behavior is harmless. Parents appease their own consciences by teasing and making light of what is actually sin against a holy God. Regardless of appearance, the teen really wants a parent who will be a parent.

Gray areas are confusing to a child. Many times, children do not know if a certain behavior is always wrong or only just when Mom and Dad get embarrassed by it. Plus, children are astute about the different situations that contribute to their punishment or lack of punishment. Parents should not let different situations contribute to different responses. For example, filthy language in a Christian home should not be acceptable, and the fact that the TV says it, and not a family member, should not make a difference. It's confusing for a child to be told not to talk that way, yet he hears the family laugh when it is on TV. Parents must back up what they say with action. We shouldn't say it if we don't mean it.

Not defining clear boundaries and living in the gray area leads to easy disobedience and an unpricked conscience because a person can't feel when he has crossed a line. That's the devil's intent with establishing gray zones. If a person fudges here or there, what does it matter? Then, the next time he fudges a little more, he never feels the smart of crossing the line.

It's dangerous to bend a rule or go outside its limits and then label the infraction as harmless. Some even go so far as to label certain actions actually within the limits of righteousness. Christians don't say, "I'm going over the line even though it's wrong," but instead say, "I'm going over the line, and it's OK. In fact, God is right here with me." This is exactly how a person ends up with a seared conscience.

It is disturbing when I see anticipation on teenagers' faces when they talk about attending rock concerts, going to Las Vegas when they're old enough, or getting a tattoo or some kind of piercing. The law of the land, which allows certain behavior at certain ages, has more weight to them than the laws of the Bible.

A lack of conscience is really a problem among numerous Christians today. These kids are constantly told by the TV that sin is OK and that it is harmless and even funny. Some Christians don't even try to hide that they go to movies that advocate these blatant sins. Lack of guilt is not a sign of righteous action, but of a seared conscience.

Children must have consequences. Without them, lessons go unlearned. Words do nothing. Just think of your own life. Words are hollow. Action talks. Consequences should be immediate for best results. Remember Ecclesiastes 8:11: "Because sentence against an evil work is not executed speedily, therefore the heart of the sons of men is fully set in them to do evil." If parents do not quickly deal with sin, their child's heart will be hardened to do evil. I have seen how delay in action first causes a snicker, then a giggle, then flippant laughter, then a comfortable feeling of invulnerability, then downright haughtiness toward authority.

Also, an authority's contemplation over how to deal with a behavior implies lack of concern. Parents need previously established consequences that can be put into action immediately.

The sad occurrence in modern America is that some parents refuse to execute a sentence and even refuse to allow schools to do so. This is not only a problem in public schools but in Christian ones as well. I have seen parents of children who have lied or cheated get offended that a teacher would even indicate that they should do something about it. They accuse teachers of judging their child. The child then walks off smiling. You would think a parent would be thankful for a helping hand to expose the sin that so cleverly hides in us all.

These parents seem to think that denying bad behavior or refusing to accept it will free their child of any guilt. This only magnifies the problem and indicates why the child so boldly ignores rules. If a child is caught at school lying or cheating, there is good indication he has done it before or will do it again. Christian parents should realize that their child has a sinful nature.

It is a great service to both the child and parent to find problems and to deal with them. To not expose the behavior is of disservice to the child because a continual "getting by with it" hardens his heart. Parents should understand this and appreciate the opportunity to teach a biblical principle to their child when sin is exposed.

Sometimes parents know their child has disobeyed or sinned, but they excuse it by saying that they didn't really intend to do it or were forced into cooperation by a peer. My experience tells me that anything I do, I had intentions first; and anything good I really didn't intend to do, I ended up not doing.

Some parents dismiss a chance to deal with sin by saying that there really wasn't enough evidence that their child was guilty. They wait until they have a full-color video of the infraction, taken in the bright noonday sun, with no shadows to imply it was some other child wearing their child's clothing. When they finally face the fact that it is their child, they justify it by saying, "She's a good kid; she just made a bad choice."

It is common behavior in today's society for passivity to be reflected in a parent's defense of their child's actions. One case in a local school involved several parents. Some football players were failing their schoolwork because of late-night carousing and drinking. The principal decided that they could not play football until their grades were brought up to passing. Parents revolted by saying, "What business is it of yours what our children do outside of school?" What kind of parent is that? Shouldn't each of them have been thankful that someone helped them see the error of their son's ways? These rebel parents will no doubt reap the fruits of their ill-advised example for their sons.

Another relinquishing of parental duty is demonstrated by parents who readily claim that their child's disobedience stems from ADD or ADHD. Some children truly have legit-imate learning problems and need medical assistance, but most children can learn to pay attention by conventional methods of discipline.

Who would ever claim their child had RFSN (rebellion from sin nature)? Parents want to hear that their child's misbehavior is not their fault and is certainly not their child's fault. The fact that the child will not sit still in class or listen to a word the teacher says is quickly blamed on something else. How far do you think that excuse would have gone with a mother in the late 1800s or early 1900s? It would not have been accepted. More children sat still and obeyed their teacher as a result. The problem of ADD could be solved quickly with correct parental guidance. Instead, we are pushing drugs down children's throats and telling them that they need extra help to act like other children.

Recently, educators are claiming that children with ADD are actually more intelligent than the average child. With that information, several adults and educators are claiming they have it too. Back off and take a look at these facts. Can a child who does not listen or obey common classroom behavior rules truly be borderline genius? Nonsense! What a ridiculous lie of the enemy to persuade people into thinking it is an honor to have a child who is plaguing the classroom. To the detriment of other children's learning, he becomes a hero.

If Ezra 7:26 were applied, results would be different. Think how those kids would sit up straight, stop talking, start listening, and therefore, know answers to the teacher's questions after reading Ezra's words: "Whosoever will not do the law of thy God, and the law of the king, let judgment be executed speedily upon him, whether it be unto death, or to banishment, or to confiscation of goods, or to imprisonment." Most children simply do not obey until there is a cost.

Instead of the biblical principle of cost, Christians are applying the world's doctrine of rewards to obtain obedience from children. The majority of children today will obey only if they agree or if it pays. Parents are not teaching obedience for obedience's sake. It is politically incorrect to say, "Because I said so." That phrase says a lot. It says, "Obey anyway." Parents feel they must explain a situation to the point where the child agrees or sees a benefit from obeying. This is in direct opposition to biblical obedience. Christians must obey, even if it costs them. Christians are called to obey even when we disagree, don't understand, or do not benefit. Jesus was obedient unto death, and He "learned obedience by the things which he suffered" (Heb. 5:8). How can this generation of children stand against persecution if they are not taught the lessons of obedience? Instead, they will succumb to the payoff that the mark of the Beast will offer.

I know of Christian parents who use vacations, money, or gifts as leverage to persuade their child to obey. We must stop and teach obedience simply because it is the right thing to do. The Bible clearly tells us that by showing favor, a person "will...not learn righteousness" nor will he "behold the majesty of the Lord" (Isa. 26:10). Many truly think their child will grow up OK by not suffering consequences. These parents think every consequence is too harsh, so they cushion them with candy, special lunches, or extra money.

I've heard of parents holding the prospects of a new car over their child's head to cause him to behave better. When there was still no change in behavior, they bought the car anyway. This is truly a display of unnatural affection. The Bible does not talk about rewarding children as a means of instruction.

Opportunity to teach children to do the right thing simply because it's right is often overlooked. At the school where I taught, we held a canned food drive every year. Each year, the contributions lessened. One year, the fun idea of creating a competition between the high school and grade school was mentioned. It was decided that the group who brought the most cans would receive a no-uniform pass for several days. That year, the younger kids brought the most cans, but it was then decided that all grades would receive the reward since all had participated. The goal was not even reached, but the reward was given anyway. At a time when children should have been taught that giving to the poor was right, we chose to make it an issue of wanting to do the right thing because of personal benefit. We abdicated our duty of teaching the principle of giving and we caused the children to forfeit any heavenly reward for giving out of a pure heart.

The Bible has clear direction for the parent who wants to hear it. Proverbs 23:13 says not to withhold correction from a child. Verse 14 says, beating him with a rod will deliver his soul from hell. Proverbs 16:6 says that "by mercy and truth iniquity is purged: and by the fear of the LORD men depart from evil." It was not wrong for parents of the past to "put the fear" into their children. I am not advocating child abuse, but I am advocating discipline with a little pain. Psalm 82:2 asks, "How long will ye judge unjustly, and accept the persons of the wicked?"

Charles Spurgeon said:

> Put poison in the spring, and it will impregnate the whole stream. Take care what you are after sir! You are twisting the sapling, and the old oak will

be bent thereby. Have a care! It is a child's soul you are tampering with, it is a child's soul you are preparing for eternity. I give you a solemn admonition on every child's behalf. Surely, if it be treachery to administer poison to the dying, it must be far more criminal to give poison to the young life. If it be evil to mislead gray-headed age, it must be far more so to turn aside the young heart to a road of error in which he may forever walk. Ah! It is a solemn admonition—you are teaching children.[8]

Time with your children is very short. Do not be the one to cause them to stumble, but lead them into the way of everlasting life and teach them the fear of the Lord. Remember, they want you to.

Chapter 2

FAMINE OF HEARING

Behold the days come, saith the Lord God, that I will send a famine in the land, not a famine of bread, nor a thirst for water, but of hearing the words of the LORD: And they shall wander from sea to sea, and from the north even to the east, they shall run to and fro to seek the word of the LORD, and shall not find it.

—Amos 8:11–12

W HAT A TERRIBLE scarcity to have the sustenance of God's Word lacking. We do not realize how dependent we are on God's mercy. What a sad predicament to be searching for truth, yet be unable to find it because God is withholding it. Daniel speaks of those in the last days who will run to and fro. He also mentions that it will be a time of increasing knowledge (Dan. 12:4).

We see how knowledge has definitely increased. Since the printing press, literature has been mass-produced, and now the Internet allows any factual question to be answered almost instantly. Knowledge about other people, their cultures, and their religions inundate our lives. Even Bibles and Christian literature is in abundance, especially in America.

The famine mentioned in Amos is not the lack of availability, but the lack of ingestion. It is a famine of hearing God's Word. How sad to have the food before you, but you're unable to eat it or you don't even want to eat it. What if you knew that the food was somewhere in the house, but you could not find it after you had looked every place but the very place it was actually located? This is a situation that calls for panic.

Flocks of Christians are searching for truth in the wrong places. They assume it's in the Christian literature, tapes, CDs, and programs, but much of that is only junk food for the soul. Then they try mixing ancient mystical beliefs, psychology, or Eastern religions with biblical doctrines. They're eating rat poison, and the hunger pains are satisfied only for the moment. They have a definite spiritual hunger, but they will not find satisfaction in the false religions across the sea. Proverbs 27:7 says that "to the hungry soul every bitter thing is sweet."

Hunger is evident, since Christians are eating. We are gluttons for sweet, tasty, non-nutritious food. Our spiritual man, too, is starving for healthy meat. It is sad that we are so full of unwholesome foods that we don't even want the meat. Since we are full of junk food, we don't even see our need for nutrition. We are seeking, but are not finding even though God's Word is right under our nose.

The period of time between the Testaments, between Malachi and Jesus' birth, is an era called the "silent years" because no inspired prophet arose in Israel. I have wondered if there is a parallel with the silence before Jesus' first coming and the silence today preceding His second coming. In the intertestamental period, there were small groups, a remnant, who resisted the influence of the worldly Greek and Roman cultures.

However, there was also a great falling away from truth evident in the writings of the Apocrypha. This was a collection of Jewish writings that were not part of the Law, the Prophets, and other writings of the Hebrew Bible. Jesus never quoted from the Apocryphal writings. Early church fathers distinguished between true Scripture and the Apocrypha. These new and popular writings contained historical and geographical inaccuracies.[1]

Deception takes a strong foothold when it is under the disguise of truth. The label may say "Christian" when, in fact, it is not. The shortage of true teaching today stems partially from a similar problem faced by the believers in the centuries before Christ's birth. Believers read the Apocrypha and believed it was the true, inspired Word of God.

Modern Christians tend to believe that any translation of the Bible is the inspired Word of God. Few compare the new translations with the old and, therefore, do not see the discrepancy, but who would not naturally think they could trust anything that said "Bible" on the cover? Satan is the master of deceit and lies. He has moved Christians from an "it is written" attitude to a "could be, might be, ought to be, should be" mentality toward God's Word.

Only a remnant knew that Jesus was the Messiah when He came to earth. Jesus asked, "Why do you not understand my speech? even because ye cannot hear my word" (John 8:43). He spoke differently, but they were accustomed to common speech. What they heard was the everyday speech of the street. They weren't hearing His Word. There was a famine of hearing God's Word and the result was ignorance.

We think, how did they not see? Bible prophecy clearly pointed out that Jesus was the Christ, but when the brain is muddled with conflicting information and "enlightenment" from other sources, it cannot see the truth clearly. Therefore, most rejected him as the Christ. Are we in the same crisis? Do modern Christians fail to see the true Christ, and will they readily accept the false one when he comes on the scene? You can bet that Satan is conditioning the whole world for that very moment. He wants no resistance so that he will be ushered in with popular consent.

Some jokingly say, "What you don't know won't hurt you." If anyone ever asks you for an example of one of Satan's lies, give them that one. To the contrary, what you don't know can and will hurt you. Do not be content with junk food from tables other than the Lord's. Seek the truth from His Word and not from other sources. Pray for discernment in a day of strong delusion.

THE ANSWER

Having a Bible is a good thing. Reading your Bible is a good thing. But, the Bible tells us that "faith cometh by hearing, and hearing by the word of God" (Rom. 10:17). That verse is the answer to our famine problem. Preachers and teachers must preach God's Word so that people will hear it. Many say they are teaching it when they are not. Many say they will teach it when they won't. In the mean time, people starve for lack of hearing truth. Whose fault is it? Those who know where the food is are not pointing it out. They are letting people search all over the house while they stand there with it in their hands. How cruel. Our job, if we love Him, is to feed His sheep. The great commission includes bringing people to salvation. We must feed them once they are in the fold. While many churches today are trying to save the world, they themselves are full of unsaved people. How can a sinking ship assist another?

Once a new convert is made in the church, it is critical to teach him and guide him into all truth. It is cruel to give someone a bite of something good, then not continue to feed him. New converts are like babies, and they need attentive care, especially in a day when deception is at its highest point. They must be told to read their Bible, but also they must hear the Word preached and taught to them. It is the Holy Spirit who actually guides us into truth (John 16:13). Yet, as a conductor, the Word allows Him to flow through truth. Faith will respond to no other sound but truth.

Hosea declared, "My people are destroyed for lack of knowledge" (Hosea 4:6). God is speaking of His people, not the world. Just when we thought we had all the answers, we see we don't know anything. Would a popular preacher respond well to a comment that he doesn't know anything and, as a result, has destroyed God's people?

Be sure you are in a church where you hear God's Word. Be like the Bereans who are mentioned in Acts. They searched the Scriptures daily to see if what they heard preached was true. Don't assume your preacher is preaching the Bible just because the sign outside affirms you're in a church. Don't assume he is preaching the Bible if he and others say he is. Remember our weakness. We are sheep who are prone to follow. Saying and doing are not the same thing. Count how many times a speaker actually uses Scripture in his sermon. If you are hearing God's Word, then pray for your pastor not to be led astray by easier doctrines and tell him you appreciate it.

THE DANGER

Little by little, Satan deceives people until they are caught in his trap. Increments of deception are presented to people. Every time we fall for it, we move down a notch toward the gaping mouth of the trap. Satan is even patient enough to wait from one generation to the next. Since the early church, each generation has lost ground. Ezekiel indicated how dangerous this is because, after a while, the truth becomes unavailable to the leader who once had it. Ezekiel 7:26 states, "Mischief shall come upon mischief, and rumour shall be upon rumour; then shall they seek a vision of the prophet; but the law shall perish from the priest, and counsel from the ancients." Satan is not satisfied with a famine of hearing; he wants the truth gone. God will allow the famine to end in starvation if we refuse to eat from His table.

Ephesians 5:15–16 warns, "See then that ye walk circumspectly, not as fools, but as wise, Redeeming the time, because the days are evil." We must be careful while there is still time. As long as people in the church are still alive and breathing, something can be done. Time is short before the return of Christ. We need to be found doing the will of the Lord (Eph. 5:17).

The regrettable shame of the church is that entertainment has substituted the hearing of God's Word. In place of hearing Scripture, jokes are inserted. In place of hearing Old Testament character lessons, accounts of family vacation or movie "lessons" are inserted. In place of hearing Bible stories and Scripture, the youth are playing foosball, musical instruments, pool tables, PlayStation 2, listening to iPods, watching movies, or throwing parties. The church shouldn't give children the world in order to convert them from it.

John Berthrong, associate dean at Boston University's School of Theology, noticed, "When I talk to students about their own sense of religious identity, I find that more and more of them have been brought up in homes that are post-Christian. So to say that they are reacting against Christianity is wrong; they've never been Christians. Even some of the ones who are Christians will say, 'But I really like Taoism and Buddhism, too.'"[2]

"The Bible and theology department at Wheaton College in Illinois," adds professor Gary Burge, "has studied the biblical and theological literacy of incoming freshmen. These students are intellectually ambitious and spiritually passionate. They represent almost every Protestant denomination and every state in the country. Most come from strong evangelical churches and possess a long history of personal devotion and Christian involvement...They use the Bible regularly—but curiously, few know its stories...."[3]

William Penn would be shocked to see how far the churches have fallen since his day. He saw the church drifting in this 1688 discourse: "Plays, parks, balls, treats, romances, music, love sonnets, and the like, will be a very invalid plea for any other purpose than their condemnation, who are taken and delighted with them, at the revelation of the righteous judgment of God. O my friends! these were never invented, but by that mind which had first lost the joy and ravishing delights of God's holy presence."[4] Do we even look at entertainment through those eyes? No, we justify it and claim it is how God really intended it to be. We claim that it is entertainment that wins souls even though there is no Scripture to verify it. Again, William Penn wrote while in prison in the Tower of London in 1688, "The pretended innocence of these things steals away their minds from that which is better…It is a liberty that feeds the flesh, and gratifies the lustful eye and palate of poor mortality."[5]

Jeremiah clarifies this problem by saying, "For my people is foolish, they have not known me; they are sottish [like a drunkard] children, and they have none understanding: they are wise to do evil, but to do good they have no knowledge" (Jer. 4:22). We don't know Him, but we foolishly know how to have fun. The church is drunk on fun and entertainment. Have you seen how Christians are wise to do evil? How about the young people? We can't deny that they are extremely wise about evil. The lack of teaching has caused an increase in sin among Christians.

Amos 3:10 explains that people are wise to do evil because they know not to do right. This is why teaching is so important. People do not naturally know how to do right. How can we claim great end-times revelation when we don't even know the basics? How can we claim a great anointing on the young people when they are wise to do evil? Are we deceived? Psychology claims that the children of today are hurting and, therefore, reaching out to the wrong things (sin) for comfort and love. No, if not taught to do right, people do wrong. Kids succumb to peer pressure for acceptance. Their flesh feels that acceptance is the most important goal in life until someone teaches them otherwise.

The Old Testament prophets were truly prophets. Not only did they see what was happening in their day, but they also predicted our day with great accuracy. Malachi 2 demonstrates how the "priest's lips should keep knowledge," and that they should "seek the law…for he is the messenger of the LORD of hosts" (Mal. 2:7). But, instead, they have "departed out of the way" and have "caused many to stumble" (v. 8). They are "partial in the law," teaching only the happy and loving side of the Bible (v. 9). They have thus "profaned the holiness of the LORD" (v. 11).

Scripture was written for our admonition and instruction. We must hide it in our heart, that we might not sin against God (1 Cor. 10:11; Ps. 119:11). We must refuse what the world offers in the way of half-truths. Psychology is full of practical-sounding answers, but they are opposed to God's Word. We must exercise ourselves unto godliness by refusing the fables of the world and giving attendance to reading, to exhortation, and to doctrine (1 Tim. 4:7, 11). Exhortation is the persuasive preaching that involves hearing God's Word and not just our reading it. It is not enough for churches to assume people are reading their Bibles. Some churches have turned aside to "vain jangling." They would rather talk about hobbies or personal experiences than the truth.

Jesus only spent time with truth while on earth. Isaiah 7:15 teaches us that Jesus ate butter and honey, which are good and not evil, so that he would know to refuse the evil and to choose the good. He gained discernment through digesting truth. We, and especially our children, need that discernment, too.

Christians ignorantly believe that to have sown wild oats as a teen has actually prepared them for the real world. This indicates an unrepentant heart and a wishing it were true in avoidance of true repentance. Romans 16:19 says we are to be "simple concerning evil." Did Jesus sow wild oats? Was He prepared for the real world? Was He prepared to take on the enemy? Was He ever deceived? Was He naïve because of His innocence? He was sinless and in all things He spoke the truth. He was a good shepherd, leading His flock by truth.

Yet, false shepherds cause their flock to be left as prey for the enemy. The sheep wander on the mountains and they scatter upon "all the face of the earth," but God will require the flock at their hand (Ezek. 34:6, 10). He will destroy the fat and the strong; and feed them with judgment (Ezek. 34:16). From this we see that shepherds are accountable. Paul gives instruction to shepherds in Acts 20:28: "Take heed therefore unto yourselves, and to all the flock, over the which the Holy Ghost hath made you overseers, to feed the church of God, which he hath purchased with His own blood." Feeding a congregation falsehood, or even half-truths, does not count as feeding the flock.

Moses and Joshua would read the entire law to the people (Exod. 24:3, 7; Josh. 8:35; Heb. 9:19). Today, preachers try to cut sermons short because the people start getting bored. It's true that they get bored, because their flesh is full of fun and entertainment and the more the flesh gets, the more it wants. However, Proverbs 28:9 warns, "He that turneth away his ear from hearing the law, even his prayer shall be abomination."

THE FRUIT OF IGNORANCE

I have even heard a pastor state from the pulpit his new "plan" for church services, specially designed by him and the elders. It included less preaching, more worship, and a more casual attire to draw in the crowds. Preachers choose to water down the gospel until it is thin and weak. It's as if they had boiled a chicken bone and fed it to their flock. The young members of the congregation don't even know it is watered down and lacking in nutritional value because they never had any nutrition to measure by.

When a person is not aware of something, such as a term or idea, it goes right over his head when mentioned. Maybe you have noticed how upon learning something new, you start to hear it afterward. You could very well have been hearing it previously, but were unaware of it. Some Christians seem totally unaware of Satan's tactics of deception.

Christians aren't aware of false teaching and, therefore, it goes right over their heads. God warns that He will send strong delusion to the point people will believe lies if they do not love the truth (2 Thess. 2:10–11). How can someone believe a total lie? That is what humans are best at. We naturally believe lies because the truth is not in us. We must work out our salvation with fear and trembling because the flesh is very weak.

Some Christian TV programs give their listeners boiled chicken bones, too. Sometimes good preachers who know the truth will waste a good hour of airtime giving advice about vitamins, exercise, or other earthly information that ought to be left to the secular programs. Our time is short, and every moment counts. We dare not think we have told all there is to tell about the Lord and complacently substitute spiritual matters with health issues that will only profit the flesh. It is not sin to talk about vitamins. They may be good for you, but it is not wise to talk about vitamins when people are starving for spiritual food. It is America's souls that are out of shape and should be attended to.

One TV program that was promoting health issues said the reason for their program was "so you'll live long and have time with your family." That's a legitimate message to our flesh, but the focus of a Christian program should not shift from being heavenly-minded to becoming earthly-minded. People naturally want to live longer and be with their family, but we must continue to preach the gospel because it is the message people need, even though they do not necessarily want to hear it. The gospel is not a healthy message to our flesh. It requires denying our flesh and even dying. It can even cost us our family (Matt. 10:37).

As a result of the famine of hearing God's Word in children's church, children are now becoming adults who absolutely do not know how to act in the church sanctuary. They have not seen correct behavior modeled because they have not been beside their parent during church. When the churches decided to have a separate service for children, I don't know. But over a period of ten or twenty years, the effects are obvious. Young adults now do not even bring their Bibles with them to church because it was unnecessary when they were in church as a child. If a Bible was needed, youth leaders provided one rather than requiring the child to bring one. It's odd how quickly Americans have succumbed to a socialistic approach, which is always easier than demanding personal responsibility.

A. W. Tozer, noted author, teacher, and pastor, clarifies the picture. He said, "The great god Entertainment amuses his devotees mainly by telling them stories. The love of stories, which is a characteristic of childhood, has taken fast hold of the minds of the retarded saints of our day, so much so that not a few persons manage to make a comfortable living by spinning yarns and serving them up in various disguises to church people. What is natural and beautiful in a child may be shocking when it persists into adulthood, and more so when it appears in the sanctuary and seeks to pass for true religion."[6]

I remember sitting in church after having Sunday school. Correct behavior was modeled by everyone in the room.

Whether I realized it or not, I was being taught how to act. I grew up knowing you don't yell, run, wear a cap, or act nonchalantly in the sanctuary. I still have flashbacks to the sting of a pinched leg if I see a child joking and laughing in church. Who would have thought a simple change in church procedure would have caused so much damage today? The devil is once again manifesting a clever tactic in deceiving the church. It is disturbing to me, though, to hear young leaders claim they now have freedom in church and that it's not rigid like it used to be. I would agree that the flesh truly has more freedom inside the church, but my concern is that it is not a good thing.

Today's youth do not even realize the need for preparing their heart before meeting the Lord. They continually hear the part about entering boldly before the throne of grace, but they do not hear the balanced perspective—that we can do that only because of grace and not because we deserve it. We can only come boldly when we understand Jesus' merit and our lack of it. Coming boldly involves humility, not haughtiness or light-heartedness.

Youth services now begin with social laughter and fun. When the band starts its first lick, kids think they are instantly in His presence. Like superstition and a magic potion, they think God is there. Some feel "hot spots," supposing they can jump in and get even happier. Their souls are starving from the lack of truth. They do not know that God's presence comes after waiting on the Lord and that "deep calleth unto deep" when pertaining to spiritual things (Ps. 42:7).

On several instances, immediately after the opening prayer, I witnessed youth leaders begin joking and laughing. Then, they would tell the children that they did not need to do a "bunch of spiritual aerobics because God will just show up because He loves you." This modeled behavior negated all Scripture on spiritual preparedness and Christian duty. Contrary to popular belief, God has requirements that must be met.

The leadership of some pastors is a picture that no young person could possibly respect. Youth leaders portray an image of gum-chewing, baby-talking, voice cracking from over-exaggeration, and off-color joking. Their main goal seems to be entertainment and laughter. Parents need to check into their child's youth group. Just because they are in church does not mean they are being led on a path of righteousness. Just because a child wants to attend a youth group doesn't mean it is edifying. Just because children are laughing doesn't mean it's funny.

Pastors who do not feed their flock cover their sermons with hype. Tozer put it this way, "We make up by sheer enthusiasm what we lack in the power of the Spirit."[7] Pastors say you are about to hear a phenomenal word. Do you? He says he had an awesome time with God. Did he? He says he strives for excellence. Does he? Don't fall for the mass enthusiasm that seems to be commonplace in many churches today. Look for authentic food and don't settle for delicious, scrumptious dog biscuits.

Evidence for the spiritual famine is seen in the shallow lives of contemporary Christians. Teachers who truly seek to teach Scripture without hype find their classes dwindling down to only a faithful few. Genuine prayer meetings are almost non-existent in today's churches. When there is a true prayer meeting, you don't hear it advertised. This is part of what makes it the real thing. Superficial Christians claim that God is in favor of "letting the good times roll." One preacher said, "Ask God for something big. Even ask for something selfish. I'm selfish. I want things, too." We Americans fail to see how blessed we already are. We are blind to the fact that most people in the world would love to live one day like a spoiled American. Why are Christian leaders encouraging us to want even more?

When we leave a church service and say what a good sermon we just heard, are we gauging it by God's Word or popular opinion? In Mark 6:12, after Jesus directed his disciples to go out and preach two by two, they "preached that men should repent." Is that what we hear today? Is that what a "good" sermon consists of, or does that run the people off? Sin should be stopped in the early stages. We must begin hearing about dying daily and repenting of every unclean thought. Preaching should tell us to take every thought captive. Waiting until sin is rampant in a church and then seeking counsel with some psychological, worldly solution is losing the war, especially young people. We cannot wait until the full-blown sinful appetites have gained so much weight that they are too big to conquer. Daily battles are what win the war. "Letting the good times roll" while sin is on the loose is dangerous and foolish.

Good teaching requires repetition. We cannot be satisfied with giving one good sermon. We must build foundations, which are currently lacking. John MacArthur, author of numerous bestselling books gives a simple solution. He said, "We must saturate our minds and hearts with the truth of Scripture, and refuse to yield to the spirit of our age. To do that, we must understand our own sinfulness and know how to deal with our sins."[8]

Chapter 3

PSYCHOLOGY

*The L*ord* knoweth the thoughts of man,*
that they are vanity.

—Psalm 94:11

Beware lest any man spoil you through philosophy and
vain deceit, after the tradition of men, after the
rudiments of the world, and not after Christ.

—Colossians 2:8

PSYCHIC ON A television talk show said, "When we combine common sense, logic, and intuition, we get our wisest answers." It is regrettable that many Christians agree with this statement. However, the wisest answers are not generated by humans. Our logic will ultimately lead us to the most unwise answers. We cannot rely on our minds.

Psychology is the study of the mind. It should have no place in the Christian doctrine. The term *Christian psychologist* is an oxymoron. Rather than focusing on God, psychologists focus on human desires and worldly appetites. It seems that "worldly lusts fill up the study, care, and conversation of wretched Christendom."[1]

Today, some preachers use psychologist Abraham H. Maslow's Hierarchy of Needs diagram, whether they know it's psychology or not. This teaching appeals to their listeners' fleshly human appetites. The chart includes the needs for basic survival: safety, belonging, self-esteem, understanding, "beauty," and finally, self-actualization. Human nature loves to hear about self-actualization. The diagram doesn't even mention our deepest need for a redeemer, resulting from mankind's helpless condition of sin. Psychologists of the past are known to be atheists and defiant to God's principles. Yet, preachers continue to use methods of psychology and preach that we must realize and fulfill our needs and, therefore, maximize our "potential."

The Bible says "take no thought for your life, what ye shall eat, or what ye shall drink; nor yet for your body, what ye shall put on....But seek ye first the kingdom of God, and his righteousness; and all these things shall be added unto you (Matt. 6:25, 33).

Modern sermons and Christian literature reflect psychologist Sigmund Freud's belief that there is the "principle of an instinctive drive in the organism to return to previous states." Christians are urging the return to a state of perfection present in the Garden of Eden, but we were never in that state and, therefore, cannot return. Adam and Eve experienced perfection, but lost it. We never had it. The new belief that we were once complete and wholesome and have been corrupted by outside influences is false. It lines up with psychology's perversion of truth.

Freud was also fond of dream analysis, something Christians are fascinated by. Our delving into this subject endangers us with strong delusion. Jeremiah warned God's people by saying, "Let not your prophets...deceive you, neither hearken to your dreams which ye cause to be dreamed.

For they prophesy falsely unto you in my name: I have not sent them, saith the LORD" (Jer. 29:8–9). The Lord definitely speaks to Christians in dreams (Joel 2:28; Acts 2:17), but the warning by Jeremiah should not go unheeded.

Ecclesiastes 5:3, 7 tells us that a dream can come from "the multitude of business" and that "there are also diverse vanities" with some dreams. The Koran is a direct result of misguided dreams. It is claimed to be the "direct transmission of the word of God revealed to Mohammed."[2] Another psychologist, Carl Jung, developed analytical psychology. The dictionary verifies his anti-biblical views by stating his beliefs about the unconscious mind and its archetypes, such as the hero and the "mother goddess."

Psychology is a rejection of God. It replaces God's Word with man's word.

> For my people have committed two evils; they have forsaken me the fountain of living waters, and hewed them out cisterns, broken cisterns, that can hold no water.
>
> —Jeremiah 2:13

Psychology is a broken cistern. Christians have forsaken God's answers and are seeking answers from man. We are like deceived atheists who believe man has the answers to his own problems. We are trusting intuition and intellect while forgetting what God says about our sin nature and that we should not lean to our own understanding.

There is no progress in following the latest trend of worldly studies. God said of His people, "But they hearkened not, nor inclined their ear, but walked in the counsels and in the imagination of their evil heart, and went backward, and not forward" (Jer. 7:24). Leaning on psychology for answers is causing the church to go backward, not forward. This is not opinion, but fact. Counselors who use psychology are "strengthening the hands of evil doers" with their false, self-centered, God-rejecting counsel (Jer. 23:14).

How is God so patient with man's continual rejection of truth? Israel went into captivity for rejecting Him. We are not as special as we think and will also see captivity if we do not repent. Christians who waste time studying the conscious and unconscious states of mind cloud their own mind from what truth really is. Eventually, they become unable to distinguish truth from a lie. That is right where Satan wants them. The Antichrist will only further deceive beaten-down Christians who have compromised truth with teachings of human ego, self-esteem, logic, and reasoning.

Preachers are trusting statistics more than trusting the Holy Spirit. They are relying on man's reasoning. Statistics say if you were abused, then you will abuse someone else. The Bible says there is hope in Christ. Statistics say people come back to your church if it's a happy place and if, as I heard two preachers say, the chairs are 80 percent full. The Holy Spirit says people will come back if He is present and if He draws them back.

The secular humanist doctrine believes that answers lie within a person's mind, but our minds must come into subjection to our renewed spirit and answers must be sought from God. Humanists believe we all must seek deeper within ourselves to find answers. They claim "everyone has the strength inside to make their dreams come true." They are wasting time, because it is not there. Bible study groups spend their time discussing each person's purpose, opinion, or past hurts. This humanistic approach relies on inner thoughts and feelings. How did Christians get so far from truth to seek answers from psychology?

Reason has always led man astray. During the late seventeenth and eighteenth centuries, the age of reason adopted rationalism and other humanistic philosophies and placed man in the position of God. Their deception has led to a dominant pattern in our thinking, today. It has placed human reason in a much higher place than it deserves. It is a mark of the latter days to see Christians swallowing the lies of human reason.

Christians argue that psychology does indeed have some things to offer. To believe that is to ignore its basic reliance on humanism. A Christian cannot attend psychology classes and be unaffected. In fact, he or she will likely succumb to the rational, logical, sensible, way of thinking portrayed in class. Of course it makes sense; it's humanism and we are humans. God says we must resist the flesh and rely on Him for answers. We must not lean to our own understanding. Psychology sounds good and even right at times, but it is wrong thinking. If we back off and look at everything taught by psychology, it is totally man-centered. If we consider our dependence on God, then psychology makes no sense at all. Focusing on God will cause psychology to appear to be the lie that it really is.

FALSE HOPE

Christian counselors have turned to psychology and have released individuals with false hope. Yet, many claim their counseling sessions are working. Those counseled feel gratified because they were able to find someone who would listen as they poured out their hurts and divulged how others unfairly judged or misunderstood them. The counselor pacifies them with encouragement of their self-worth and value and does not point to the person's need to acknowledge and confess sin.

There is a difference between pain from past hurts and pain from one's own sin. Rarely do modern counselors instruct their couch-warmer to repent of his own sin. It seems all problems now are the result of mistreatment. Psychology ignores our basic sin nature, which is self-centered, covetous, envious, bitter, and easily offended. Instead of asking forgiveness, a person is told he needs to forgive others. This is definitely a biblically advised action, but psychology shifts a person's focus away from his own sin when pointing the finger so readily at others.

The only "sin" mentioned by psychology is the sin of unforgiveness. Why has this not been eliminated with all the others? It is because pointing to unforgiveness infers the problem is someone else's fault. If there is nobody to forgive, a person has to face his own self-centered nature. Once again, Satan puts a clever twist on Scripture by causing Christians to think they have done all to obey God when they forgive others.

We take it too far when we teach one principle to the detriment of others. Some, if not all, people have had devastating hurts in their childhood, but our answer is in Jesus, not in dwelling on how we were wounded. Did Jesus ever minister to past hurts? Did He ever heal people from rejection? One reference to pain in relation to the past is given in John. The disciples asked Jesus about a man blind from his birth. They asked, "'Master, who did sin, this man, or his parents, that he was born blind?' Jesus answered, 'Neither'" (John 9:2–3). He explained that the reason was so the "works of God should be made manifest" in the man (John 9: 3). It had nothing to do with the man's past.

The modern perspective of pain and suffering is distorted. The Christian once saw pain as an opportunity to learn. Songs formerly reflected that. The hearty attitude of former Christians thanked God for the mountains and the valleys. As Paul said, "I know both how to be abased, and I know how to abound: every where and in all things I am instructed both to be full and to be hungry, both to abound and to suffer need" (Phil. 4:12). Yet, today, we feel held back by our "valleys" and only view them as an obstruction to real life.

Satan has so cleverly brought psychology into the church. It seems he didn't have a hard time doing it. Psychology not only stirs up our sensitivity to pain, but then only tries to stick a wet Band-Aid on it. The Lord reminds us in Isaiah 30:1, "Woe to the rebellious children…that take counsel, but not of me; and that cover with a covering, but not of my spirit, that they may add sin to sin."

Christians enjoy counseling sessions since they gain the opportunity to talk about themselves. They go to several counselors until they find the one with remedies they want to hear. Psychologists advise their listeners to do whatever feels right and encourage them to be the judges of their own circumstances. This is to advise against the Bible and encourage men to do whatever is "right in his own eyes" (Judg. 21:25). They are told "peace, peace; when there is no peace" in their situation (Jer. 8:11). Most, then, go about their life committing the same sins and even adding other sins because they have been told their problem is all someone else's fault.

> Were they ashamed when they had committed abomination? Nay, they were not at all ashamed, neither could they blush.
>
> —Jeremiah 8:12

The basis of our trouble and bad behavior is not someone else's fault. Humans are not a hurting crowd, but a sinning one. Trouble is rooted in sin. Pain, in general, has resulted from sin. True counsel shines the light of truth on a person's life and reveals the distortion and disease of our hearts. If something genuinely unfair has happened to us to cause fear and mistrust, we must still turn to Jesus for help and not our mind's rationale. Our minds tend to nurture the wound and make it even more tender. While psychology keeps the wound tender, Jesus is able to heal.

Christian counselors are not advising repentance. Neither are they warning of resulting judgment. Psychologists are prophesying lies of peace in His name (Jer. 14:14). Church counselors, corrupted by psychology, sway with situation ethics and offer fickle advice. People are tossed to and fro with every wind of doctrine and, in the end, add sin to sin because of faulty counsel. Psychology tells Christians that their motives aren't as bad as they thought. They are urged to find someone from their childhood who can be charged for their weaknesses. Usually, it is the parents who catch the blame.

Psychologists urge people to break away from the lies of their parents and to say good-bye to their past. Satan is in every corner trying to establish this lie. He knows that once the old is thrown out, the new is more readily accepted. Americans are quickly accepting the deception that their parents' strong Judeo-Christian principles have hindered them and have held them back from reality.

Pastors use psychology as they appeal to our fleshly desire to hear that we have been made a victim of someone else's abuse. We hear we must deal with these hurts rather than being told to deal with sin. The opposite was taught in churches of the past. They taught that we must deal with sin, not hurt. Today, we are referred to counselors rather than the altar. We are pressed to forgive those who have done harm rather than consider asking forgiveness from others.

Do You Want the Truth?

Some church counselors are not using psychology. These particular church counselors are, in fact, telling the truth about a person's situation and are suggesting repentance, patience, trust, and prayer. But many today refuse to hear. If a person does not heed this godly counsel, he is in a serious predicament. He may not understand why his problem gets worse.

> Such as sit in darkness and in the shadow of death, being bound in affliction and iron; Because they rebelled against the words of God, and contemned the counsel of the most High.
>
> —Psalm 107:10–11

Because of more flattering results, Christians are refusing godly counsel and choosing psychology instead. However, the Bible warns, "They that observe lying vanities forsake their own mercy" (Jonah 2:8). Refusing the right answers causes a person to harden his resolve against truth, and he will find it leads him to a place he never intended to be. As Proverbs 29:1 says, "He, that being often reproved hardeneth his neck, shall suddenly be destroyed, and that without remedy."

Isaiah 59:8–10 explains:

> The way of peace they know not; and there is no judgment in their goings: they have made them crooked paths: whosoever goeth therein shall not know peace. Therefore is judgment far from us, neither doth justice overtake us: we wait for light, but behold obscurity; for brightness, but we walk in darkness. We grope for the wall like the blind,

and we grope as if we had no eyes: we stumble at
noon day as in the night; we are in desolate places
as dead men.

Psychology leaves no room for godly judgment. It gropes
in the dark corners of human reason for answers and refuses
the answers of the Bible, which are viewed as intolerant,
narrow-minded, and finger-pointing. Therefore, the results
of psychology are false peace and unsolved problems, leaving
those in its path as dead men.

The Pain Epidemic

Today, there is an excusing of sin. Psychology in the church
protects areas of weakness and sensitivity. It tells the person
he is wounded and needs healing. Church members do not
question this since the word *healing* implies biblical healing.
Psychology and many church counselors urge their clients
to think and talk about that area of pain they have always
protected. Yet, Charles Spurgeon does not call it pain. He
calls it sin. He pointed out in a sermon entitled "For the Sick
and Afflicted" that "even thus you do not like to search in a
certain quarter of your nature; it is a very tender subject—
something you feel very grieved about when anybody even
hints at it: it is just there that the sin is harbored."[3] There
are, of course, other types of pain, but Spurgeon's take on
the matter is one that is very rarely heard today.

We feel we must be treated with indulgence for our weaknesses. I have continually heard youth pastors telling young

people that their weaknesses were related to pain. Children did not hear that they were related to sin. We excuse our weaknesses as resulting from mistreatment or bad experiences in our life. Preachers are now saying that Christians divorce because their "heart has been broken." Not many preachers are saying that high divorce rates in America are a result of selfishness.

There once was a day when preachers stressed that in marriage there was no way out and that the commitment was for better or for worse. Now, "worse" is not acceptable, and a person's need for happiness and fulfilled dreams override their vows.

Preachers say people are hurting because their dreams and false expectations have been crushed. We do not hear how false expectations are usually self-centered and that they should die. How many enter a marriage relationship with false expectations for their spouse's happiness? I have never heard anyone say, "I am so disappointed in my marriage and want a divorce because my mate just didn't get everything he expected from me when we married."

Another proliferation related to the pain epidemic is the continual moans we hear from children. As a teacher, I heard constant concerns with being tired or not feeling well. Their symptoms were extremely minimal, yet they begged to go see the nurse or to call their mothers to come and take them home. Most children would consume at least one painkiller per day as part of their daily diet. A generation of quitters is soon coming to adulthood. Personally, I do not remember once taking an aspirin or any other painkiller while at school. Our school didn't even have a nurse. Can you believe I lived to tell about it?

Billy Graham has spoken of his childhood and how his family had no indoor plumbing, radio, or television. He said he worked from three o'clock in the morning until the sun went down. His mother would fix breakfast every morning at five thirty. He said he and his siblings were content. Yet today, he said, television cameras would be on the scene to see their lives as abused and neglected. He said he didn't even realize they had it so bad off.

Excuses of having it rough were not allowed in those days. Instead, accountability was taught to America's youth. If a person did not do his chores, he remained hungry that day or he received a reminder behind the wood shed. He knew it was his fault and nobody else's. Children weren't even allowed to open their mouths with excuses. There was no time to waste on that.

If we were serious about teaching what God's Word says about accountability, children would be more content. They could have the perspective of the older generation, who was easily encouraged rather than discouraged. When a person focuses on how bad things are, they become disheartened. When a person has been told he has been mistreated, something in him believes it. That something is a self-centered ego. We are misled when we are told our problems are related to someone else or to our circumstances. Then, we notice this is untrue when problems remain after we have been left alone. Difficulties linger even after the "abuser" is gone.

Mankind must acknowledge his own personal sin. Through repentance, fleeing temptation, and ignoring lusts, a person can find peace. If counselors directed their instruction toward the idea that we, too, are capable of the same behavior as our pain-inflictor, we could forgive more readily. If psychology's claims to low self-esteem were true, we could actually forgive without any prompting because we wouldn't even care if we were mistreated, but therein lies the proof that low self-esteem is not the problem. People do care if they are wronged and are sensitive about it because "no man ever yet hated his own flesh" (Eph. 5:29).

I have seen in youth services how psychology's influence has diverted times of repentance into times of selfish contemplation. When rare moments of quietness would occur, the youth leader would guide the child into dwelling on how he had been hurt, rejected, or stressed out. He would ask for those who wanted prayer to come forward. Many readily responded. After the service, the adults felt it was a wonderful time spent with the Lord because so many kids had gone forward for prayer. Why do we not realize that to go forward for someone else's sin is much easier than going forward for our own sin? There is a difference.

The popular gospel heard by our youth is one that implies Jesus is only a Savior from troubles, sadness, loneliness, despair, pain, and suffering. Scripture says He came to save us from sin. However, Jesus did say, "Come unto me, all ye that labour and are heavy laden, and I will give you rest" (Matt. 11:28). But, many today do not see that we can be heavy laden with the burden of sin. God definitely is our

Healer and Comforter, but He came primarily to save us from sin. I am not writing to ignore the issue of abuse, but to address the issue of avoiding sin.

There is a difference between our feigned insecurity and repentance's unselfish pleading. Jeremiah demonstrated this when he said, "We lie down in our shame, and our confusion covereth us: for we have sinned against the Lord our God, we and our fathers, from our youth even unto this day, and have not obeyed the voice of the Lord our God" (Jer. 3:25). This humility is lacking in today's shift toward psychology. Where do we hear of Christians realizing their unworthiness and congregations falling on their face in repentance?

The truth is, everyone has been mistreated by someone. There are people with genuine hurts and wounds. Some people have been sorely wounded and terribly hurt. They truly need comforting.

The trend I am condemning is a wallowing in self-pity and immediate blame on the past among church members. This natural tendency is encouraged by psychology's teachings. The answer is not in petting a wound. Rather, the need is for the true medicine, which stings. This medicine is called truth.

If it is true that today people's wounds are deeper than they used to be, then we need even more truth administered. Part of the truth involves the advice to "get over it." Our wounds need to dry up. When the scar is left, there should no longer be sensitivity. The pain should be forgotten when it is handed over to God. A person who truly trusts God with his hurt can genuinely forgive and forget.

Psychology focuses on a process rather than a solution. It focuses on the pain rather than the healing. Christians are being counseled for years for something that should be dealt with in two months or less. Most hurts can even be solved with one trip to the altar. Other hurts involve confession of one's own sin or rebellion. But, Satan coaxes Christians to spend hours of thought, conversation, and even prayers focused on their hurts and feelings.

Dwelling on certain hurts makes them more hurtful than they really are. Our perspective of pain is not always the right one. Most hurts are seen through eyes of selfishness. In the mean time, we are not thinking of others and are far from thinking about God. Psychology's focus is on humans. Satan knows what he is doing, yet we don't seem to have a clue.

Preachers waste precious time talking about a man's need for honor, a woman's need for security, a child's need for acceptance, everybody's right to be happy, and the need for human value and worth. These were once labeled desires of the flesh and preachers taught that they should die. Christians were not taught to focus on them. In modern times, though, it is the major focus of sermons. We all have needs, wants, and desires; but God said, "They that are Christ's have crucified the flesh with the affections and lusts" (Gal. 5:24). Dead men don't feel pain. A dead man doesn't need to be told to shut up because he keeps talking about his pain.

Easier but Costly

Satan would love to groom a generation so sensitive in their flesh that they would never want to feel uncomfortable. In this condition, they would be less resistant to his ultimate plan. Sensitive, tender flesh easily opts for comfort and an easy way out of adversity. Sensitive flesh would never resist the Antichrist when he is purging those who resist him.

As a result of psychology's influence, Christian parents guard their children from any form of rejection. Modern children are too sheltered from hurts by their parents. They do not realize that their kids need to experience it, especially if they are to walk a Christian life in an ungodly world. Rejection is what Jesus said we could expect. Instead, Christians think rejection is worse than any disease. They avoid it, rebuke it, and therefore, compromise with the world at every turn when they refuse to suffer rejection.

The more material wealth a person has, the less content he is. Why is that? It's because the flesh is never satisfied. The more it gets, the more it wants. Many "hurt" people in the counselor's chair are unhappy with their lives because they have too much. Can a person have too much? Of course. It's called being spoiled. It's a fitting word because it's not unlike what happens to old fruit. It's ugly, it stinks, and it draws flies. A person would be happier and less accusing if he had lived with some rejection or had suffered lack. Remember the story previously mentioned about Billy Graham?

Humanistic psychology's belief of internal goodness tells us we deserve wealth and that we deserve better than what we have. It feeds the greed in us all. Many are choosing to swallow the lies of modern psychology and feel that their desires are legitimate and that all their appetites deserve sympathetic attention.

Why are Christians seeking to deal with wrong behavior (sin) in the church with a handbook other than the Bible? How can congregation members show up at counseling sessions and agree with what they've been told from a psychologist? People do not know God's Word, nor do they seem to care. They would much rather be petted and receive sympathy than hear about repentance and obedience. Most people want instant answers, and they are not willing to wait on godly counsel (Ps. 106:13).

Certain people would reject counsel advising them to wait on their spouse and patiently pray. Today, when a person has made up his mind about getting a divorce, he finds the counselor who agrees with him. Have you noticed the number of church counselors who tell their clients to go ahead and get a divorce because they understand the hurt is too bad. The Bible says pain is not the issue. Obedience to His commandments is the issue. We should obey God no matter how much it hurts. He doesn't even promise that obedience will remove the pain. Martyrs learned that firsthand. They died, anyway. Would we rather do it God's way or man's? Most are choosing man's way because it is so much easier.

Some are teaching that the strongholds mentioned in the Bible are actually wounds from early lies you've been told by your parents or other authority figures. However, the real lie is from that teacher, not the person's parents. In our culture's rejection of so-called lies from the past and lies from child-hood, people are wholeheartedly swallowing the lies of today. Strongholds are sin, not hurts. Second Corinthians 10:5 mentions these strongholds as being "imaginations, and every high thing that exalteth itself against the knowledge of God." Christians have been fully convinced that what holds them back is fear, insecurity, or mistreatment. In reality, it is sin, rebellion, disobedience, and selfishness that hold the Christian back. Christians have the answers to their prob-lems, but are refusing to implement them because they are too difficult to confront.

While faithfully attending psychology classes, a certain Christian was trying to attain a counseling degree. In a conversation I had with this person, we discussed giving counsel to people. I tried to understand the predicament of being a psychologist and a Christian and said that at least a Christian counselor has the answer and can tell a person about sin. The response from this psychologist and another co-worker in the room was that it was not ethical in coun-seling to talk about sin because it does not allow the client to come to his own conclusion. I was told a counselor cannot offer direction to that end. Does psychology outweigh God's great commission? What a rip-off for the client. The Chris-tian counselor has the answer, but refuses to give it. So, psychologists cannot offer true answers that will really help because the person may not believe it will help? They have to think of it themselves? People can do that for free. That must be why they make so much money in requiring continued attendance since the problem is never dealt with.

Because the world is so heavily influenced by psychology, we Christians think we must get involved, too. There is no difference between a church using psychology to solve problems and a church using a Ouija board, crystal ball, the Koran, tarot cards, or the Satanist handbook. Christians influenced by psychology are not far from fortune telling, urging their client to be encouraged because they see only good in their future and for them not to worry about past mistakes.

> He blesses himself in his heart, saying, I shall have peace, though I walk in the imagination of mine heart, to add drunkenness to thirst.
>
> —Deuteronomy 29:19

Compromising Christians are the delight of Satan. He'll have them on his front lines leading others astray down the road to delusion. When the foundation of any teaching is not rooted in God's Word, it is not worthy of our time. The fruits produced from roots that are embedded in lies are also lies. Can a corrupt tree bring forth good fruit? No, a corrupt tree cannot bring forth good fruit (Matt. 7:18). Satan has come into the church through psychology. Those who seek to bring only its good and leave the bad outside do not realize that there is no good in it. We must stop getting blind-sided by Satan as he persuades us into thinking there is some good in everything and certain things are harmless if used only on a small scale. Look at history to see how a nation goes downhill. It's not overnight.

While man thinks he is improving, he is quickly sliding in his depravity. Yet, psychology tells us that we are naturally good. It teaches us that our natural drive and motivation is for goodness. It claims that everyone's ego must be praised. Is an ego a good thing? This belief is also in line with evolutions' doctrine because they both allege that all things are progressing and getting better. This slanted perspective is easy to fall for, but damaging in that it is far from truth.

A handbook of psychology for pastoral counselors included this explanation under the heading "original sin:"

> No reputable psychologist would hold the ancient theological theory that sin is passed on from generation to generation....Our inherited drives, for example, are our equipment. As such they are amoral....So long as there is this disparity (for which the individual person is not responsible) there is more than a myth in the doctrine that we are not easily made into saints.[4]

Original sin is a theory? Our inherited drives are "equipment" and are indifferent to morality? It's a myth to believe people cannot easily be made into saints? To believe people are "easily" made into saints implies the road to eternal life is broad and the road to hell is narrow, but that is not what the Bible teaches. How can we agree with a doctrine that denies the truth of original sin? How can we counsel while believing humans have no sin nature? How can we compromise by believing humans do have a sin nature, yet still rely on psychology? The internal root of human problems is denied in psychology and supplanted with reasoning that the root is external, environmental, or caused by someone else.

LIES ARE NOT TRUE

Psychology tells us that we are in no need of improvement. Praise is freely given and is not always based on merit but on just *being*. Unmerited praise breeds laziness, and we are seeing just that trait in today's children. Children think they have already arrived at a state of greatness because they constantly hear praise and even receive medals for mere attendance. This impedes motivation to do better. Children see no need to try because reward comes for both trying and not trying.

If a child notices that he is not so great yet continually hears that he is, he becomes depressed and discouraged because "greatness" is not all it's cracked up to be. Our children need the honest truth. The truth is that humans are not great and that worth comes only from Jesus. The answer is Jesus plus nothing.

One pastor on a television program said that God wanted to heal wounds and hurts. Then she said God was coming back for a pure and spotless bride. The implication was that the bride would be cleansed of hurts, not sin. Did this pastor believe there was no sin nature in need of cleansing in order to be presented as Christ's bride? That would be the likely interpretation of young people, especially, since they have not heard otherwise. What a perversion of Scripture and a negation of Jesus' death and resurrection. It is error to think we are only dirty because someone else hurt us.

Hurt feelings are a major focus of psychology. One particular pamphlet distributed at a women's retreat listed classes offered that weekend. From healing after abortion to surviving cancer, hurts were covered. When that many women get together, wouldn't it be a great opportunity to open the Bible and learn about the Lord? We are currently shifting our focus away from God and onto ourselves. Studying His Word may not appear to solve "hurts," but it really does. All those attending classes could have been healed in one class about Jesus. The Holy Spirit receives an invitation when Jesus is the focus. In a moment, the Holy Spirit is able to blanket every person in an entire group with comfort.

Since so much credit is given to human feelings, some church doctrines are now being written that oppose God's Word. They implement psychology's solutions instead of biblical ones. Some churches grant approval of divorce based upon "emotional abandonment." The world labels "alien-ation of affection" as an ample reason for divorce. What's the difference? Worldly church policy now overrides God's counsel.

Psychology deals wrongly with human behavior. Its perspective is erroneous in that unacceptable behavior is blamed on society rather than on our sin nature. The Bible is very clear about what causes problems in life. It is not the outward influences, but the inward problem of sin. Mark 7:15 clearly states, "There is nothing from without a man, that entering into him can defile him: but the things which come out of him, those are they that defile the man."

This weakness causes us to have three enemies, according to the Bible—the world, the flesh, and the devil. The Bible doesn't say our parents, society, or our environment are our enemies. Psychology is in direct opposition to the Word of God. It is an "opposition of science" that Timothy was warned about by Paul (1 Tim. 6:20).

Another pathetic principle of psychology is to say that all of our actions and reactions springboard from these hurts and needs. We blame our fit of anger on the fact that we are hurting, in spite of the fact that the person we just hit is the one bleeding. We steal candy as a child because we want acceptance from our friends. One Christian speaker said she went to parties when she was a teenager to avoid being with herself. Does any of these reasons conjure up sympathy for the transgressor? Yes. Does this point of view reflect that people have a rebellious, sin nature? No. Two psychologists on television asserted that a tantrum is a cry for help. I guess they haven't witnessed some of the tantrums I've seen. The fact is, human nature sins, and when given the opportunity, it sins again. We hit people, steal, lie, cheat, gamble, lust, etc. because we are selfish and our heart is desperately wicked. To gain sympathy for manipulators, controllers, murderers, wife abusers, child molesters, robbers, sluggards, and liars because they are the ones hurting is ridiculous. Yet, we Christians are doing just that.

Instead of admitting jealousy, one pastor alleged "insecurity" that his dad never took him fishing. He said he was insecure when he saw his friend's new fishing pole. Another pastor's sermon outline defined *covetousness* as an unhealthy need for things to make up for a lack of a secure, nurturing relationship. Either he added his own psychology or he had a humanistic dictionary. My dictionary says to covet is simply to long for something belonging to someone else. There is a difference in wanting something because you want to be nurtured and wanting something because someone else has it. One sounds innocent, the other selfish. It's a simple twist, but it is a devastating twist because the focus shifts from truth to a lie, from a sinful sinner to a hurting victim.

A youth pastor told the story of a kid who held a gun to his head and pulled the trigger in front of his parents. The gun was empty. The pastor sympathetically declared, "He just wanted to be noticed." Is it not cruel to do that to your parents? We don't seem to consider that the teen may have been wanting to scare his parents because he thought it would be funny. We do not consider the likelihood of his being a defiant rebel refusing to submit to his father's will. None of these options seem to be mentioned in many churches. So, prayer for this individual is not for repentance, but for better parents. Satan not only grins to see this diversion in prayer but actually releases a satisfied giggle.

I have heard youth pastors say time and time again, "Some of you are chasing relationships so hard because you need security and approval." Christian parents even think this is true and agree that this counsel is really helping their teen, but they do not see the dangerous focus on the flesh. They see no resulting change in their teens, but they feel it could be worse if they weren't attending such a "wonderful" youth group. I say it could be better if their teens were hearing more about Jesus and less about themselves.

Christian teachers use psychology studies to tell their students about brain research and how the brain develops from childhood. They speak of the importance of love and touch and comfort. Who would argue with such a tender message? Beware of modern brain research, because it is trying to prove one thing. It tries to prove evolution is true. Evolutionists believe the human brain is now evolving, rather than the body. We cannot trust research that implies newfound states of "higher consciousness." Recent studies are pointing toward higher ability levels in the human brain. They are claiming sixth senses and quantum leaps in the evolutionary cycle. Beware! Even ADD has been attributed as an incredible gift rather than a hindrance because new research claims there are genetic mutations in people with ADD.[5]

Today, praise is given when energy, creativity, and humor are allowed to run wild. Where did Jesus praise energy, creativity, or humor? Where did He praise lack of restraint and a person's running wild? This teaching sounds valid, but it is not. Let's not be gullible in believing goodness resides in our souls as a driving force that unleashes our potential through "unrestricted" actions.

Another influence from the influx of psychology into our culture is when parents feel strongly that their daughters must spend quality time with their fathers or they will likely seek love "in other places." What a diversion from truth.

Notice the shift of focus to human answers and the subtle excuse for one's own shortcomings when young. As a result, fathers are taking their daughters on "dates" and buying them everything they want, coddling them at every turn. They are surprised when this does not solve the problem.

In fact, teenage pregnancy among Christians is, in fact, very common. Psychology needs to be rejected and parents need to direct their daughters to the love of Christ. When that is found, she will remain true to her heavenly Father, not her earthly one.

Psychology's humanistic slant claims that shortcomings and other adult attitudes are determined by the amount of parental approval received during childhood. It stresses the importance of human approval in every area of life. However, the Bible does not teach that our assurance is in human affirmation. Christians should be taught by church leaders that their ultimate goal is in seeking affirmation from their heavenly Father, which only comes through Christ.

We find in the book of Isaiah that the focus is on God and not on man.

> I, even I, am he that comforteth you: who art thou, that thou shouldest be afraid of a man that shall die, and of the son of man which shall be made as grass.
>
> —Isaiah 51:12

Jesus is able to comfort us because He was "despised and rejected of men; a man of sorrows, and acquainted with grief" (Isa. 53:3).

Psychology will lead Christian counselors to advise their "hurting" victim against having any guilt, but notice how the lack of guilt correlates with innocence. Christians view guilt as wrong. Guilt is, in fact, a good and healthy feeling. Without it, we would all have very few friends. Children in our modern churches are being conditioned to think that guilt is of the devil. What a progression of our depravity to not only sin, but to sin and have no guilt. This is the tonic for a seared conscience. Satan loves for Christians to erase the guilt factor.

In one particular chapel service I attended, the teacher said to the children, "Go back in your mind's eye and find the first time you felt fear." She continued to tell them that the fear began with a lie. They were told to tell the enemy to leave them alone. This process was designed to erase any fear. Children who had disobeyed a parent and remembered their "fear" of getting caught were consoled. Their healthy fear was stagnated, never to be nurtured into a fear of the Lord.

When a person believes that answers to life are resident within his own soul, he then desires to tap into that "energy source." Beware of the practice when counselors or teachers instruct you to close your eyes and go back into your memory to evaluate the past. It is not a biblical practice, but a pagan one. Dwelling on human thoughts and inner feelings is not edifying.

Others tell their listeners to close their eyes and imagine whatever they would like to have. The person is encouraged to imagine his biggest dreams. Children are constantly being told to "follow their dreams." Then, just like television programs and commercials proclaim, we Christians believe that if we want it, we can have it. Human intuition, gut feelings, and first thoughts that come to mind are all sought by modern Christians. Nobody seems to notice their reliance on fallen humanity rather than on God. The deception here is in thinking once a person receives Jesus into his life, he automatically can trust his intuition. Our flesh remains untrustworthy. Man's spirit must be nurtured with Bible reading and prayer. The longer a person spends with God, the safer he will be. To know what God says is to know His Word. God never suggested that we rely on gut feelings.

THE DEVASTATING RESULTS OF BELIEVING LIES

The repercussions of this fatal move toward rejecting Christ, our Rock, will be devastating. Saul died for his transgression against the Lord by seeking ungodly counsel (1 Chron. 10:13). In the song of Moses written in Deuteronomy 32, God abhorred His people because they were "unmindful" of the Rock that begat them. He called them children in whom was "no faith." God was "provoked to jealousy" because they were a "nation void of counsel" and understanding. Their enemies became their judges. He warned that their "foot would slide in due time" and that their "calamity" was at hand. The warning was that the Lord would judge His people. Today, we too have rejected the counsel of God. We are seeking answers from Christianity's enemies, Jung and Freud. They have become our judges.

It is sobering to know that God gives people up to their own hearts' lust and allows them to walk in their own counsels (Ps. 81:12). If psychology is what we want, He will let us have it. We cannot passively say He will guide us into truth when we are not seeking it. Our attitude of "don't worry, be happy" will be one of our greatest regrets on judgment day.

Christians everywhere are easily accepting humanistic psychology's motto that "everyone comes from a dysfunctional family." Well, if a person is human, something was dysfunctional the moment he was born. That's a given, if it has to be labeled. We could also argue that no family is dysfunctional because that's the way human families function, given their weak covering, called flesh. Why have churches decided to dwell on dysfunction so much? Is it because we are teaching humanistic psychology?

Humanism's intent is to erase any traditional, Christian beliefs, but it cannot accomplish this task overnight. The first step to wiping out this belief system is inculcating society with the idea that the past may hold mistakes and that they are the reason for dysfunction.

If psychology can successfully cause people to doubt their parents' instruction and feel betrayed by people of their past, it can then successfully cause people to embrace new teachings that are neither traditional, nor Christian. The page has to be erased before new writings can be put on it. Psychology is erasing Christians' minds from facts about right and wrong taught to them by their parents and traditional churches.

God, not humans, gets the last word by saying only "a small number" shall escape the sword, and they "shall know whose words shall stand, mine, or theirs" (Jer. 44:28).

Chapter 4

COMPLACENCY

He that justifieth the wicked, and he that condemneth the just, even they both are abomination to the LORD.

—Proverbs 17:15

A COMPLACENT CHRISTIAN IS one who is sluggish in his duty and lacks responsibility. He is self-satisfied, lacking in self-criticism, and is content with his walk in Christ. He does not live with an expectancy of Christ's coming. In short, he does not resist the devil. He lives and lets live.

One of the main culprits used to kill a Christian's mind-set for duty is the psychology teaching against "performance." Christians now fear they are performing when that is really the enemy renaming their obedience. But, Christians must be soldiers. Paul told Timothy in 1 Timothy 1:18–19 that he must "war a good warfare; Holding faith, and a good conscience; which some having put away concerning faith have made shipwreck." The action suggested in these two verses is to "war" and to "hold." It requires courage, boldness, vigilance, and strength. On the other hand, it's easy to "put away" our duty, our weapons, and our faith. We must keep holding the fort and not be complacent Christians.

In war, a complacent soldier can jeopardize the whole war. If he is told to guard the entrance to the camp and does not, the enemy can get in. If he is told to chase the enemy down and does not, the enemy can get away.

A soldier must be alert, active, reactive, and refuse to be casual in dealing with the enemy. Good defense is not casual, nor complacent. Resistance against any force must be stronger than the opposing force. Satan is never casual or half-hearted in his assault. In fact, when he sees neglect in opposition, he comes in with relentless attacks.

In a spiritual sense, it is true that our resistance against Satan is already stronger since we have Jesus on our side and we can claim the victory has already been won. Modern preaching and teaching seem to emphasize this victory without mention of the problems that remain as long as we are alive in the flesh and alive on the earth. Until we are in the grave, we must be soldiers who take our earthly duty very seriously.

Christian children are growing up believing that there is no obligation to resist evil and that all things just naturally work together for good. They do not hear that "good" only works out for those who love God and are called according to His purpose (Rom 8:28; 2 Tim. 1:9). They do not hear the difference between God's purposes and their own. Working out God's purpose and not our own involves a struggle. It is a spiritual contest.

One young senior in high school commented that "God causes truth to go forth through ungodly people, too." Our children are so bombarded with evolution-based thinking that they believe good will naturally happen. They do not worry about contending for truth or the outcome of the future because they are taught in the world and inside the church that even without a struggle, goodness and profitable results will always occur. A Christian lady told me while trying to demonstrate her carefree, happy life that if she needed to know anything, God would tell her. Is that an attitude that does not fear deception or realize the weakness of the flesh?

There is a struggle for truth. It can be hindered and even squelched if we do not stand up for it. It is not a responsibility we should take lightly. However, we are not left to ourselves to defeat Satan. We can look to Jesus as our guide. He is our general, and we must obey His orders. We must see life on earth as a war zone and realize that there truly is a battle for truth. If we see no battle, we will never put up a resistance. Until Christians see the conflict, they will continue to feel content and complacent. Until we awake to the fact that we are bombarded with principalities, powers, rulers of the darkness, and spiritual wickedness, we will continue to feel unthreatened and content (Eph. 6:12). As long as our comfortable lifestyle does not look to be in jeopardy, we will continue to be undisturbed by the conditions around us.

We have lived with unholiness for so long, we have come to view it as natural and even expected. We are not frustrated when we see unfaithfulness in our politicians, teachers, or friends. We are not disappointed to hear our pastors telling small lies or failing to stand up for truth.

Christians do not want to know about spiritual attacks on their families. They will agree that the devil, in general, is against their family, but deny it when faced with specifics. When a particular movie, TV program, video game, or even school curriculum is brought to light, they refuse to confront the problem. They don't want to see it because it requires action.

Immediate justification arises in their insistence that the named program or game is not really influenced by Satan. They believe there is a big gray category for movies and games and that, even though they violate Christian principles, they do little harm. Christians are justifying Satan's crafty devices in the name of "everyone is doing it."

The devil loves it when Christians have a vague concept of him. Like in war, if soldiers continue to generalize where the enemy is located and fail to pin him down to a certain area, he will never be caught. Some Christians feel it is too radical and paranoid to name specific movies as being demon-inspired, but cautious people don't go to sleep when the enemy is on the loose. Of course, the secular TV media will always point to Christians as being paranoid or radical to bridle them. Our complacency must stop, and in spite of name-calling and ridicule, we must stand up for truth and stand against the enemy.

I have talked to some Christians who look very uncomfortable and look away when the sinful parts of movies or video games are mentioned. They choose to overlook those parts and just "glean the good." That is exactly what the devil wants. While you're gleaning, you're getting contaminated, indoctrinated, and even more calloused to sin. Christians should immediately and adamantly refuse to attend a movie or participate in any program that has been previewed with the filth and profanity that so many contain. Instead, we get caught up in the storyline or we are partial to the lead actor/actress and just simply overlook the impurities. We even justify the filth because there are actually good parts in the movie. Because one guy prayed or one lady forgave her sister, the movie gets a stamp of approval.

Are we just ignorant to the tactics of the enemy? Do we think like a mouse approaching a trap that we can glean the good and walk away only with the cheese? If we can't see down the road to where all the off-color language, thoughts, and actions are leading, we are deserving of what awaits us. While we are complacently agreeing with the enemy by not resisting him, he is leading us into a trap. If he can just sear our conscience until sin doesn't even feel like sin, Satan can advances his troops. He is patient enough to wait as long as it takes. He'll wait until he has a completely calloused, oblivious group of participants to help him in his grand end-times scheme. With this generation, he feels that his waiting has paid off.

Feeling secure and being complacent is only a feeling. Relying on those feelings and not facts, is unwise. Satan wants the Christian to feel secure in his sin. When a person is comfortable, he won't usually change. On the other hand, if a person feels guilty or insecure, he may want to change. Feeling comfortable in sin is Satan's goal for the Christian. When a person is comfortable and feels no guilt when participating in sin, that person is deceived. When he has no prick in his spirit upon seeing or hearing sin, he has a calloused conscience.

Satan will be able to employ a person who is totally unreceptive to the Holy Spirit. That person will be an available tool for further deception and hardening of the hearts of others in their sin. David Jeremiah wrote in *Escape the Coming Night* that "to believe the solemn truths of prophecy and then make our way complacently through a world of sin and shame is not merely unfortunate, it is criminal."[1]

It is dangerous in these last days to be complacent Christians. Deception is at an all-time high. Evil men and seducers are waxing worse and worse, deceiving and being deceived (2 Tim. 3:13) If we claim peace and safety from the enemy, then sudden destruction will surely come and we will not escape (1 Thess. 5:3). A live frog in a pan of water is unsuspecting of his death by degrees as the water slowly reaches boiling. So have increments of sinful living dulled our senses. We do not realize that each degree of sin is headed toward death and destruction. Our consciences are so dulled and calloused that we are not feeling the heat. William Penn concluded that it is the "design of the devil, where he cannot involve and draw into gross sin, is to busy, delight, and allure the minds of men and women by more seeming innocent entertainments, on purpose that he may more easily secure them from minding their duty and progress and obedience to the only true God, which is eternal life; and thereby take up their minds from heavenly and eternal things."[2]

How have Christians reached this point of gullibility? We have done it through our lack of love for the truth. French philosopher Blaise Pascal said, "Truth is so obscure in these times and falsehood so established, that unless we love the truth, we cannot know it."[3] To love the truth involves seeking after it. It involves reading His Word and finding a preacher that preaches it. It's a fight. We must seek it with effort, not complacency.

WRONG ACTIONS AND COMPLACENT INACTION

Our actions of self-fulfillment and our inaction in standing for truth proves our complacency. We seem content with the amount of truth we already know. Polls have indicated that fewer than half of Christians use the Bible as a source for answers in life. Most base their decisions on pleasing results and make choices that involve the least conflict.

> For when we ought to be teachers, we have need that one teach us the first principles of the oracles of God and we are become such as have need of milk, and not of strong meat.
>
> —Hebrews 5:12, author's paraphrase

Instead of reacting to life based on the truth of the Bible, we choose the childish, conflict-free route.

However, it requires conflict to obey God's commandments and conflict to disobey the desires of the flesh. This childish approach is not only in congregation members, but also among church employees. I wonder how many church employees choose to avoid conflict by telling small white lies. Do they feel a twinge of guilt afterward, or does everyone do it? Do church secretaries say, "He's not here right now," when the pastor is just around the corner? Do preachers say, "I'll be on vacation all next week," when that is not exactly the case? Is integrity and honesty implied in churches, or is it real?

Do we ever question comments from the pulpit? Do we ever seek out answers from God's Word, or do we trust a man to get truth for us? Christians relied on the church for answers in Europe in the sixteenth century before Martin Luther exposed its error. Many Christians, then, could not even read the Bible and trusted church leaders to tell them what it said.

What was then considered to be a restraint on freedom is now seen as a privilege. Now we view overhead excerpts of Scripture as someone doing the work for us. We are glad we don't have to bother taking a Bible to church. We wonder how people in the Dark Ages could believe their pastor when he told them they could buy their salvation with pieces of paper called indulgences. Do we wonder why Christians believe similar lies from the pulpit today? Are the people of the Dark Ages who had no Bible printed in their language more accountable for truth, or are we more accountable, who do have the Bible printed in abundance in our language?

Complacency is not hard to detect in the modern Christian. When questions about God's Word do arise in our hearts, we have opportunity to search for truth. Instead, we find it easier to opt for the tanning bed, a day at the spa, or a special day of shopping or golf.

What about the Sabbath? Do we remember to keep it holy? Do we set aside time for God only? Do we train our kids on a daily basis that prayer before meals is important? (See 1 Timothy 4:3; Romans 14:6.) What about prayer in public? Do we as Christians witness to the world with the simple act of praying in restaurants? We fear how it looks and listen to lies from Satan advocating complacency. We are not in the habit of praying, and we just "keep forgetting;" but it is never too late to begin. Satan loves complacency in everyday activities. In fact, if the children are not trained now, Satan will be able to bring them even stronger delusion when they're grown.

Some Christians interpret having a good time with Christian friends as having spent time with God. Some Christians are content because they attend church and even a small group every week. However, until we walk away from these meetings affected by God, the time spent there profits little. All our righteousness is as filthy rags to God. A content, self-satisfied walk is no good. When we are not affected by God's Word, we leave the meeting and immediately start to consider where we will dine. We turn on the radio for news or entertainment. We may start talking about something unimportant. On the other hand, an affected Christian will not resist spiritual matters and will strive to be significant for the Lord's sake.

When Christians say they have spent quality time with the Lord, it's not always true. We settle for flowery words because deeds are too costly. We ought to write down how we spend twenty-four hours in a day and by the end of the week or month see just how much time is actually spent with God. It doesn't count if it's only under a label of time with God. A meeting of Christians may be just that, with no actual encounter with God. Are we Christians in name only? Is our time actually spent in prayer, fasting, and the Bible, or with the Internet, television, and friends?

The regretful consequence of being slothful is that it leads to even more laziness. Once a rock starts rolling downhill, it picks up momentum and then it's hard to stop. Gravity pulls toward laziness. Proverbs 19:15 says, "Slothfulness casteth into a deep sleep; and an idle soul shall suffer hunger." Our complacency doesn't stop with our sitting down. It leads to lying down, then sleeping. As a result, our spiritual man suffers. We find ourselves "eating" things we never would have a year ago because we are suffering from hunger and are too lazy to "eat" from the good table provided for us by God's Word.

We must remain standing! We must learn our lessons about lying down. Our nation is now killing approximately 3,700 babies each day through abortion because we haven't stood.[4] We must have a zeal for righteousness. Our enemy has an agenda and intends to use his zeal to accomplish it. Until Christians resist with equally intense determination, we will suffer great consequences. Resistance takes effort, not complacency. When we decide to wage war, we can stop the enemy in his tracks.

In our complacency, Christians have failed to take the Bible literally. We have overlooked the importance of how God's Word stands alone. We do not need supplemental materials to study truth. We feel we must look up the words to see what the "real" meaning is, so we look in a man-made Bible dictionary. Shouldn't we prefer God's Word over man's? Do we truly believe we are holding God's Word in our hands, or just a fair rendition of it? We must trust the Lord to have preserved His Word throughout all languages and stop trying to better it. We are straining at gnats and swallowing camels in our search for truth in every place but where it really is. The Bible says what is says and means what it means.

If we would have our Bibles in hand at a Bible study and not a book written by a man, then maybe we would learn more about God and less about ourselves. Christian books are not necessarily wrong, but a lot of Christians need to study their Bibles first. If we were studying the Bible on our own at home, then a Bible study using a good book could bring edification. However, many Christians never open their Bible and then attend a Bible study where they don't open one either.

I have heard comments of how we as Christians should read Milton's *Paradise Lost* in order to know what is in it. This was recommended since "most Christians quote it instead of the Bible anyway." Why add to the problem? One Christian said she read Milton's poem every year. The reaction to this by another Christian was, "Cool." Are we impressed if someone reads *Paradise Lost* but unimpressed with those who spend time reading the Bible?

There is irony in our complacency. We uphold the very things we say we reject. While attending a National Honor Society meeting for a Christian high school, I saw how the students were honored for their character, scholarship, leadership, and service. One student who was being honored commented in his speech that he would "make this short" because he knew everyone wanted "to go home and watch" the last episode of a certain television program known for its indecency. This student was being honored for character, and he was bold enough to admit he watched a filthy TV show? Evidently he wasn't trying to hide it from his parents, since they were in attendance, too. Those present only laughed at his comments and did not see the irony.

Why don't we care about right and wrong? Why don't we care about the dire signs of Satan's influence? I have heard disputes over doctrine end with, "If God did or didn't, who cares?" Don't we as Christians care? Do we readily admit that we don't care because searching it out is too difficult and may require precious time away from fun and entertainment?

Modern teachings promote feelings of complacency toward truth. Preachers and teachers try to comfort their listeners with notions that God does not expect them to be perfect. They preach how to escape the "ought to" mentality, but Jesus' perfection should always be our goal, whether we achieve it or not. Jesus said, "Be ye therefore perfect, even as your Father which is in heaven is perfect" (Matt. 5:48).

We must not lower the standard with comments like, "Don't worry, you don't have to be perfect," because that is not what the Bible tells us.

Ignorance will not be counted as innocence on judgment day. We are accountable to know right from wrong. Just because we aren't aware of a sin doesn't mean consequences will be overlooked. We are required to know God's Word since we have been given it freely in America. To whom much is given, much is required. (See Luke 12:48.) We cannot assume that just because we are Christians, we will not make errors.

To continue our daily lives with the attitude that we are only doing what the Holy Spirit approves of without searching it out is an arrogant approach. We should question our motives, question our actions, and question our decisions. We must live our lives in fear and trembling because we may be ignorantly violating God's holy law. I am speaking to happy, carefree, complacent Christians, not those who already live in humility.

Christian children are not being taught in their services to question their motives because of a sin nature. Instead, they are encouraged to let their motives and ideas escape freely and taught to believe they have pure motives because they are the youth of a new and better generation. This is error.

To commit a sin unknowingly is still a sin. The sin is in not knowing since Bibles are available and no law prohibits reading them. James wrote, "Therefore, to him that knoweth to do good, and doeth it not, to him it is sin" (4:17). There's no reason for us to be ignorant of God's Word. Just because we do not feel the guilt does not mean we are innocent. That should not be our gauge. I have heard Christians tell of their tampering with worldliness and casually say, "I didn't feel corrupted." Does that mean they were not corrupted? Our feeling about a situation has nothing to do with it. In fact, we are deceived when we do not feel guilty. Hitler didn't feel guilty, either.

The purposes for knowing God's commandments are written in Psalm 19:11–14:

> Moreover by them is thy servant warned: and in keeping them there is great reward. Who can understand his errors? cleanse thou me from secret faults. Keep back thy servant also from presumptuous sins; let them not have dominion over me: then shall I be upright, and I shall be innocent from the great transgression. Let the words of my mouth, and the meditation of my heart, be acceptable in thy sight, O LORD, my strength, and my redeemer.

We learn from the psalmist that we are capable of "secret faults" that we don't even know about. We have a natural tendency to be presumptuous about our relationship with God. We naturally feel better than we are.

This downfall of man contributes to our inability to deal with things that are serious. Complacency is common among Christians who believe Jesus' return is not in the near future. We and our children especially have been encouraged to dream big by society and pastors alike. We feel nothing will stop us from having all we want. We do not want Jesus to interfere by taking us to heaven. Life is too good, and we don't see how it could get any better. We have all the money, time, and gadgets anyone would want. But, of course, we would like more. God tells us we are to "love not the world, neither the things that are in the world…For all that is in the world, the lust of the flesh, and the lust of the eyes, and the pride of life, is not of the Father, but is of the world" (1 John 2: 15–16). The attitude in many churches is, "Please, Lord, don't come quickly."

William Penn nailed it with this comment:

> Thus are their minds employed, and so vain are they in their imaginations, and dark in their understandings, that they not only believe them innocent, but persuade themselves they are good Christians all this while, and to rebuke them is worse than heresy. Thus are they strangers to the hidden life.[5]

Leonard Ravenhill said, "We do not have revival because we are content to live without it."[6]

There are complacent excuses for why Jesus is believed to be delaying His coming. I heard from a youngster who hoped Jesus would linger in heaven that, "The gospel hasn't been preached everywhere, yet." This comment was given while I was teaching about Africa and the small villages hidden in the jungle. However, the gospel has already reached every nation (Rev. 14:6). We always use that reference as a condition to be met before the rapture and do not hear of the likelihood of it as a condition to be met before the second coming. Conditions are ripe for the rapture. It is feasible that the gospel could then spread everywhere in the tribulation by God's 144,000 evangelists.

People who complacently think they have all the time in the world to prepare for Christ may not know that:

> There shall come in the last days scoffers, walking after their own lusts, And saying, Where is the promise of his coming? for since the fathers fell asleep, all things continue as they were from the beginning of the creation. For this they willingly are ignorant of….The Lord is not slack concerning his promise…but is longsuffering to us-ward, not willing that any should perish, but that all should come to repentance. But the day of the Lord will come as a thief in the night.
>
> —2 Peter 3:3–5, 9–10

We should be living for His coming. If today's Christian truly believed Jesus was coming at any moment like he or she believed the sun would come up tomorrow, there would be marked differences in their actions, speech, dress, and focus.

As mentioned in the previous psalm, many of us are guilty of presumptuous sins. We take for granted a relationship with God, assume He is our friend, and presume all is well. With today's "I'm worth it" mentality, presumption is even encouraged. We tell ourselves what we wish were true and therefore justify sin while living with false peace and comfort. We start to believe that God created us to live a simple, cozy life of satisfaction and pleasure.

We idly neglect the duty to deny ourselves and our own fleshly desires. We are lethargic to live righteously before God as a witness to a sinful world. First John 1:6 tells us, "If we say that we have fellowship with Him, and walk in darkness, we lie, and do not the truth."

Proverbs 1:20, 22–25, 27–29, 32 warns of the following:

> Wisdom crieth without.…How long, ye simple ones, will ye love simplicity?…Turn you at my reproof…Because I have called, and ye refused; I have stretched out my hand, and no man regarded; But ye have set at nought all my counsel, and would none of my reproof.…when distress and anguish come upon you. Then shall they call upon me, but I will not answer…For that they hated knowledge, and did not choose the fear of the Lord.…For the turning away of the simple shall slay them, and the prosperity of fools shall destroy them.

Wisdom cries out. Do we refuse to hear? Do we not see how we are walking on the edge of a cliff with our American Christian conceit? We should fall to our knees in humility for our lack of action and vigilance. We must ask God to "teach us to number our days, that we may apply our hearts unto wisdom" (Ps. 90:12).

I have counted the minutes that actually go into speaking truth in some church services, and it is very, very minimal.

These churches have chosen to load their services with video advertisements, funny skits, more singing, and even sports activities. In the mean time, another week goes by and the congregation is not fed much truth, if any. Usually an hour or two is set aside for a church service. In an hour service for children, I have seen the first five minutes used for jokes; the next ten minutes used to talk about the speaker's week, with comments about unmentioned sins laughingly disguised with "I won't go into that;" then the remainder of time filled with references to film clips or movies for a "life lesson." Only one or two scriptures were actually quoted. Sometimes these scriptures are used out of context and even misquoted.

One well-known guest speaker took the time to gather clips from a secular movie and used them to teach how words of teachers can absolutely destroy you and how the teacher in the movie was fighting for her student's soul. He pointed out how "it will destroy you if you gain your worth from other people." Once again, children were led to think about themselves and their self-worth. They were not taught how to consider the aspects of the heavenly realm. It's easy to see how a monthly and even yearly diet of that kind of "church" will no doubt starve its listeners. If the speaker and the listener truly loved truth, there would be a demand for it, and, as a result, it would be taught.

The same teacher who used the actual movie clips ended his "sermon" with the comment, "I love to go to movies. I love to go because I look for a place where God will speak to me and change my heart." Guess what? God doesn't speak to us through movies that were designed in Hollywood by ungodly, lustful producers and actors. God doesn't speak to us through corrupt channels. God speaks to us through truth. God doesn't use fortune tellers, Ouija boards, or movies. However, there is someone who can speak through those channels. If you're convinced you've heard from God at a movie, consider that your soulish feelings and emotions were touched, but by another spirit.

COMPLACENT ABOUT MOVIES

In the Faith section of a local newspaper, a subtitle read, "Group studies classic movies for life's lessons."[7] This group of people spent the summer watching classic movies and tried to attain spiritual edification from them. Each movie taught a different lesson. One viewer commented that "so much of what's in the Bible" can be found in "something that's similar or applicable to the movies." Another member combined study of the Bible with movie watching because it was "a fresh way to examine familiar concepts." He continued that "everyone has studied the Bible. We all know it. But it's hearing something new from someone else" that impressed him. If everyone knows the Bible, ask your neighbor or someone at the post office to quote just one verse from each book. Can he even name the books of the Bible? What about the Ten Commandments?

What a shame that we Christians even try to compare movies to the Bible. What a mockery of the pure, living Word. There is no comparison. Movies are as far from the

Bible as a burned-out match is from the sun. There is a vast difference. Why do Christians continue to call evil, good? As for hearing from "someone else" and a "fresh" view of life, beware who you listen to.

The notion that God will speak through anything and everything is an error that is invading society. New and modern teachings lead people to believe everything is God and that all is one. When we say that God speaks through everything, we are saying that everything is truth. Jesus told Satan to "get behind" Him when Peter spoke untruth (Matt. 16:23). We need to resist the devil and his lies, not complacently call them good.

Complacent Christians choose to believe God will speak to them on the run because they do not want to take the time they need to spend with Him and His Word. However, God is not shallow, and He has designed spiritual communication to be intense and weighty. He said in Psalm 42:7 that "deep calleth unto deep." Answers to life's questions are not lying on the surface. They must be sought with effort through prayer and meditation on His Word.

Jesus said that His sheep would know His voice. If Christians label several voices as being the voice of God, they are deceived. The more voices we listen to, the less distinct God's one true voice becomes. God has one voice, and it does not come through impure channels. Even if a movie quotes Scripture, remember Satan quoted Scripture to Jesus when he was being tempted.

God used a burning bush and a donkey in the Bible, but they are neutral entities with no agenda. However, movies have creators with agendas. They are not godly ones. (I am referring to Hollywood movies, including Disney films, and not necessarily ones promoted by Christian companies.)

Another participant in the "summer of spiritual growth through movie watching" commented that she had never seen most of the movies because, she said with a laugh, she "was brought up Baptist." She warned that it was the movie of today that "you have to be afraid of." Well, the Baptists and other Christians of the past saw that their "movie of today" was also dangerous. Most Christians in the 1940s and 1950s could see the tragic door that the movie industry was opening, and churches preached that its members should avoid them.

How did we come so far from the classics to the perversion of today? It's because we took that first step. The English poet Alexander Pope clarified this problem when he wrote, "We first endure, then pity, then embrace."[8] He was right. Through time we have managed to become desensitized to movie smut. Today's Christian jeers at the wise Christian of the past while proudly marching off to another irreverent movie. Is it better to resist the small offenses of past movies or to embrace the large offenses of today's movies? Who should jeer at whom?

A. W. Tozer wrote of entertainment that:

> For centuries the Church stood solidly against every form of worldly entertainment, recognizing it for what it was—a device for wasting time, a refuge from the disturbing voice of conscience, and a scheme to divert attention from moral

accountability. For this she got herself abused roundly by the sons of this world. But of late, she has become tired of the abuse and has given over the struggle.[9]

We have fallen from the standard. I have even seen justification for movies in the Christian bookstores. Some books claim to state valid, rather than invalid, reasons for our love of movies and fairy tales. In reality, the basic reason we love movies and fairy tales is because our flesh loves entertainment. We love to avoid truth, and as Tozer said, we want to silence the disturbing voice of conscience.

The Bible warns of the last days when people "will not endure sound doctrine; but after their own lusts shall they heap to themselves teachers, having itching ears; And they shall turn away their ears from the truth, and shall be turned unto fables" (2 Tim. 4:3–4). Isn't this exactly what is happening in the church? There is a turning from the truth and a turning unto movies because they satisfy the itch of our ears. If something looks or feels good, we claim it is good.

I heard a high school student talk about a movie saying, "I know it wasn't right, but it was neat." Jesus warned us to "judge not according to the appearance, but to judge righteous judgment" (John 7:24). We should place righteousness at the forefront of our decisions. We shouldn't judge according to visual appeal or other allurements.

In an article by Richard Winter in Charles Stanley's magazine *In Touch*, Winter claims, "Not unlike drug users who develop a tolerance and need larger doses to achieve the same effect, we, too, have developed a tolerance for amazing events as well as for entertainment itself." He also stated, "When stimulation comes from every angle, people reach a point of being unable to react with much depth to anything. The boredom we feel today is probably due to overload even more than underload."[10] I know of one Christian parent who rented seven videos for her family for one weekend. Do you suppose that on Monday they were walking closer to the Lord or were more in touch with the world?

The local and national newscasts once delivered news about real situations. Now the news has allocated a spot for what's happening in Hollywood, killing legitimate news time with celebrity birthdays, the latest film titles, and the best fashions. Are Christians complacent enough to spend their time caring about this unprofitable information? Jesus confronted the same error with this rebuke: "Ye are they which justify yourselves before men; but God knoweth your hearts: for that which is highly esteemed among men is abomination in the sight of God" (Luke 16:15). I appreciate my dad for using that verse in teaching me and my siblings to avoid the popular way. Do Christians today ever really consider that "popular" things are an abomination to God?

Television programs and commercials are very persuasive, too. They can make a garden burger look delicious. Beware as you casually and comfortably sit in your home watching a seemingly harmless program. The devil knows when your armor is hanging in the back room and when you are tired and don't feel like fighting. Begin watching programs with alertness to the devil's tactics.

On primetime sitcoms and dramas, I have seen several casually placed statues of Buddha, restrooms marked with unisex symbols, and even a gentle song in the background of a popular crime scene drama declaring New Age philosophy.

I have observed Christians' complacency in not criticizing blasphemous cartoons because they "just don't see them as that bad since they're cartoons." So, can boys draw indecent pictures, as long as they don't look at real photographs? Doesn't God look at the heart?

How can we continue to defend the desensitization to evil that is taking place in our country because of movies and TV programs? We are complacently ignoring the promotion of world religions, homosexual lifestyles, occultism, reincarnation, pornography, profanity, blasphemy, mythology, and evolution, to name a few. Teenage stars mock authority, use God's name in vain, and make fun of Christians. Then these rebels are exalted as the heroes at the end of each movie. Like pork barrel laws in which politicians add small attachments to the main idea, the devil adds his perversion to a storyline and is satisfied to have his "law" passed.

Christians attending these movies seem clueless that they are laughing at inappropriate language and moments of indecency. We don't even recognize that our emotions are being pulled in favor of the mistreated homosexual or against the judgmental do-gooder. We pay money and support Satan's agenda, which is aimed right at us and our families. It is evident that the character of Americans is disintegrating quickly. One day, we say, "I would never," and the next year we are doing it.

Consider this: are movies designed to spread the gospel or promote holiness? Then, consider that God may not be speaking to us through them. What is the motive behind them? If a producer has no motive at all, will a good movie naturally evolve? Will good come from evil? No. Will good come from nothing? No. Evolutionary teachings have done more to influence our thinking than we think. It wasn't designed to just make us believe monkeys are smart. It is a direct attack on truth and God's Word.

Seldom do movie-makers have the intention of including God unless it's for blasphemy, deception, or ridicule. I have heard the comment that movie producers only want to make money and nothing else. Well, consider what sells and what doesn't. Betty Wein, former *Morality In Media* senior editor, indicated what is happening when she said, "The pornography industry and exploiters of sex and violence in the mainstream media stand ready to leap parasitically on the back of every new high-tech advance."[11] When will we get it?

Christians are complacent about the indecency in movies because they have heard from their pastors and teachers that lust is normal and that their desires, needs, and search for significance must be fulfilled. Some pastors imply lust is a man's most noble attribute. Therefore, Christians' consciences aren't even pricked when they see scenes that only seem to prove mankind was designed to be happy in his drive for gratification.

Movie producers really do have intentions, and they strategically design movies to support their intentions. Even if they are not aware of all their intentions, they are still driven by the non-neutral force of evil. If a man walks in the dark, there is no light in him (John 11:10). Luke 11:23 says, "He that is not with me is against me: and he that gathered not with me scattereth."

Satan has an agenda, and he is not complacent. He uses the most effective devices available. Therefore, the motive behind movies is to desensitize us, to make us laugh at inappropriate times, and to cause us to sympathize with the "sinner." Why do we continue to participate? How is God so longsuffering and full of mercy?

I even heard from the pulpit, "I watch movies. The Holy Spirit is with me at all times. I love movies and golf." What a far cry from the preachers of the past who advised against movie-going. The Holy Spirit is probably not "with us" in the movie, but "the eyes of the LORD are in every place, beholding the evil and the good" (Prov. 15:3).

Some Christians adamantly defend movies as being "Christian" when there is no evidence for it. Many try to parallel movies with the Bible, but this is unwise. *Star Wars* has been applauded for illustrating the contest between good and evil. It is quite clear that "the force" within its characters is not a representation of God or His power as defined in the Bible. Therefore, this movie is a representation of evil fighting evil. *The Wizard of Oz* had a good witch and a bad witch.

Witchcraft is made up of black magic and white magic. Both are evil. For the most part, Christians don't give credibility to the parts of movies that are rooted in centuries-old black magic. We tend to undervalue evil and even ignore it.

The "good" side of evil is always appealing and never as scary as the "bad" side, "and no marvel; for Satan himself is transformed into an angel of light" (2 Cor. 11:14). In *Star Wars*, the ugly, demonic, scary-voiced characters appear to be the nice guys only because they are fighting against the *really* ugly, demonic, scary-voiced characters. If Satan can get the viewer to cheer for the lesser evil, he is content to get the cheer. Some Christians feel the Force is even a representation of the Holy Spirit! Why do we differentiate between evil and more evil and not between evil and holy?

God tells us in 1 Timothy 4:7 that we are to "refuse profane and old wives' fables, and exercise [ourselves] rather unto godliness." We need to find truth from the Bible, not from stories, fables, and movies. Actually, truth is not in stories, fables, and movies. We are, in fact, told to abstain from even the appearance of evil (1 Thess. 5:22).

Do Christians really see the danger in movies and TV programs? Do we believe there is no agenda for destruction of morals and the traditional family? Do we believe that our defiled ears and eyes will not destroy our homes? Do we recognize the filth coming from our own defiled mouth after watching so many hours of garbage? Our speech is definitely affected by movies.

One result is the continual use of God's name in vain among Christians. The writer of Psalm 119 prayed for God to turn his eyes from beholding vanity (Ps. 119:37). Isaiah speaks of the Christian who walks righteously and speaks uprightly. He that "stops his ears from hearing blood, and shuts his eyes from seeing evil; he is the one that shall dwell on high" (Isa. 33:15–16, author's paraphrase). James tells us that the tongue is a world of iniquity, and it defiles the whole body (James 3:6). Our testimony will be affected if we talk like the world and use its profanity, gossip, and disrespect. We should be sobered by the following verse in the book of Psalms:

> Thou givest thy mouth to evil, and thy tongue frameth deceit. Thou sittest and speakest against thy brother; thou slanderest thine own mother's son. These things hast thou done, and I kept silence; thou thoughtest that I was altogether such an one as thyself: but I will reprove thee, and set them in order before thine eyes. Now consider this, ye that forget God, lest I tear you in pieces, and there be none to deliver. Whoso offereth praise glorifieth me: and to him that ordered his conversation aright will I shew the salvation of God.
>
> —Psalm 50:19–23

We forget how serious the holiness of God is. He is of "purer eyes than to behold evil" and He cannot look upon iniquity (Hab. 1:13). We think He doesn't care that we are complacent. Evidently, we do not foresee a day of reckoning. If we sow to the flesh, we shall of the flesh reap corruption (Gal 6:8). We will give an account for every idle word in the day of judgment (Matt.12:36). There are no gray areas with God. As A. W. Tozer stated, "We cannot act apart from the concept of right and wrong."[12]

We should be like David, who purposed his mouth not to transgress (Ps. 17:3). He prayed for the Lord to set a watch before his mouth and to keep the door of his lips (Ps. 141:3). He said he would take heed to his ways that he sin not with his tongue and vowed to keep his mouth with a bridle, while the wicked were before him (Ps. 39:1). Job would not have attended our movies because he "made a covenant with his eyes" saying, "Why then should I think upon a maid?" (Job 31:1).

We should "let no corrupt communication proceed" from our mouths, "but that which is good to the use of edifying, that it may minister grace unto the hearers" (Eph. 4:29). Notice the goal of no corrupt communication. We shouldn't allow ourselves a margin of error. Our worldly actions grieve the Holy Spirit (Eph. 4:30). We forget, or maybe have never heard, that a perverse tongue is a breach in the spirit (Prov. 15:4). How can Christians be led by the Holy Spirit and hear Him speak when we are saying things we should not say?

"Let us cleanse ourselves from all filthiness of the flesh and spirit, perfecting holiness in the fear of God" (2 Cor. 7:1). We should "present our bodies as a living sacrifice, holy, acceptable unto God, which is your reasonable service" (Rom. 12:1). We should be thinking on things that are true, honest, just, pure, lovely, and of good report (Phil. 4:8). There are so many verses on this subject that we Americans should be ashamed of our complacency. God means business.

We cannot claim more revelation and "enlightenment" in these last days when the deeds of godly men of the past put ours to shame. Our corrupted speech and actions put a vast gulf between us and our ancestors. We must recognize that we are the temple of the living God and we must come out from among the things of the world. We must be separate ourselves and touch not the unclean thing so that God will receive us and be a Father to us (2 Cor. 6:16–18).

Eli's house was judged forever because of iniquity and because his sons made themselves vile, and he restrained them not (1 Sam. 3:13). We cannot abdicate our responsibility to our children. It has been documented that by high school graduation, a child will have watched 18,000 hours of TV, but spent only 13,000 hours in class. If a child attends a house of worship one hour a week for 18 years, he or she will have spent only 936 hours in church. It is very important what children are hearing in those 936 hours. It does not benefit them if it is the same as what they are hearing in the world.

Tell your kids to turn off the television. Tell them no when they just have to see the latest movie. I am thankful for having a mother who would not allow our minds to be polluted with certain television programs. I now have great memories of playing outside with my sister and neighborhood friend. Thanks to a mother who was concerned about television's influence, I fondly reminisce of jumping on the trampoline, watching the trees change color, smelling the lilacs, and hearing the birds sing. Children today miss out on these small blessings because they are glued to the TV.

God's grace teaches us that in "denying ungodliness and worldly lusts, we should live soberly, righteously, and godly, in this present world; Looking for that blessed hope, and the glorious appearing of the great God and our Savior Jesus Christ; Who gave himself for us, that he might redeem us from all iniquity, and purify unto himself a peculiar people, zealous of good works" (Titus 2:12–14).

We should reduce our interests to a few. We shouldn't waste time learning cute stories, the latest blonde jokes, or Internet puns. We must learn to pray and read God's Word. If we think it is boring in comparison, we need a change of heart. We must practice obedience, honesty, and humility. Pray for a focused heart and a single eye that is turned to Jesus. Don't allow your mind to become scattered with roving thoughts. Concentrate on spiritual matters of substance. We must reach the point where we can honestly say, "There is none upon earth that I desire beside thee" (Ps. 73:25).

Chapter 5

A SEARED CONSCIENCE

Now the Spirit speaketh expressly, that in the latter times some shall depart from the faith, giving heed to seducing spirits, and doctrines of devils; Speaking lies in hypocrisy; having their conscience seared with a hot iron.

—1 Timothy 4:1–2

ALL PEOPLE ARE born with a conscience. All are born with a knowledge of right and wrong and the ability to feel guilt for wrongdoing. It would be very difficult to teach a child right from wrong if he didn't already have an innate sense of it. Doesn't it help when detecting something is amiss just to see the guilty expression on a child's face? That little look is healthy for you, and it is healthy for him. It is a warning that should not go unheeded.

Society argues that feelings of guilt are harmful and should be avoided, but guilt is not an unhealthy feeling. A feeling of condemnation is unhealthy, but there is a difference between the two. Where would we be or what would we being doing without a conscience?

Our consciences are not necessarily a correct gauge when detecting right from wrong. People set their own gauge through decisions they make. We as Christians must remember to daily set our gauge with the standard of the Bible. Catholics teach that the conscience must be "educated."

Just because we feel something is right does not mean that it is. Our consciences can be corrupt. As mentioned in the opening verse, our conscience can be misled by seducing spirits and doctrines contrary to God's Word. Because of our lack of inborn holiness, our sin natures naturally steer our consciences off-course. If we notice the different standard levels of consciences among people, we can see clearly that human conscience can be wrong. To let our conscience be our guide, as the world teaches, is to trust our soulish sin natures and to put faith in our humanness. We cannot let our mind, our will, or our emotions guide our consciences. Only through the "renewing of our minds," may we "prove what is that good, and acceptable, and perfect, will of God (Rom. 12:2).

Some feel it is wrong to eat meat, while others do not. Others feel it is right to recycle, while others couldn't care less. Some murderers feel it is not wrong to murder. Other murderers feel the guilt. It doesn't matter what each person thinks is right; it matters what is truly right and that our standard lines up with what is always right, and that is Scripture.

To live otherwise is to live under the standard of doing whatever is right in our own eyes (Judg. 21:25). Today's culture clearly lives by that standard. "If it is right for you, then who am I to judge?" is a common phrase. But living by that standard is no standard at all. Our society and even Christians are living just where Satan wants us. He knows that no standard leads to no guilt, which leads to a hardened heart.

This generation of young people must not continue to see the lack of standards among Christians. Without the deterrent of parental and church fortitude, this generation will readily agree with anything and everything without guilt. Because of the influx of worldliness today, parents should be working double-time at home to teach Bible standards. Sadly, this is not happening. Many are not even teaching their children at all, leaving the job to the church, who is also woefully behind in their pursuit of God's commandments.

We must be vigilant to the wiles of the devil and be sensitive to the Holy Spirit. He must be the guide of our consciences. If we ignore God's standard, we will end up with a seared conscience calloused beyond feeling. A callous is not sensitive. It doesn't even realize when it is pricked. We can become calloused to the true measure of holiness. Our daily justification of little sins leads to justification of larger ones. The Bible warns us that this behavior leads to a hardened heart. When people continually justify sin and refuse to listen to correction, they become hard-hearted. God speaks in the book of Zechariah of His people refusing to hearken to Him. They pull away their shoulder and stop their ears. As a result, their hearts became as an "adamant stone" (Zech. 7:11–12).

Christians, too, can become hard-hearted, and we can become calloused to sin. To avoid this catastrophe, we must see sin as God sees it. Romans tells us it is "exceedingly sinful" (Rom. 7:13). Sin must appear to be sin and not a "fun" expression of ourselves or a "harmless" one-time event. Sin works death and is, therefore, extremely serious. We see cyanide as harmful. We sure get nervous when bombs or chemical weapons are mentioned. Why don't we get on red alert when sin is in our lives?

In Ephesians, God warns us to "walk not as other Gentiles walk, in the vanity of their mind," whose understanding is darkened and who are ignorant and blind to God's standard. He continues to warn that these people are "past feeling" because they have "given themselves over unto lasciviousness" and "uncleanness" (Eph. 4:17, 19). We must fear becoming beyond feeling. There are those who feel something is wrong when it is not and others who feel something is right when it is not. But, to be beyond feeling one way or the other is worse.

Our culture is breeding an environment that is past feeling. The boundaries are being removed and people are even praised when they overstep an old boundary into "freedom." Have you noticed how there is no shame in Hollywood? How they refuse to blush (Jer. 6:15)? They rejoice at evil and delight in the frowardness of the wicked. They not only sin, but have pleasure in others who sin, too (Jer. 11:15; Prov. 2:14; Rom. 1:32).

We must not omit God's standard and do the same. Does our conscience react when wickedness is praised on television in the form of an off-color joke? Do we respond with guilt or do we respond with pleasure when sinful delights are mentioned? Are we unfeeling to filthy comments or blatant homosexual affections? The question is, are our consciences seared?

Leprosy is a disease that represents sin in the Bible. People with this disease are numb to any feeling because their nerves are desensitized. They do not even know when their fingers fall off or when a rat is nibbling at their toes. That clearly illustrates what sin does to us. We become so numb to sin, we don't even realize it is destroying us. We do not even realize that rats and other little demon destroyers are attracted to that type of person because desensitized flesh stinks.

A seared conscience precedes seven things that God hates—yes, hates. It leads to a proud look, a lying tongue, hands that shed innocent blood, a heart that devises wicked imaginations, feet that are swift in running to mischief, a false witness that speaks lies, and being one that sows discord among the brethren (Prov. 6:16–19). Being insensitive to the holiness of God will cause a person to do all these things without guilt.

These activities are common in our culture today, but Christians do not usually commit these acts. However, are Christians close to committing them when they laugh at them? Are they one step closer if they give no reaction at all when they see and hear about these abominations?

Are we guilty of the fourth one? Do we devise wicked imaginations? Do we think evil thoughts? What do we think about when we lie down at night? Is it all right to think certain thoughts because nobody knows what we're thinking? Do we feel fantasy is harmless? I really don't want to know what Christians are thinking, but we better pray for a sensitive conscience that pricks the living daylights out of us when we go places in our minds that we shouldn't. Satan knows what he's doing. We may be clueless, but he knows that wicked actions start in the mind. If we think we can keep them confined only to our minds, we are deceived. In fact, we are sinning already. Without even committing the act, it is active in our hearts (Matt. 5:28).

Why do Christians avoid being shocked when we are in the presence of sin? Does it make us look on top of things if we act like we can handle it? To avoid seeming prudish or like those mocked on prime time, do we act like it's no big deal? If we fly off the handle about some sin in the church, would we appear legalistic or self-righteous? I know of a youth pastor who told the kids that he couldn't be shocked. He wanted to appear to be a tough guy that was never caught off-guard by their sinful inventions. He constantly seared their consciences by making light of all types of sin, not just the little things. Why do we think it's embarrassing to be sensitive to sin? Why do we claim Christians who are sensitive (usually older people) lack freedom in God? Is it possible the devil is smiling while we are frolicking along the path toward more abomination and evil?

We eat from the table of sin when we continually partake of filthy movies, television sitcoms, and late-night garbage. Even if the movie is 95 percent "clean," it's the 5 percent that's searing us over. Oh, Satan is clever. The Lord says, "For my people is foolish, they have not known me; they are sottish children, and they have none understanding: they are wise to do evil, but to do good they have no knowledge" (Jer. 4:22).

The question was, are our consciences seared? The answer is yes. We have become so accustomed to garbage that we do not even realize a violation has been made. We are beginning to think a little fornication, a little covetousness, a little foolish talk, and so forth is harmless, and as long as temperance is applied, we can manage it. But Ephesians 5:3–4 tells us that fornication, uncleanness, covetousness, filthiness, foolish talk, jesting should not even "be once named" among us. We've come a long way from the true godly standard set forth for us in God's Word.

As modern Christians, we are also guilty of sinning "willfully after we have received the knowledge of the truth" (Heb. 10:26). We know certain things are wrong, but we do them anyway. Are we so calloused we just do it and say, "Oh well, I'll just ask for forgiveness later"? Some Christians don't want to hear teachings on what is wrong in God's eyes because they do not want to be held accountable for it. That is a definite sign of an insensitive conscience. We should be searching Scripture to find out how we are displeasing God and to find which commandments we are breaking. When we find out, we need to repent and stop.

If this all sounds too rigid, remember that all things are lawful, but all things are not expedient, nor do they edify (1 Cor. 10:23). Let's not go too far in one direction claiming freedom when we are cautioned in God's Word about certain things that are not suitable, advisable, or that hinder our Christian walk.

God looks at the motive of our heart.

> Unto the pure all things are pure, but unto the
> defiled is nothing pure…They profess to know
> God; but in works they deny him.
>
> —Titus 1:15–16

If we were truly pure-hearted, wouldn't worldliness affect us? It affected Jesus. He wept because of what He saw. He was entirely without sin. His words were "pure words, as silver tried in a furnace of earth, purified seven times" (Ps. 12:6).

I have heard Christians talk of vacationing in Las Vegas or New Orleans. I have heard them say they do not feel guilt when walking into a liquor store. Does the lack of guilt mean we are innocent, or does it indicate the presence of an insensitive conscience? Does it mean the Holy Spirit isn't even there to convict? I've heard Christians claim that body piercing was "not a Christian issue." I've heard Christian teens use vulgar language then ask, What did I say? or, How is that a bad word? Either they knew it was wrong and were trying to justify it or their conscience was so numb they didn't even feel guilt for using it.

What if we do something we think is right and it is actually wrong? The children of Israel were told by God to make a trespass offering even when a sin was committed through ignorance. Leviticus tells us that a man "certainly trespassed against the LORD" even though "he wist it not, yet is he guilty, and shall bear his iniquity" (Lev. 5:17, 19). Even when we don't know it's wrong, it still counts as wrong.

Billy Graham talked of a time when he was a boy and his mother gave him iodine instead of cough medicine. She thought it was cough medicine. Graham said she was "sincerely wrong." The men who flew into the Trade Center sincerely thought they were achieving eternal life. They were "sincerely wrong." The road to hell is many times paved with good intentions, but Christians are responsible to know what is right and what is wrong, especially in a land where Bibles are abundant.

We must call sin what it is. We would never feed our children rat poison, because we know rat poison is bad. We see it for what it is. We would never wallow in cow manure because we see it for the filthy, germ-infested sewage that it is. Wait a minute. People, for the first time in TV history, readily wallow in cow manure; put maggots, roaches, and worms into their mouths; or even drink blood—all for the sake of reality television fame. That is becoming common behavior, and the shock of it is already wearing off. Soon a person will be considered an out-of date dinosaur if he is unwilling to participate in such pagan rituals. What a piece of work Satan has completed on our consciences. He knows that physical participation is the first move toward mental justification. Do you smell the burn of the hot iron?

A FALSE FRONT

Those who have not yet fallen for blatant filth are many times lured when something smells sweet, looks good, or is side-splittingly funny. This can be a cover for what is truly intended. Remember, one of Satan's tactics of deception is to act as an angel of light. Christians should see beyond a false label. We should know that looks can be deceiving. The

Bible is clear in telling us what contaminates, but we choose to swallow filth anyway. We are guilty of judging by the clean, enticing label. We pull our shoulder away from God and refuse to hear what He says. We don't want to know the truth.

When we laugh at the purposefully planted jokes that degrade Judeo-Christian values or uplift homosexual life-styles, we are participating in sin and not seeing it for what it is. It's toxic, and it's killing our consciences. It is especially harmful to our children. We must wake up, stop laughing at inappropriate times, and turn the TV off. We can teach our children several lessons at one time if we would just turn off the television in disgust or walk out of the movie theater when everyone is watching. Who cares if people roll their eyes? Be willing to risk it for righteousness sake. Can we claim we would never be pressured to stand in line to accept the mark of the Beast when we will not even stand against a crowd in a movie theater?

Observe how Hollywood always masks evil with humor. People will notice if you're the only one not laughing. If a Christian stands strong, he might possibly attract a sinner to the stability of his standard. We are the salt of the earth and must act like the preservative that it is. If for only one reason, do it for your children. They must be taught to hold the line because they are living in a day when the enemy is gaining ground.

Most Christians have their own standard for movie viewing. Some accept two or three vulgar words. Others accept more obscenities and a few inappropriate scenes.

Most accept the fact that God's name is being taken in vain constantly. To draw a clear line would cause a person to miss out on nearly all movies. In the area of movies alone, haven't our consciences become seared? Do we even hear when God's name is taken in vain? Does it affect us? Do we justify it just because it's so common?

Christians should not trust labels on movies, whether G, PG, PG-13, or R, since the standard of movie producers has fallen year by year. I have heard Christians defend PG-rated movies, saying there was nothing bad in them. Then, when viewing them for the second time, they exclaim, "Oh, I forgot about that part." How can we forget? If a person ever ate excrement, decaying road kill, dog vomit, or gangrene from an elephant wound, wouldn't he remember? Our consciences have become more numb than we realize. John MacArthur points out that "the Bible reveals that most of us are far more guilty than our own hearts tell us."[1] To treat our consciences flippantly is spiritual suicide. Paul wrote of those who, by rejecting their consciences, suffered shipwreck in regard to faith (1 Tim. 1:19).

It is very alarming how easily Christians laugh at carefully designed punch lines. Does Hollywood just accidentally get it right with the timing? It is more likely they have attempted several takes until the impact of the unseemly behavior has full potency. Think of the damage to our nation's conscience committed by movies alone. How can we continue to participate and fund the pipeline of sewer pouring into our nation?

Ezra rent his garment, "plucked off the hair" from his head and beard, and sat astonished when he heard that the people of Israel did "not separate themselves from the people of the lands, doing according to their abominations" (Ezra 9:1, 3). He saw sin for what it was. Are we ever astonished? Do we just recklessly avoid all shocking sensations, hoping one day they will completely go away? We think there is safety in a silent conscience when it is the most treacherous possible thing to have.

To not have a conscience is like a pilot without a control panel. Without one, he cannot detect when he's losing altitude and he doesn't know how close he is to the ground. It's also like a ship that is taking on water, but there is no signal on the panel warning the captain because the wires have been cut. All of the panel instruments indicate normal conditions. We are in the same boat. We ought to be in a state of alarm. Instead, we have chosen a flippant, relaxed attitude toward sin.

The church has abdicated its duty of teaching children how to be separate from the world. The modern church is striving to look and act like the world with its programs, events, and especially its slang. With the lack of foundational truths being taught, treason to God's kingdom has been cultivated. I have seen that many children who graduate, even from a Christian school, quickly become an instant prop in the scenery of the world whether at college or at their jobs. Teenagers who are supposedly free from their parents soon take up drinking, smoking, multiple piercings, bad language, and tattoos, to name a few issues. They are unable to be separate from the world. They easily conform. They even believe they can witness while partaking in sin. Who ever told them this wasn't true?

Be aware of how culture is trying to ease our consciences. New books and movies are stressing the lie that everyone is going to heaven because a loving God would never allow anyone to go to hell. New philosophy pacifies people into thinking everyone fulfills his or her purpose in the end. These lies tell people that even though they may think they have messed up, it will really turn out all right. New teachings are claiming that all people are connected and the stories of the world are one. But, God says there is a difference between the man who has accepted His Son and the one who hasn't.

Countless people believe that all people are good down deep inside underneath their hurt feelings and that everyone will go to a "safe place" when their life on earth is finished. Television appeases the conscience by showing that even after committing crimes, the main characters are basically good people. We hear that if a "life lesson" is not learned on earth, someone from the past will meet us in heaven to teach us that valuable lesson. *The Five People You Meet in Heaven*, a book by Mitch Albom, was made into a movie of the same name. The movie claimed that the people one man met in heaven after he died "made all the difference" and that "in heaven, there is no judgment, but rather an opportunity to examine our lives."[2] Doesn't this ease people's consciences and cause them to postpone dealing with sin? Life lessons are not determined after death. They are determined before death. Satan knows it's too late if a person waits until after he dies to get things right.

The worthwhile lesson we fail to hear is that the only way to heaven is through Jesus. By accepting Him and rejecting our sin natures, we have hope. The regret, the weeping, and the gnashing of teeth will be overwhelming for those who realize they failed to learn that valuable lesson while on earth. Satan wants people to throw off accountability with the belief that all can be fixed after they die. Too late! He has tricked them again.

We must saturate our minds with God's Word and stop filling it with toxic waste. It will make a difference in our speech, our attitudes, and our impact on others. If our right eye offends us, we must pluck it out (Matt. 5:29). God is clear about drastically ridding ourselves of fleshly desires and explains how it is better to go to heaven without those things than to hell with them. We are without excuse because He has told us very clearly in His Word what is expected of us.

Chapter 6

UNBALANCED TEACHING: PART 1

Woe unto you, scribes and Pharisees, hypocrites! for ye
pay tithe of mint and anise and cumin, and have omitted
the weightier matters of the law, judgment, mercy, and
faith: these ought ye to have done, and not to leave the
other undone.

—Matthew 23:23

W E NATURALLY FOCUS on outward appearance
more than on the weightier matters of being a
Christian. Certain teachings in the church may
not necessarily be wrong, but particular points may be exaggerated while others are trivialized. Overemphasis of these teachings to the neglect of their counterpart causes churches to be unbalanced.

We hear that living for Jesus gets better and better, but we aren't hearing that that truth applies to our inward man and not our outward man. Second Corinthians 4:16 says, "For which cause we faint not; but though our outward man perish, yet the inward man is renewed day by day." We need to know that it gets worse and worse for our flesh.

We hear that being a Christian makes life easy because He helps us, but we don't hear that Christianity can make life harder because we have to stand apart from the world and be rejected. We teach the part about the Bible tasting sweet, but leave out how it can be bitter to the belly. (See Revelation 10:10.)

The modern church emphasizes man and his needs rather than focusing on God. One church's weekly bulletin boasted that their desire was "to make people 'priority one,' as Jesus did in His ministry." We naturally agree with the idea that people are important to Jesus, but we fail to see that Jesus' first priority was the Father, not people. A. W. Tozer noted, "The gospel in its scriptural context puts the glory of God, first, and the salvation of man second."[1] God was God without ever having created man. We tend to think the Bible is about man and his relationship with God, and that's as high as we can manage to extend our thoughts.

Balanced teaching is similar to the chemical makeup of salt. Two ingredients are necessary to be effective. Salt is composed of sodium and chloride. Separately, they are poisons. If one is taken and not the other, it can be deadly. They must be combined to provide the healthy effect intended. We must obey Jesus and be the salt of the earth and teach all the doctrines of the Bible. If we decide to only teach part of the gospel, the cost will be high.

GOD IS LOVE

It is true that God is a loving God and His love surpasses all others, yet that is only part of God's character. If we teach only that He loves and do not mention His hatred of sin, the imbalance will lead to error in our thinking. This teaching seems to be prominent in churches. There is an effort to offset what is considered to be harsh teaching from the past. Pastors feel their flock has been bombarded with thoughts of an angry God, and they are trying to erase that picture. They have reasoned it to be a wrong picture of God. In their effort, they have swung too far to the other side and are failing to maintain a balance. Paul reminds us, "Behold therefore the goodness and severity of God" (Rom. 11:22).

One Christian teacher on television went so far as to say, "If God is love, then love is God." John did say that God is love (1 John 4:8). But, as Tozer said:

> Had the apostle declared that love is what God is, we would be forced to infer that God is what love is. If literally God is love, then literally love is God, and we are all, in duty, bound to worship love as the only God there is. If love is equal to God then God is only equal to love, and God and love are identical. Thus we destroy the concept of personality in God and deny outright all His attributes save one, and that one we substitute for God. The God we have left is not the God of Israel; He is not the God and Father of our Lord Jesus Christ; He is not the God of the prophets and the apostles; He is not the God of the saints and reformers and martyrs, nor yet the God of the theologians and hymnists of the church.[2]

Children are being persuaded by this new slant and even believe it is wrong to mention God in any other way than as loving. But, God has many attributes and love is only one of them.

Another reason why pastors and teachers are neglecting to teach about God's wrath, judgment, and hatred of sin is because they want Christians to be happy and lighthearted. They don't want an atmosphere of heaviness or regret. But, think how detrimental it would be if a doctor decided to tell his patient, who was dying of cancer, only the positive side of his health. He would be told that his blood pressure was fine and his cholesterol great, and then he would go home "happy" yet ignorant of the true condition of his health. By churches omitting truth, Christians are being misled about the true condition of their souls.

How can we deny that we live in a world of decay? When misled Christians experience hardships, they become even more unhappy because they have not been told the truth about suffering. We are having epidemics of depression partly because Christians are not being told the truth about life. Instead, they are being told to focus on love and happiness in this life, and when they see it's not always possible, they feel tricked by God. They've really been tricked by unbalanced teaching.

At Easter, when churches are expected to have above-average crowds, one preacher was quoted in a local newspaper as saying, "We're not looking for a lot of decisions for Jesus Christ or re-commitments." He continued, "What we do expect is people to walk away and say, 'You know, that was a good experience. That's not the boring church I remember as a child.'"[3] How unfortunate that a preacher put a "good experience" above salvation. How erroneous to feel that childhood experiences like altar calls, recommitments, and confrontation of sin are boring and to be avoided in the church today.

Our assertion of God's love and nothing else causes us to avoid conflict and persecution. We are trying to show the world that the Christian life is only a happy life of love. We strive for our children to be accepted, popular, and happy. We forget how Jesus gave His back to the smiters and hid not His face from shame and spitting (Isa. 50:6).

Preachers are not telling their flocks about the cost of discipleship and the cost of sin. We only hear over and over how God loves us. Love and tolerance cause people to believe there is no real enemy and, therefore, no battle. They do not even resist the devil because they feel God's love envelopes all circumstances. They feel that only good can happen to them.

The consequences of sin are downplayed while God's love is continually the focus. Not many are preaching the salvation message to sinners concerning sin. A sinner needs to hear about sin before he is converted. That's a simple realization. Still, it is overlooked by preaching that tries to draw a sinner only by saying he is loved. As a result of imbalance, the sinner rarely hears about sin. It is critical for a sinner to understand his violation against a holy God. He must understand his sin nature to attain true salvation. He assumes he already has salvation with this one-sided teaching. He is told that he just has to realize he is loved.

Jude 22–23 tells us that some are saved with compassion while others are saved with fear. Compassionate, loving, kind words should definitely be a part of a church service. But, leaving out the half involving fear leaves out half the possible salvations. A preacher must preach God's Word and lean not to his own understanding (Prov. 3:5).

In Malachi 2:17, the prophet tells God's people that they had wearied the Lord with their words. They answered, like us, "Wherein have we wearied him?" He then replied, "When ye say, Every one that doeth evil is good in the sight of the Lord, and He delighteth in them; or, Where is the God of judgment?" We are doing the same by telling people that God delights in us no matter what we do. We do the same when we imply there is no God of judgment. God is weary with the modern church. As we teach and preach, we cannot assume all have received the secure love that is only in Christ Jesus (Rom. 8:39). Children and newcomers to church must hear both sides of the gospel: "Behold, therefore the goodness and severity of God" (Rom. 11:22).

Such unbalanced teaching fits nicely into the world's doctrine that everyone is a child of God. We also hear, "God is not a God of rules or a God of dos and don'ts." Nobody dares to stand up and say, "Excuse me, but God is a God of rules. He hates violation of those rules because it is a sin to disobey them." Children hear about love without the qualifications. Jesus said, "He that hath my commandments, and keepeth them, he it is that loveth me: and he that loveth me shall be loved of my Father, and I will love him" (John 14:21).

In our teaching of God's love, we are failing to understand it fully. If we would teach the other attributes of God, we could learn much more about His love. The fact that He is holy, self-existent, self-sufficient, and omnipotent reveals to us that He does not need man but loved man enough to die for him. The fact that He is a God of justice and sovereignty indicates that He loves us enough to be fair and not let evil overcome good. The fact that He is a God of wrath shows us His love most of all. He sent His only begotten Son to receive the wrath that we deserved for our sin. How can we measure that kind of love?

Grace vs. Law

For there are certain men crept in unawares, who were before of old ordained to this condemnation, ungodly men, turning the grace of our God into lasciviousness, and denying the only Lord God, and our Lord Jesus Christ.

—Jude 4

There has been an attempt in churches for the last decade or more to swing the pendulum away from hard, brow-beating sermons. Preachers today do not want to be associated with the fire-and-brimstone preachers of the past. In this attempt, the pendulum has swung too far. The danger is to the children. It causes an unhealthy understanding of God when children only hear soft sermons and even hear mentioned that hard ones are not of God.

The error is a "Go ahead and do it, then ask forgiveness" mentality. It is taught that grace will ultimately cover sin, so you might as well commit the act, even when you know it is wrong. This teaching takes the facts about grace too far. The fact that grace is a free gift that covers sin is not an entitlement, a license, to sin nor an excuse to be void of good works.

The teachings today have been taken so far that they are erroneous. It is like taking the fact that bleach whitens teeth to the extreme by drinking a gallon every day to make them even brighter. That goes beyond clean and into the zone of erosion, and the bleach has been applied to areas it was not intended to help.

God's grace is sufficient without our adding to it. Grace is not meant to give ultimate freedom to a person and make him absolutely free from all obligation and duty. It is not intended to exempt the receiver from all the effects of sin. It also does not apply to those who refuse its conditions (the unsaved). We are neglecting to teach that there are consequences for sin. As a result, we are teaching an idea that sin will not hurt us. This causes many, especially teens, to indulge.

True grace increases conviction of sin. A person who is sincerely saved realizes his unworthiness to receive grace. True grace makes a person's conscience more sensitive. Grace tends to make us watch our hearts more carefully. The heart of someone who is genuinely sorry is like a burn victim who is thereafter terrified of the thing that once hurt him. He fears sin and its consequences.

True grace enables us to live a life of obedience and holiness. "Let us have grace, whereby we may serve God acceptably with reverence and godly fear," wrote the author of Hebrews 12:28. Notice the word *acceptably* in that verse. There is an acceptable way to serve God and an unacceptable way, just as there is an acceptable way to apply grace and an unacceptable way to apply it.

With true grace, we are more certain of our deliverance from eternal punishment, but we are more aware that we don't deserve it. Christians struggle with what grace really means. Some denominations have no security because they are too aware of their failures, while others have no security because they are not even aware of their failures. A balance is important to the security of the believer. We must be aware of our failures and be willing to call sin a violation against God while at the same time admitting it is by God's grace and not anything else that causes us to receive salvation.

It is true that we are justified freely by His grace (Rom. 3:24). It is true that by grace, we are saved through faith, not of ourselves, but as a gift of God (Eph. 2:8). It is also true that where sin abounds, grace does much more abound (Rom 5:20). We often hear the truth that we are not under the law, but under grace (Rom. 6:14). The natural reaction to this is, "What shall we say then? Shall we continue in sin, that grace may abound?" The Bible answers, "God forbid" (Rom. 6:1–2).

If we are truly dead to sin, how can we continue to live in it? (Rom. 6:2). This is the part that is left out of our teaching. All of the focus on freedom and liberty is omitting the fact that we are not to continue sinning so grace may abound. Dead to sin means we don't feel the desire for it and, as a result, stop doing it.

There is also imbalance in the misapplication of grace as an automatic ticket of forgiveness to be applied before or after a deed has been committed. Remorse for sin is numbed with the effect of "free" forgiveness. The numbing affect gives liberty to do things we normally wouldn't do because it really doesn't count when it's free. One youth pastor who usually did not miss an opportunity to appease guilt told the youth group, "Whatever you do, grace is there. It's no big deal." So, Jesus' death was no big deal?

We neglect to teach that we must unite with Christ in His death and resurrection and, therefore, be made free from our former enslavement to sin. God looks at the heart, and the heart of a truly converted person wants to please Him and is not under the law of having to please Him.

This person says, like the psalmist, "My soul hath kept thy testimonies; and I love them exceedingly" (Ps. 119:167). We are freed from sin and do not have to serve it once grace is applied to our life (Rom. 6:6–7). We are no longer under the law of sin and death. We have a new outlook on sin and how it displeases a holy God.

If a person has no change in his outlook toward sin, reconsider his conversion. False conversions put an end to the prickings of the conscience, especially when the person continually hears he need not worry about sin now that he has grace. Counterfeit repentance does not cause a person to flee his lust. When there is no accountability for change in our churches and the teachings tell the new convert that he does not need to worry about anything, it is not likely he will change.

Out of balance teachings on grace lure the believer or nonbeliever into the realm of corrupt thinking. Since there is an accompanying belief attached to this new kind of grace that teaches nothing is forbidden with God, preachers jokingly imply that, of course, he and his flock "want" to drink, smoke, and commit fornication or adultery. The Bible teaches us that a true believer does not desire to commit those acts because he is a new man. When we continue to tamper with the idea of sin and refer to it laughingly or in a joke, we are misled into thinking that, while under grace, we can play like we're committing those acts.

Notice how many times preachers who tamper with sin jokingly in their sermons or refer to acts unashamedly end up in a shameful scandal.

> But every man is tempted, when he is drawn away of his own lust, and enticed. Then when lust hath conceived it bringeth forth sin: and sin, when it is finished, bringeth forth death.
>
> —James 1:14–15

Grace misapplied casually assumes sin is less serious than it really is. Christians are beginning to brag that God will use "anyone" to do His work. The youth are being told that He especially uses those who have led a really corrupt, rebellious life. They believe this because of the example given to them by youth leaders and pastors who were once extreme rebels. These rebels spend most of their sermon time bragging about their past, unknowingly glamorizing it to their young listeners.

God can truly use anyone He pleases, but it is misleading to imply more godly work can be done when a person knows what he's dealing with, having experienced it himself. This advocates worldliness, which the Bible clearly condemns. If it didn't matter whom God chose for a job, why would He say that while man looks on the outward appearance, He looks on the heart? (See 1 Samuel 16:7.) Why would He say that when a man is faithful over a few things, He will be made ruler over many things? (See Matthew 25:21.) Character counts, and we must tell our children.

I once received a Christian e-mail that listed Bible characters and their "areas of weakness." It told the reader to stop making excuses for why God wasn't using them because "God uses anything." The difference between weakness of the world versus spiritual weaknesses is not made evident to today's churchgoers. God strengthens us through weaknesses that men shun and these do not pertain to sinful weaknesses. First Corinthians 1:27 says God chooses the weak things "of the world" to confound the things that are mighty.

The emphasis of that e-mail and many sermons is in reverse of what it should be. Instead of an over-emphasis of God's use of "weak" people, churches should preach about God's employment of people who are strong in Him. In fact, God uses our weaknesses in relation to our flesh's starvation, neglect, and denial. A person who is weak in his flesh is spiritually strong in Christ. There is a big difference in what is true and what is being preached in many churches.

By saying God used Noah, who got drunk at least once in his lifetime, we should say God used Noah's strength of obedience to God in the face of 120 years of ridicule. Instead of saying God used Jacob because he was a liar, we should say God chose Him because of his patience and obedience. Patience and obedience are "weaknesses" of the flesh because strong flesh is impatient and strong-willed which, in turn, are "strengths" in the world.

Instead of encouraging disobedience among young people with the story of Samson's rebellion, the other side should be told that God had chosen him from birth to keep the Nazarite vow. In fact, Samson's sin almost caused him to blow it. In the end, he died because of his disobedience. His sin didn't clinch a deal with God, as one-sided teaching implies.

We know the Bible says that when we are weak, He is strong. Second Corinthians 12:10 speaks of Paul being weak from infirmities, reproach, necessity, persecution, and distress. God used Paul, and He used those weaknesses of Paul's flesh. Hebrews 11, the chapter that lists heroes of the faith, speaks of those who "subdued kingdoms, wrought righteousness, obtained promises, stopped the mouths of lions, Quenched the violence of fire, escaped the edge of the sword, out of weakness were made strong, waxed valiant in fight" (v. 33–34). Strong faith and weak flesh brought on the valiant works mentioned in this chapter. This is what is meant by God using our weaknesses. Another explanation is that when our flesh is incapable, God can show Himself strong because it is obviously not the person's strength.

We are not teaching the consequences of sin to this generation. Is it any wonder our children are committing sinful acts in higher percentages than ever in recorded history? We are actually encouraging sin by referring to it as a light matter and saying God will compensate us and "use it" in the end.

One youth leader taught a high school chapel service on the subject of grace. He taught only one side of grace. It was like he was just giving them chloride without sodium. He said that when he was young, he would go out drinking, "all in fun, you know." Then he told them if they had gone too far with their boyfriend or girlfriend they were not disqualified with God. He talked about approaching the throne of grace boldly without the mention of God's holiness. Teen rebels in that chapel service walked away actually comforted in their sin. As with David, sexual sin does not disqualify a person, but young hormones should not be encouraged. The prophet Nathan told David, "By this deed [his adultery with Bathsheba and the strategic murder of her husband] thou hast given great occasion to the enemies of the Lord to blaspheme" (2 Sam. 12:14). David's sin also resulted in the bitter fruit of grief and regret. These results should be pointed out to our children.

Children are being taught that sin is not so bad if temperance is used, but temperance is supposed to be applied to lawful actions, not unlawful ones. They are told that real error is in sinning often, but sinning once or twice is all right and nothing to worry about. They are told God dislikes bad "habits." They are told God understands that people will always sin a little.

Sadly, children interpret this as freedom to sin. They think the error is in getting caught. Notice how it is uncommon, today, to hear an offered apology until a person is caught. Then sincere and regretful apologies are freely offered, oftentimes with tears. When a child hears wrong teachings in church over and over, it is like feeding him poison. They need to be taught about the heartbreak and devastating results of sin and how it all starts with the little things.

Christian children are boldly using grace as a license to sin. They believe they can sow some wild oats in college then come back prepared to be a youth pastor. Satan loves for children to think that Christians automatically return to church after sowing wild oats, but he knows most people stay in the world once they go out into it.

Today, children lack guilt and even feel a great entitlement to be "God's favorite." Their plan is to do great and popular things for God, no matter what sin they've committed. Those preachers who continue to be "partial in the law" and "cause many to stumble at the law" and continue to corrupt the covenant will be made "contemptible and base before all the people" (Mal. 2:8–9).

Praise God for His great forgiveness. Where sin abounds, grace much more abounds (Rom. 5:20). But there is another side. Experienced adults know this side. Children need to be forewarned of the price of sin. The Word of God, in balance, is a great deterrent to sin.

We are seeing the grace of God turned into lasciviousness because of the unbalance. It is one of the signs of apostasy in the last days (Jude 4). How can we deny the flippant attitude toward sin and the continual sinning with no remorse?

Christians have told me that God will forgive them if they commit an act that they know is wrong. God can forgive, but we must take seriously the Scripture that warns:

> If we sin willfully after that we have received the knowledge of the truth, there remaineth no more sacrifice for sins, But a certain fearful looking for of judgment and fiery indignation, which shall devour the adversaries. He that despised Moses' law died without mercy under two or three witnesses: Of how much sorer punishment, suppose ye, shall he be thought worthy, who hath trodden under foot the Son of God, and hath counted the blood of the covenant, wherewith he was sanctified, an unholy thing, and hath done despite unto the Spirit of grace?
>
> —Hebrews 10:26–29

It is very, very serious to use grace as an opportunity for the flesh. God gives grace to the humble and resists the proud (James 4:6). We cannot proudly boast of grace. If we are proud, we do not realize that we are stacking up judgment, and not grace, on our side. What a sad day when a person realizes how wrong he was. This situation will most likely befall our children.

As time goes by, we are hearing less and less balanced teaching. More and more sermons are filled with human-focused stories that appease the conscience. Children who have only been fed one ingredient and not the other are now in college or in young adulthood. Ask your children what they think about sin and grace. You may be shocked.

Abraham received grace because he believed and "staggered not at the promise" (Rom. 4:20). He was strong in faith and it was imputed to him for righteousness (Rom. 4:22). Grace comes through faith (Rom. 4:16). We must have faith to believe. To believe is to obey. The proof of our belief in God is obedience to his commandments.

> He that saith, I know him, and keepeth not his commandments, is a liar, and the truth is not in him.
>
> —1 John 2:4

So, we see how dangerous it is to teach that grace means you do not have to keep God's commandments.

We are falsely interpreting the fact that we are not under the law to mean we are not under obligation. Jesus said, "If ye continue in my word, then are ye my disciples indeed" (John 8:31). He also said, "Whosoever committeth sin is the servant of sin" (John 8:34).

Jesus also said that we would be able to know Christians "by their fruit" (Matt. 7:16). This is not told to the children.

They are oblivious to the requirements of the Christian life that bears fruit.

So, we see that works have something to do with our duty as Christians, and yet it is all about grace. Only faith can understand that truth. A holy life is evidence of saving grace. Jonathan Edwards asserted that a holy life is the "greatest of all signs of grace, both as evidence of sincerity to others and also as proof to our own consciences."[4] New teachings on grace, as mentioned earlier, throw out the law as being null and void.

However, we fail to see that God's demand for holiness is even greater in the New Testament. There, the Ten Commandments become a matter of the heart and not action only. We have greater responsibility under grace than we had under the law.

Is the law a bad thing? What does Scripture say? Romans 8:3 says the law was weak. But that's not the whole message, though some preachers stop there. Reading further, we see that its weakness was due to human flesh, in that we couldn't keep the law. Our flesh caused the law to be weak. To teach that the law was weak and stop there is to teach only one side of the coin. It leaves out the fact that "the law of the Lord is perfect, converting the soul" (Ps. 19:7), and that "if there had been a law given which could have given life, verily righteousness should have been by the law" (Gal. 3:21).

However, the law was not weak in Jesus. He "condemned sin in the flesh: That the righteousness of the law might be fulfilled in us, who now walk not after the flesh, but after the Spirit" (Rom. 8:3–4). "The law is holy, and the commandment holy, and just, and good" (Rom. 7:12).

The law was made to expose sin. Jesus came to eliminate sin after it was exposed. Jesus did not come to destroy the law, but to fulfill it by destroying the sin that it had exposed. (See Matthew 5:17 and Romans 7:7.) We are unable to receive grace until the law reveals the sin that grace frees us from. Many today receive no grace and therefore no salvation because they do not come to grips with their own sin, as pointed out by the law.

> For the law of the Spirit of life in Christ Jesus hath made us free from the law of sin and death.
> —Romans 8:2

Many times when the Bible speaks of our being free from the law, it's from the law of sin and death. When we are led by the Spirit, we are not under that law (Gal. 5:18). Being led by the Spirit produces these fruits: "love, joy, peace, longsuffering, gentleness, goodness, faith, Meekness, temperance: against such there is no law" (Gal. 5:22–23). There is no law against doing the right thing.

A person lives a life of freedom when he is living a right life. There are no laws saying he cannot do what is right. He is free to do right by his own choices. Otherwise, he does what is wrong and obeys the desires of his flesh. That is not really freedom, but bondage to the slavery of sin.

God made humans with the ability of choice, and by an act of our will, we can do the right thing. We do not, however, know what is right and what is wrong until it is pointed out to us.

The law is a schoolmaster telling us we have sin. Whenever we recognize our violations, we can be led to Christ. Otherwise, we see no need for Him. The law brings us to Christ so that we may be justified by faith (Gal. 3:24). After we have faith, we don't need the force of the law because we are then able to walk by the Spirit. We will not fulfill the lust of the flesh (Gal. 5:16). We now are by our will obligated to a law of righteousness.

We must see both sides of this issue. It is true that we do not have to obey God's laws to receive salvation. First of all, it has been proven man cannot obey all of God's laws, and even one offense brings guilt in all areas. But, it is also true that if we have truly received God's grace and freedom from sin, we will want to keep His commandments. We are able to choose obedience when we are under grace, whereas the law requires it. We are not under the law because forced obedience is bondage, yet we are made free when we want to obey. In the new covenant of grace, the Lord puts His laws in our mind and writes them in our hearts. (See Hebrews 8:10 and Jeremiah 31:33.)

Modern Christians tend to be biased in their thinking and throw out anything associated with the word *law*. With over six hundred commandments in the Bible, why do we think we can cancel out that much when we say, "Throw out the law"? There are many commandments in the New Testament for Christians.

The imbalance in our teaching is throwing the baby out with the bathwater. Christians do not feel obligated to obey the laws written in their Bibles. Their disobedience causes them to be under the very law they claim freedom from. First Timothy 1:9 says that the law was not made for a righteous man, but for the lawless and disobedient. Claiming freedom while still fulfilling the lusts of the flesh is no freedom from the law at all. Only a life of righteousness gives a person freedom from the law as God intended.

Christ redeemed us from the curse of the law (Gal. 3:13). Sin is that curse. The law gives sin strength to condemn our flesh (1 Cor. 15:56). Our flesh naturally does things that are contrary to the law (Rom. 7:18, 22–23). For us to be free from the curse, we must die to our flesh and live with Christ.

> For he that is dead is freed from sin.
>
> —Romans 6:7

This is what is truly meant when Christians are said to be under the New Testament and not the Old. Hebrews 9:17 explains it by saying, "For a testament is of force after men are dead: otherwise it is of no strength at all while the testator liveth." We can live in the New Testament, free from the law of the Old Testament, when we die to ourselves, which involves obeying laws that our flesh hates. The new covenant is no longer about right and wrong. It's about a spiritual life of righteousness and godliness, which has no room for wrong (sin).

We are now under a new law. Which law? The law "of works? Nay: but by the law of faith" (Rom. 3:27). According to Scripture, we are under a new law of faith. We are made just by this law. After Paul was saved, he saw the two laws warring against each other (Rom. 7:23). However, today, we aren't hearing this viewpoint because we've been told we are not under law.

When we are saved, "do we then make void the law through faith? God forbid: yea, we establish the law" (Rom. 3:31). How can we establish the law if we don't even know what the law says? Satan would love for us to be ignorant of the law and therefore oblivious to our sin. We should stop shunning the laws that point out our sin. We must be made aware of our sin by reading the Bible. If we want to continue pleasing God, we must study diligently to see if what we are doing is wrong. We must seek to obey the principles God designed for every situation.

If we believe not Moses' writings, how shall we believe Jesus' words? (See John 5:47.) The law was given to men by Moses, but it originated with God. The law represents the will of God for man. "There has been no abrogation of the principles of morality contained in the law," noted A. W. Tozer.[5] Violation will always brings its own penalty.

The danger of teaching only freedom from the law without teaching that the Spirit now leads us into obedience under a new law is a belief that there is no standard. We are already seeing chaotic results of having no standard in the world. Children are bombarded by worldly propaganda stating there is no standard of truth. We are seeing what

Habakkuk saw. He observed that when the law was slacked, judgment did not go forth, and the wicked compassed the righteous (Hab. 1:4). Let's pray "that the righteousness of the law might be fulfilled in us, who walk not after the flesh, but after the Spirit" (Rom. 8:4).

RELIGION AND TRADITION

If the foundations be destroyed, what can the righteous do?

—Psalm 11:3

There is an unbalanced teaching in many churches that portrays religion as a bad thing. Of course, when referring to the dead, lifeless, rote rituals of certain church practices or the pharisaic spirit that condemns others as being of less value, it is bad. Religion is also bad when associated with false religions, such as Islam, Hinduism, Buddhism, or Christian Science. But, religion is good when it is the true religion of Jesus Christ. James explained what a Christian must do who practices religion. He said, "Pure religion and undefiled before God and the Father is this, To visit the fatherless and widows in their affliction, and to keep himself unspotted from the world" (James 1:27). True religion is not something to avoid.

For years, people were considered religious if they went to church regularly and talked about God or the Bible on any day other than Sunday. It was considered a compliment to be called religious. It was a term relating to virtue and honesty.

Now, Christians hear the word and either laugh in ridicule or frown at the image of a harsh, hate-filled, narrow-minded person. This is much like the picture the world has always had for religion.

Somehow, we've joined the world in its mockery of religion. We especially mock zealots, as some pastors and teachers disapprovingly associate religion with piety. With their body language and jokes about avid Bible readers and sticklers for truth, they cause their audience to automatically decide they never want to be like the religious or pious. The dictionary defines *piety* as "devotion and reverence for God or an act which shows this quality."[6] I ask, why do Christians think this is a trait to be ashamed of? Where can you find a genuine, pious person today?

This doctrinal shift did not take decades, like most. It happened sooner. Error flourishes with one-sided teaching. Always hearing the same thing about something or someone is very persuasive. It is much like the propaganda used by Hitler against the Jews. Eventually, the disillusion cannot be erased because the masses are fully persuaded by the lies.

It seems churches are ashamed of their relationship to the word *religion*. They want to be associated with more in-style terminology. When looking up the words *religion* and *irreligion* in the thesaurus, I would much rather be associated with *religion*. Compare words like faith, theology, divinity, truth, doctrine, confession, and piety with ungodly, doubt, unbelief, atheism, materialism, infidelity, paganism, and anti-Christianity. How in the world did *religion* become a bad word?

Two TV preachers talked about how boring sword drills were when they were young. They even said they "didn't do any good." This rationale has led to neglect in the area of religious foundational learning in children today. Churches have now decided to fill the void with movies and entertainment. Scottish-born Presbyterian author and pastor David H. C. Read wrote, "The vacuum left by the waning of religion in Western countries has been filled by an army of superstitious cults and beliefs."[7] The door is flung wide open to new and deceptive teachings as soon as the old system of Christianity has been thrown out and perceived as outdated. Satan is very clever. No wonder our forefathers called Satan "the Old Deluder."

Having a religion is simply believing in something. How can Christians say they believe in God and at the same time say they aren't religious? A Christian's belief is in Jesus. Martyrs of the past died for their religion. In the past, laws were passed by Nero and others to condemn the Christian religion. We are Christians because of our religion. We are Christians because of our belief in Jesus.

I've seen a bumper sticker that read, "When religion ruled the world, they called it the Dark Ages." There, again, is only one side of the story. The false, ungodly church ruled the Dark Ages, not allowing people to read the Bible for themselves. True religion did not rule the Dark Ages. It was when the printing press was developed and people could read the Bible in their own language that the Dark Ages ended. So, religion was actually the reason the Dark Ages ended. Can we continue to eat this lopsided diet? No, and our children certainly cannot. They are not receiving the foundation of solid truth. Partial truths are producing a deceived generation.

If we are saying *religion* is a bad word because it represents legalistic people who have their noses in the air, then what is the new word for us? *Christian* is still a good word, right? Have we begun disguising our Christian label, too, with Bibles that look like magazines or even pocketbooks and attire that looks like "Monday clothes" instead of "Sunday clothes"? Is our language any different from Hollywood? Do we want a label that is different than the average person, or do we want their label? William Penn observed, "By thy heart growing carnal, thy religion did so too; and not liking it as it was, thou fashioned it to thy liking; forgetting what the holy prophet said, 'The sacrifice of the wicked is an abomination to the Lord.'"[8]

The world would love nothing more than for true religion to die. Media liberals are now blaming Christianity as being the catalyst for all past and present conflict. They feel that peace would result if only Christians would cooperate and agree to embrace other beliefs. They believe world harmony and an end to future hostility would take place if Christians weren't so obstinate. I agree that spiritual turmoil is at the base of all wars, but the world's objective is to lay blame on Christians rather than placing responsibility with those men and nations who have risen up against righteousness.

I understand that the world wants to kill "religion," but I'm curious as to why Christians are going along so easily.

Saying that religion needs to die is apostasy in its sharpest form. We have fallen so far from what we used to be. As a young nation, America unanimously passed the Northwest Ordinance in 1787, which charged, "Religion, morality, and knowledge being necessary to good government and the happiness of mankind...."[9] Satan wants to do away with religion, especially the stubborn Christian one, and, as a result, establish his new world system. We will more readily accept a new "religion" if we throw out the old one first. Praise the Lord that we have been assured the gates of hell shall not prevail (Matt. 16:18).

That brings me to my second point in this section: tradition. It is true that we are to forget those things that are behind us and reach for those things that are before us (Phil 3:13). Once we have set our hand to the plough, if we look back, we are unfit for the kingdom of God. Tradition is sometimes bad, but that is not the whole story.

Traditions of men are not necessarily good, but godly tradition is always good. As the result of unfair teaching from only one perspective, godly tradition is being cast aside for a new, modern, "better" way. Jesus denounced the Pharisees "for laying aside the commandment of God" and holding fast the "tradition of men" (Mark 7:8). Second Thessalonians 2:15

tells us to stand fast and hold the traditions that we have been taught. This speaks of godly traditions.

Godly tradition nurtures each new generation. Parents in the Old Testament era were told to teach their children the Lord's words when they sat in their house, when they walked by the way, when they lay down at night, and when they got up in the morning. They were told to write them on the doorposts of their houses and on their gates so that their days would be multiplied (Deut. 11:19–21).

We are far from following their example, but we did try for a while, at least, to put God's commandments on display at schools and other public places. Those are now gone, and that was even a far cry from having them written on our doorposts at home. Psalm 78 stresses the importance of making known "sayings of old" (v. 2) to the children so that the generation to come might know them and that "they might set their hope in God" and "not forget" His works (vv. 6–7). The psalm also speaks of not hiding the parables and dark sayings of old from the children. Is it too late to convince Christians that "old" can be good?

Remembering the past is not a vain effort. Memorials are necessary to remind us of important, past events. We remember history not only for the sake of the dead, but also for valuable lessons. We can see what can be avoided or, in some cases, see what must be repeated. Jews remember feast days and observe them in their "generations by an ordinance for ever" (Exod. 12:17). Christians have holidays that they observe by tradition, and it is necessary, especially for teaching children, to keep those holidays.

Psalm 44 speaks of remembrance: "We have heard with our ears, O God, our fathers have told us, what work thou didst in their days, in the times of old....For they got not the land by their own sword...but thy right hand, and thine arm" (vv. 1, 3). Tradition and stories from old can be a testimony to God's goodness.

How many television programs make fun of parents that say, "When I was a little kid..."? Teenagers roll their eyes when they hear this and expect to have to listen to yet another boring tale. That's not funny, nor is it biblical. The older people are supposed to be teaching the younger ones. Children should be listening and learning from their parents' experiences quite often.

It is the common attitude, even among Christians, to be ashamed of our parents. Why are we ashamed of our parents and the older generation, when most parents of the past raised their children to have purpose. They sacrificed for their children to have not only physical needs met, but they took the time—yes, the time—to teach and build character, too. Most wouldn't even have thought of dropping their child off at a neighbor's house, day care, or grandmother's house just so they could get their nails done or take a break. As a whole, they took the responsibility to raise their children.

Yet, rebels of today think the old way was devastating. Selfish thoughts tell us that we were denied a good childhood because it consisted of discipline. We haughtily reject the old school and decide to let our children live a less rigid life to spite our parents. If only we could see Satan with his teeth shining in a satisfied grin.

So many Christians have bought this new mind-set. They feel that anything associated with tradition is oppressive. Freedom is now the pursued goal of life. This is clearly manifested in churches trying to have their atmosphere reflect a casual, non-traditional setting. They continually say, "Come as you are" or, "Just be yourself," with no indication that the gospel is all about changing people.

One day as I was teaching school, a Messianic Jewish lady told those around her that she had recently asked her father why they, being Jewish, celebrated Passover with a place set for Elijah. Then she commented, "You know, that's the danger of tradition." That same day, which was Passover, the school held a chapel service. We had communion with fluffy loaves of leavened bread, and I thought, "You know, that's the danger of not knowing tradition!" Passover is also called the Feast of Unleavened Bread, but who knew or even cared that day? First Corinthians 5:8 reminds us, "Therefore let us keep the feast, not with old leaven, neither with the leaven of malice and wickedness; but with the unleavened bread of sincerity and truth." We could have shown the students our sincerity about Passover by observing traditions of the Bible, but our flippant attitude about tradition just added to their flippant attitude toward another chapel service.

We cannot get around the fact that Christianity and the Bible are filled with tradition. There is no new way to worship or new technique to live by. It was all written long ago, and it has all been recorded in the Bible. Peter speaks of those who speak evil of the way of truth and for us not to follow them (2 Pet. 2:2). Pastors mock tradition by degrading the disciples in their sermons and saying, "Peter really struck out there." If Peter struck out, then we're not even in the game! Does ridicule of godly men from the past make us feel superior? Does it make us look better? Be careful when listening to one-sided teaching about disciples. It is true they were common, uneducated day-laborers. But, they were not common in the area of obedience, devotion, and willingness to be set apart. They certainly made mistakes, but we should not use them to justify our own sin.

Once while I was teaching fourth grade, an obedient, sweet student told me that all he would want if he were stranded on an island would be the New Testament. I pondered why he did not say the Bible. After listening to comments throughout that year and the next, it dawned on me that the children thought the Old Testament was bad and old. They saw a vast difference between the testaments rather than the unifying principles of God's faithfulness. Biased teaching had slowly but surely indoctrinated them to shun the Old Testament. Satan is patient enough to let Christianity die little by little.

Tozer summed up the completeness of the Christian Bible by stating:

We should banish from our minds forever the common, but erroneous, notion that justice and judgment characterize the God of Israel, while mercy and grace belong to the Lord of the Church. Actually there is, in principle, no difference between the Old Testament and the New. In the New Testament scriptures there is a fuller development of redemptive truth, but one God speaks in both dispensations, and what He speaks agrees with what He is. He has always dealt in mercy with mankind and will always deal in justice when His mercy is despised.[10]

One real danger of our making *religion* and *tradition* unsavory terms is that it falls right in line with society's attempt to redefine traditional institutions. New definitions for marriage, sex, and gender are on the forefront of the battle lines. We must stand strong for traditional values and definitions like never before. If all our children are hearing is that tradition is bad, they will easily change "old" definitions and even think they are doing the right thing because they learned it at church! Let's not mislead them any further. If we remove the foundations, the logical result is downfall.

Many adults who come into a church today have only tasted church when they were a child. That taste was actually a seed. We have avoided watering that seed and seek to conjure up a new experience. If only we would sing a traditional hymn to bring them immediately back to the last time they were convicted. Without saying fast, happy songs sung to the beat of a drum are wrong, the error is more in the overall way we mimic the world's music and remind people of the songs heard in such places as nightclubs and rock concerts.

Modern thought argues that any grownup must have had a bad experience with religion as a child, but we fail to realize that our new perception is more wrong. It is more likely that the older a person is, the better his religious experience was as a child. Church once was a place of reverence. If only we could meet someone who was two thousand years old. He could really tell us how it should be done.

> For the time will come when men will not endure sound doctrine; but after their own lusts shall they heap to themselves teachers, having itching ears; And they shall turn away their ears from the truth, and shall be turned unto fables.
>
> —2 Timothy 4:3–4

In our rejection of tradition, we have embraced our culture's falsity, fantasy, and fables.

Today, fables are constantly being written. They appear on colorful paper and portray colorful, fun-loving characters with a light and happy atmosphere. Fables lure with lies of an easier, less costly road. It's a road that offers peace and prosperity. Fables are stories that are not true but sound true and very good. According to Webster's Dictionary, a fable is a story in which the characters are often animals gifted with speech and other human traits; "a falsehood."[11] The movie industry is able to make one argue that the fable is true to life, but the Christian should only be concerned with real truth. Especially, concerning children, we should teach them with true stories, not fiction.

It's important to note that Jesus used parables, which may be defined as a story designed to teach a moral by suggesting a parallel, with the unsaved rather than using them to teach His disciples.[12] (See Matthew 13:13.) As we teach children, it's important to keep the world's fantasy separate from the reality of God's Word so that they will not be confused when the world tries to declare the Bible to be make-believe.

> Therefore, brethren, stand fast, and hold the traditions which ye have been taught, whether by word, or our epistle.
>
> —2 Thessalonians 2:15

Legalism

> Thou hast commanded us to keep thy precepts diligently.
>
> —Psalm 119:4

According to Webster's dictionary, the definition of *legalism* is a "strict adherence to requirements of the law…without regard to the intention of the law."[13] The primary intention of the law is not to bring us to salvation but instead to lead us to the acknowledgment of our sin. A legalist believes his precise obedience to the law will bring him salvation. He does not even see his own sinfulness. He obeys because he feels he has to, not because he wants to. His obedience is accompanied by pride because he thinks his righteous acts make him good. His pride is presumptuous because he thinks his goodness will gain him salvation. Jesus told His disciples to beware of the leaven of the Pharisees. Leaven is a representation of sin. The Pharisees' sin was not a sin of obedience, but of pride and confidence in the flesh.

The Pharisees tried to obey every law, but they could not meet all the requirements of the law all the time because of the weakness of their flesh. God requires obedience to His laws, but provides grace because of our weakness. Without grace, everyone would go to hell. Grace is the only thing that provides salvation. It's not our works that enable salvation, because we cannot obey the law.

The fact that grace is readily available does not give us an excuse to sin. (See Romans 6:1–2.) A person with a heart that is obedient and submitted to God receives His grace and, like Paul, strives to obey God's commandments. He sees there is a warring in his members pulling him toward sin, but he wants to avoid sin and sees obedience as a choice rather than coercion from God.

The new twist in church teaching focuses on the Pharisees' obedience to the law and accuses anyone who strives to know and obey God's laws as being legalistic. What was once called holiness is now called legalism. Contrary to new teaching, a Christian's goal should be righteousness.

The sin of a legalist is not the striving for obedience, but the pride of trying to prove to himself that he is good. The law does not bring salvation, but it does bring the acknowledgment of sin. How clever Satan is to make Christians stop reading the law so that they will be ignorant of right and wrong. Without the obstacle of stubborn Christians in his way, he can smoothly work out his new system with new definitions for what is right and wrong. When nobody stands against him, he can accomplish his goals.

We would not know about sin without the law. Jesus fulfilled the law by taking it a step further. He made obedience to His laws a matter of the heart. Jesus made our righteousness possible. He brought salvation by bringing a change of heart. We cannot change our hearts without Him. He is our salvation.

The Pharisees added to the law by claiming it brought salvation. We are just as guilty of wrongdoing when we subtract from the law and do not allow it to convict of sin. Today, unbalanced teaching focuses on the Pharisees' strict obedience rather than their pride. As a result, Christians now see the law as something to avoid and even disobey. This is subtracting from the law, and it leads to lawlessness.

One day while teaching school, a student explained to me his fasting regimen during a time when everyone at the school was fasting, as designated by the pastor to begin the New Year. The student said, "I fast lunch every now and then. I still have snacks, though. I don't want to get into legalism. It's really cool." He told me this as he was sitting in detention for having disobeyed a school rule. I'm sure his flesh was really being denied when he fasted a meal after snacking on French fries, candy bars, popcorn, and chips. Even though he had neglected obeying basic school rules, he felt quite clean since he was fasting a meal every now and then.

This student's priorities were out of balance. Just as Pharisees overlooked the importance of the law and how it pointed out their sin rather than gave them occasion to boast, lawless people today overlook its importance, too. Jesus warned of "omitting the weightier matters of the law, judgment, mercy, and faith" while paying attention to other things. He said we should not only do our duty as Christians, but we should not leave other things undone (Matt. 23:23).

Lest we rise up in pride, Jesus also said in Luke that we should realize that we are "unprofitable servants," even after we have done that which is our duty (Luke 17:10). In other words, we never have occasion to boast. When we say we don't have to obey God's laws because we are covered by the blood or by grace, we are missing the point. No, we don't have to obey, but when the blood is truly applied, we should want to obey.

Satan would love for Christians to think obedience to God's Word is legalistic and wrong because he knows obedience brings glory to the Lord. He also knows that Proverbs 28:4 says, "They that forsake the law praise the wicked: but such as keep the law contend with them." Our flesh should die in obedience so that we can demonstrate God's glory and grace in our lives. We must show the world that it is possible to be different and that a person can be unaffected by temptation because of Jesus' grace, not his or her own goodness.

I have seen many, many instances where Christians seek to bend a rule or throw in an exception to avoid appearing legalistically obedient. They either subtract from the law or add to it to make it work for their unique situation. The very thing they are trying to avoid—legalism—is what happens in their actions because they forget the intent of the law and make it look like they are obeying it. Pride gets in the way of obedience.

Churches are not teaching what legalism really is. If it is legalistic to be obedient, then why don't Christians unfasten their seat belts every other day. "Oh no, that would be dangerous!" is our reasoning, but it is even more dangerous to sin than to drive without a seatbelt. Why do Christians get furious at their teenagers when they put too many friends in the car with them? Because man's law forbids it and because it's dangerous. Why do Christians fear their children's exposure to the sun, but do not fear their exposure to the world? We should be more protective of our spirit than our flesh.

We Christians are legalistic about man's laws. We are diligent in wearing seat belts, never talking with our mouths full, and keeping our tires inside yellow lines. But, we take God's laws lightly and at our convenience. We claim God's love outweighs any demands on our flesh. We are told happiness is more important than any struggle required to do the right thing.

We would angrily protest if we did not receive our paycheck on the day allotted. Why not give some grace and skip a few paydays? Nobody accuses their accounting department of being legalistic about getting paychecks out every single time.

Take time to notice how modern Christians' priorities are out of place. God's law forbids sin because it, too, is dangerous. Why can't we take His law as seriously as we take man's laws? Why don't we try to obey God every time in all things?

The tolerance teachings of the world have squelched the Christian's desire to adhere to rules. It seems intolerant to stand your ground and not compromise. Where can you find a person who will not give in to circumstances or peer pressure? That person is not easily found today. Jesus was that person. He never compromised or caved in to common teachings aimed at ridiculing truth. We should seek to be like Him. He did not once bend a rule or disobey. He applied all rules exactly the way God intended them to be applied.

If strict obedience to the law, rather than pride, really were the sin of the Pharisees, all scriptures on diligence and obedience should be thrown out. To the contrary, Paul wrote to Timothy that he should "follow after righteousness, godliness, faith, love, patience, meekness" and to "fight the good fight of faith" (1 Tim. 6:11–12). He continued to say, "Keep this commandment without spot, unrebukeable, until the appearing of our Lord Jesus Christ (1 Tim. 6:14). Notice how this strict advice is from the New Testament.

With grace we are able to obey. With a change of heart we can lovingly and thankfully obey a forgiving Father who sent His only Son. The Pharisees obeyed God, but without grace and without love. They sought to be clean for selfish reasons. On the other hand, the tolerance movement today claims to love, but ignores the principle of obedience to God's rules. David Jeremiah stated in his book *Escape the Coming Night* that "where doctrine is present, without love, it is legalism; where love is present without doctrine, it is humanism."[14]

In the humanistic world, absolutes are considered to be unloving. Churches are following this humanistic doctrine in their unbalanced teaching of legalism. They are annihilating the absolutes of God's laws. Christians don't want to be labeled as intolerant and stubborn or look unkind, uncaring, and against everything "good;" but we should never try to please the world with our actions. In fact, if we are doing our job, we will make the world angry with us. They might even want to crucify us. The world hates a standard, and will take it out on the standard-bearer.

I hear of persecution in other countries, but I rarely hear about it in America. Satan has persuaded us, like the world, that holding fast to God's law is intolerant and wrong. He has convinced us that a traditional, Scripture-quoting, uncompromising Christian is something to be avoided and even ashamed of.

Satan would love nothing more than to dissolve all absolutes. He has gained much ground by persuading Christians to think gray is OK and that black-and-white thinkers are legalistic, intolerant, and arrogant. His ultimate goal is to dissolve the notion that God is God. Why can't we see the danger of abdicating Christian principles in the name of tolerance or in the name of avoiding so-called legalism?

At least the church of the past was known for obeying the Ten Commandments. The new church's attitude toward strict adherence to rules has caused many to not even heed those basic ten. How many Christians do you hear taking God's name in vain? You may notice this is prevalent, especially among young people. Is the sabbath day set apart and remembered as holy, or is it just another common day? What about the commandment that requires children to honor their father and mother? Many would have to admit this to be a rare occurrence.

Is violation of the seventh commandment prominent among Christians? That was an easy question. Adultery is very prevalent among Christians, especially under the innocent label of remarrying after a divorce. (See Matthew 5:32; Luke 16:18; Romans 7:3; and 1 Corinthians 7:39.) This is one way Christians add or subtract from the law to fit their own situation. Is the commandment against coveting committed by Christians? Is it innocent when preachers continually talk of their desire for material goods?

Since the Pharisees' sin was pride rather than obedience, we must refocus our teaching on the importance of obedience to God's laws. Our obedience is the best indication of our sincerity to Him and of our taking grace seriously. If we are truly repentant when we come to Christ, holiness should be our main priority. Just as action in marriage proves a person's love, action in our commitment to Christ proves our love for Him. Our action proves our heart's genuine desires. If we want to do the right thing, we will. If we don't want to live righteously, we won't.

> Whosoever abideth in him sinneth not.
>
> —1 John 3:6

The Pharisees lacked an internal experience with God, yet performed outwardly as if they had. So, it was fake. How much more fake is it for us to claim to have had an internal experience when there is no expression outwardly. Jonathan Edwards said:

> We hurt our religion when we dismiss what Scripture insists is most important, while we emphasize revelations and emotional impressions. We don't want to be legalistic, we say, nor governed by the old covenant, and so we spend all our time analyzing our emotional experiences thinking that we will find the evidence of grace here in these extraordinary signs and wonders. We pride ourselves on our discernment and wisdom, but all this is actually darkness and delusion. Remember

what Scripture says: 'Every word of God is pure: He is a shield unto them that put their trust in Him. Add thou not unto His words, lest He reprove thee, and thou be found a liar.[15]

Edwards found people seeking grace in emotional experiences rather than in a changed life. Today, we find the same. But, grace is found in the pure life of a Christian. Grace at work has evidence. A saved person acts more godly than he did before he was saved. There is a change of heart, a change of character, a change of thoughts, and a change of motivation.

Some of the Christians who are speaking against legalism are, in fact, deeply entrenched in it. Legalistic Pharisees assumed that once sin was committed, it could be undone by a righteous act that would outweigh the previous wrongdoing. Today's legalists, however, believe grace is the undoing of unrighteousness. Using grace as an object of "undoing" sin is legalism at its core. It ignores the intent of grace.

Christians are readily committing sin with plans of asking forgiveness later. Most Christians, like Pharisees, do not even see themselves as sinful because of their ability to apply grace. It is not common to see Christian humility, but a boasting of freedom from the law. This is taken a step further in today's young Christian. Their proud and arrogant attitudes are obvious. Because of our unbalanced teaching, children do not feel sorrow for sin and, in most cases, do not even try to avoid it. However, grace is given to the humble, not the haughty. (See James 4:6.)

Jesus told the Pharisees that they were "shutting up the kingdom of heaven against men" (Matt. 23:13). We are doing the same by not allowing the law to point out sin. We cannot lead men to Christ without the law of God. The law is our schoolmaster. Excuses for disobedience on the basis of freedom from the law will cause deep regret that cannot be undone when the kingdom of heaven is shut and hell's mouth is wide open to receive those who have been deceived.

Chapter 7

UNBALANCED TEACHING: PART 2

For so is the will of God, that with well doing ye may put to silence the ignorance of foolish men: as free, and not using your liberty for a cloak of maliciousness, but as the servants of God.

—1 Peter 2:15–16

FREEDOM

A FEAR OF LEGALISM has swung Christians to the extreme of using their freedom for a cloak of maliciousness. Freedom from the law does not mean there are no boundaries for the Christian. In fact, we are free from the condemnation of the law, not the limits of the law. Unbalanced teaching has not taught this subject properly. Adults who hear this imbalance tend to throw out any previous learning about biblical servanthood and Christian duty, while children, who have no foundational teaching to throw out, are readily accepting the concept that rules don't apply to Christians.

This newfound freedom is the foundation for rampant lawlessness. It is very ironic how many are claiming freedom and abundant grace and pardon while continuing to commit sin and disobey God's commandments. Jesus said, "Whosoever committeth sin is the servant of sin" (John 8:34). Peter said of false teachers, "While they promise them liberty, they themselves are the servants of corruption: for of whom

199

a man is overcome, of the same is he brought in bondage" (2 Pet. 2:19).

Our freedom lies in the fact that we have been made free from sin not free to sin. Some are now claiming we have gained freedom to be ourselves. In a Christian's new freedom, he actually becomes a "servant of righteousness" (Rom. 6:18). Servanthood, duty, and obligation are a part of Christianity. Liberty is even a law within itself. James speaks of the "perfect law of liberty" (James 1:25). If we abuse this by claiming we have no obligations, we can be a stumbling block to new converts and even embolden them to do evil. (See 1 Corinthians 8:9–10.) This very problem is active among young Christians.

> But whoso looketh into the perfect law of liberty, and continueth therein, he being not a forgetful hearer, but a doer of the work, this man shall be blessed in his deed.
>
> —James 1:25

In other words, good works bring blessing. Unbalanced teaching assumes we have freedom from righteous deeds, but with our freedom comes responsibility, not irresponsibility. If a person still desires freedom from laws and restraints, he is not truly a converted Christian. Conversion results in a new desire to obey laws and to live within safe boundaries. It is the rebel who wants freedom from laws.

Christians gain the freedom to make the right choices. Our freedom in America is based on the fact that we are free to do the right thing. The law will not hinder us if we are doing the right thing. There is no law saying we have to do the right thing, but if we do the wrong thing, the law will be applied. Peter Marshall stated, "What we need is not law enforcement, but law observance. In a modern society there is no real freedom from law. There is only freedom in law."[1]

Under grace, we can do the right thing by choice. We are free to deny ourselves. We are free to fulfill our duties as parents, neighbors, and Christian citizens. Our freedom should be used, not denied. We have an obligation as Christians. We must choose rightly, be responsible, and realize we are accountable for our actions.

The Lord gives us true freedom. After all, "Where the Spirit of the Lord is, there is liberty" (2 Cor. 3:17). Liberation from the bondage of sin is the most satisfying condition for a human. True freedom is in Christ. A realization that Jesus bore the burden of our sin on the cross and has justified us by His blood is true freedom from sin. When we are free from the bondage of sin, we are free to do the right thing. That kind of liberty is where the Lord is.

A. W. Tozer noted, "The important thing about a man is not where he goes when he is compelled to go, but where he goes when he is free to go where he will."[2] Jesus gives us the choice. We can do what we want when we are saved. If we are truly converted, our hearts will want to please Him. We don't always please Him, but our heart's desire is to please Him. When a Christian wants to go to a bar, watch filthy movies, talk like a sailor, live like the world, or fulfill the lusts of the flesh, he is not truly converted, nor is he free.

Yet, modern Christians are claiming unconstrained freedom to do just that. Ironically, the new definition of freedom in churches today is the foundation for rampant lawlessness. The imbalance in this teaching is actually a direct misapplication of the word. We are not free to sin, but free from sin. This teaching will bring unpleasant repercussions, especially for the next generation. Already this generation is coming to adulthood feeling no guilt when involved in drinking, gambling, fornication, body piercing, tattooing, profanity, selfishness, or lying, among other things.

Initially, we do not see that Christians are saying they are free to sin, but in reality they are saying just that when they commit these acts and have no guilt while doing them. We've been taught that if it makes us happy, pursue it. We are lovers of pleasures more than lovers of God. Young adults go to church services, attend youth groups, and have a form of godliness. But, they are denying the power of godliness (2 Tim. 3:4–5). They do not reflect the freedom to be godly, but rather the freedom to commit and therefore be enslaved to sin.

I have heard groups of Christian teenagers talking about gambling, drinking, getting a tattoo, and other such activities. They feel they are bound to the law of the land with age limits, but they see no law from God concerning these sins once they reach the adequate age. They have been taught that they are free from the law. They think the sin of committing these acts is in disobeying man's law, not God's. When they reach adulthood, they fully intend to gamble, drink, and get a tattoo and feel guilt-free while doing it. Paul warns us in Galatians that we are not to use our liberty for an occasion for the flesh to commit sin (Gal. 5:13).

The writer of Psalm 119 vows to keep God's law continually and to walk in liberty because he seeks God's precepts (Ps. 119:44–45). There is liberty in seeking to obey God's laws. That's the counterpart to the teachings on freedom and the part of liberty that we are not hearing.

Certain revelings and instances of people "letting loose" have been cropping up in church under the label of "freedom," and they have been perceived as virtuous occurrences. Christians claim that our wild nature is an honorable trait. Others say even God is wild at heart. New definitions for the word *wild* do not change the fact that it is an untamed, unrestrained, undisciplined, fleshly trait that must die in the presence of the Almighty.

The danger in this new thinking is that it is identical to the world's mentality. A humanistic value from the Enlightenment era was that more freedom is better. We have to be careful that we do not align our doctrine with teachers of the rebellious Enlightenment. Even though the Enlightenment began nearly three centuries ago, its beliefs are strong today. Hannah Arendt explains in her book *The Origins of Totalitarianism* that:

> Modern man has come to resent everything given to him, even his own existence. In his resentment of all laws merely given to him, he proclaims openly that everything is permitted and believes secretly that everything is possible...This is why the worst among us are full of passionate intensity while so many of the best lack all conviction. For unless the best among us intervene, the worst shall bring to fruition that technological totalitarian tyranny.[3]

Proclaiming everything is permitted causes us not to take a stand against things that were once outlawed without question. If we do nothing while wicked men "take the liberty" to bring the totalitarian tyranny of a new world system, we will be overtaken. The rule of bondage by the Antichrist is something we cannot fathom. God warned His people through Jeremiah that they were not hearkening unto Him in proclaiming liberty, and therefore, He would proclaim a liberty for them "to the sword, to the pestilence, and to the famine" (Jer. 34:17). We must see the danger in taking our freedom too far.

Worship

> But in vain they do worship me, teaching for doctrines the commandments of men.
>
> —Matthew 15:9

Worship is necessary because God requires it. Balanced teaching on worship is critical if we are to worship Him in spirit and in truth. Satan would love to corrupt the heart of worship, and he is the master of counterfeit worship. Something counterfeit looks real, but it is not. We cannot worship the way we want, and we must not believe we are free to worship how we please.

Dr. David Jeremiah wrote, "I don't think the evangelical church as a whole comes even close to worshiping God."[4] Christians are deeply entrenched in what pleases man rather than what pleases God. Paul asked in Colossians, "Wherefore if ye be dead with Christ from the rudiments of the world, why, as though living in the world, are ye subject to ordinances, (Touch not, taste not; handle not; Which all are to perish with the using;) after the commandments and doctrines of men?" (Col. 2:20–22).

Churches think they are following Scripture in their worship when they actually way out of balance. Certain Scriptures are taken out of context and misapplied. For instance, many churches stress dancing is important to the Lord because David danced before the Lord. That is only part of the picture. If dancing before the Lord is mentioned in the Bible, then dancing is permissible, but we must look to see what conditions invoke it. David danced as he rejoiced and praised the Lord for accepting his second attempt at bringing the ark of the covenant back to Israel.

To say David was undressed, as many say, is totally against what the Bible teaches. Second Samuel 6:14 clearly states he was wearing a linen ephod while dancing, which represents righteousness (Rev. 19:8). That scripture has been completely overlooked. Michal did not approve of his worship because she was the king's wife and kings were not to humble themselves in worship to anyone. She had pride. Worship requires humility. David lay aside his kingship as an example of what Jesus would later do when He came to earth as a man.

David said while worshiping that he would become even more vile, undignified, and humble in his worship to God. To misapply "undignified" as being stripped naked opens the door for what we already see in some churches in the way of total vulgarity and wantonness in the worship services. In the name of freedom, people worship without restraint to the flesh while they flutter wildly and bebop to a worldly beat. They mistake feeling for worship.

David's dance occurred after a momentous challenge in his life. There was critical significance in the transportation of the ark of the covenant back to Israel.

There is also an imbalance in the new songs we are hearing. The Bible talks about singing a new song in worship. (See Psalm 33:3; 40:3; 96:1; and 98:1.) I have found as I get older that certain experiences with the Lord prompt me to sing a "new" song from my heart to Him. I can sing "Amazing Grace" with new understanding as I grow older, and after learning the story of the man who wrote "It Is Well With My Soul," I sing it with new understanding. New revelation causes us to sing a new song unto the Lord. It comes from the heart.

To teach that a new song requires writing a new ditty every month or writing something that isn't even in the Bible is another misapplication of Scripture. The push for new songs seems to be the excuse for throwing out hymns from the past and replacing them with songs that contain modern language, phrases, and even slang spellings and pronunciations. Tozer noted, "If you give yourself to the contemporary fare of music that touches the baser emotions, it will shape your mind and emotions and desires, whether you admit it or not."[5] Tozer also gives insight by saying that the new songs are "saccharin ballads" that "clutter" Christianity.[6] Amen!

We are singing sing songs without theological content and without well-composed music. Congregations are not questioning the songs with very little scriptural validity. The music in church took a marked downward turn when we started singing about ourselves rather than the holy attributes and ways of God.

Some churches today call their worship services "celebration" services. It is a good thing to worship God with a "joyful noise," but there is balance in also knowing the scripture that informs us to make a "solemn sound" (Ps. 92:3). Adoration, awe, and true worship of God as the holy, sovereign, almighty, omnipotent Holy One has given way to celebration. A party atmosphere has replaced what was once called holy.

This concept of celebration is heavily emphasized in the world. Advertising campaigns, birthday parties, anniversaries, extravaganzas, commemorations, bonfires, fanfares, festivals, and holidays celebrate. But, to celebrate is not to worship. We are called to worship. We do not easily see this error because the Bible does teach that the Israelites celebrated feast days. Celebration is not wrong, but celebration should never replace worship.

Furthermore, there is a difference between the Israelites' celebrations and our celebrations today. In some cases, celebration has become entertainment-oriented. Our celebrations focus on people. Entertainment has crowded out valuable worship time and diverted our attention away from the Lord. There is a great difference between entertainment and worship, between the church's modern celebrations and true godly devotion.

Another misconception is for Christians to think God needs our worship. Many new songs focus on the idea that God needs us to fulfill His desires or even to fulfill the prophecy of His coming. Some sing that the more God is worshiped, the bigger He becomes. Others sing that God's strength is measured by human strength and that we must be strong so that He will be strong. Our worship does not attribute majesty to Him. God needs no defenders. He is God without us, and numbers do not add to His authenticity.

Songs portraying us as a mighty army or as history makers are not wrong, but it is shaky ground for those who have not even gone through boot camp. The writer of Psalm 119 said, "My lips shall utter praise, when thou hast taught me thy statutes" (v. 171). Children must learn the principles of Christianity before real worship can take place. They need to learn surrender before they learn how to be a warrior. They must also learn servanthood before they learn leadership. Children sing proudly that they are "warriors" when they don't even know the first thing about fighting battles or even the existence of an enemy.

One youth pastor asked the youth in his church, "Is there anyone who needs a lesson on how to worship?" Then he answered his own question with, "You've been beaten down and hemmed up by hard sermons. You've heard it all. I've heard it all twice." He was only adding to their complacency about learning more about the Bible, their victim mentality, and their pride of knowing all they needed to know about worship. The truth is that most young Christians are woefully ignorant of true worship.

Children are too often encouraged that anything goes in worship. They are told God accepts anything as long as the label reads "worship." There is absolutely no fear of the Lord or true reverence when children approach Him this way. They see Him as just another dispenser of goodies who must be worn down with their flattery and begging.

Some new worship songs cause saints to court Christ as they would court someone in a carnal romance. Children and young adults often see no difference between true spiritual adoration of a sovereign, holy God and a carnal love affair with someone their equal. Modern Christians readily recognize Jesus' manhood but refuse to see His deity. Too often, they associate Him with any common relationship. They see Him as an equal. But, the fact that He, who is God, would die for our worthlessness shows greater love than any romance or earthly relationship could attain. It is great love because we are not His equal. He loved those of much less significance than Himself.

In teaching that anything goes in worship, we do not teach that a person must "come clean" before approaching the throne. Repentance and humility are necessary on a daily basis, not just at our conversion. God will not answer certain questions until we deal with certain issues. If we regard iniquity in our heart, the Lord will not hear us (Ps. 66:18). The wise A. W. Tozer points out, "No worship is wholly pleasing to God until there is nothing in me displeasing to God."[7]

With the wrong focus, we get away from true worship. We become flippant as we throw a party on Sunday mornings. We are not producing Christians who worship in spirit and in truth. Our youth's attention is for successful people, rich athletes, and movie stars. So, many center their church services after them. Even our homes are not set apart unto God. Our entertainment is shallow and perverted. "Christian" has become a tolerant, loving, palatable label that people are called under to have fun in Christ. Meanwhile, Christ is calling us to carry a cross.

It's All About a Relationship

For whosoever shall do the will of my Father which is in heaven, the same is my brother, and sister, and mother.

—Matthew 12:50

According to this verse in Matthew, obedience is the prerequisite to a relationship with Christ. Churches highlight the importance of relationship, but this teaching has become very skewed.

We tell people, "God is seeking a relationship with you." But, we must understand that God does not seek our relationship for His sake. He seeks it for our sake. According to Tozer, "To believe in Him adds nothing to his perfections; to doubt Him takes nothing away."[8] God says, "If I were hungry, I would not tell thee" (Ps. 50:12). Modern Christians tend to see this relationship as a partnership, but with God, we should see that we are nothing and He is everything.

It is true that we, the church, are the bride of Christ, and He loves us very much. He even delights in His saints (Ps. 16:3). However, our understanding of this love and this relationship is crucial to our comprehension of the whole subject.

We must understand the covenant between Christ and the Father. Man had no part in appeasing God's anger at

Calvary. Our relationship with God pales in comparison to the relationship between the Father and the Son. (See Luke 10:22 and John 1:18.) It really isn't about us.

Churches focus so strongly on this word that we see it in church ads that read, "It's not about religion; it's about relationship!" We hear that it is the main purpose behind life groups, cell groups, home groups, Sunday schools, and church services. Nine out of ten preachers will mention it as priority in the Christian life, yet they do not emphasize obedience to God's Word, our witness to the world, or missionary work. They just put "relationship" at the top of the Christian's list. Why so much emphasis on this word? Who would question its importance? Who would go against mainstream Christianity and teach something else as having more value to God?

Everyone seems to seek a relationship with popular, affluent people. It is common to seek relationships with important people. But, there are requirements for true relationship and only a few gain that place. When that place is achieved, a person is finally seen as an equal. It is presumptuous for people to think they are friends with someone when they are not. It is even more presumptuous for us to think we are capable of having a quick and easy relationship with God. God is farther above us than any movie star or athlete could ever be. It is so much harder to gain access to

Him than to any movie star, or even the president. However, when a relationship with God is established, through Christ, it is never one of equal status. There is one God and none beside Him (1 Sam. 2:2; Deut. 4:35; Mark 12:32). He is the Most High (Ps. 91:9; Dan. 7:22; Acts 7:48). Even though Jesus is fully man, He is also fully God and therefore our Master and head (Matt. 23:8–10; 1 Cor. 11:3). We are joint-heirs with Christ, counted as sons, whereas Jesus is the Son of God (Rom. 8:17).

Worship will be directed toward God and His Son throughout eternity. We, as worshipers, will not share in receiving worship since Jesus alone holds the "name which is above every name" (Phil. 2:9; Eph. 2:21).

The error with the word *relationship* is that it causes us to think we are in an equal partnership with God. Satan is so clever in making something look harmless and even godly when, in fact, it is not. The only reason we can fellowship, come in contact, or get near God is because Jesus was willing to be the mediator to span the infinite gulf between God and man. Friendship is reserved for only a few. Jesus said in John 15:14, "Ye are my friends, if ye do whatsoever I command you." Only Moses and Abraham were called friends of God in the Old Testament. Yes, we can have contact with God, but it is not cheap. It is not an easy-come, easy-go relationship.

The price Jesus paid was very high to gain our access to God. The imbalanced teachings of our relationship with God does not point out the expense of Jesus' life and death. His life on earth was a life of sacrifice. He became a man acquainted with sorrow and grief. God stooped low to become a human. He didn't come and live a comfortable life of a rich man who accepted glory and honor. Instead, He suffered rejection that ended in His bloody death.

Contrary to modern thought, relationship is not what we should primarily seek. That is a diversion to our true purpose. We are to be servants of God, not equals. While Jesus was preaching one day, the multitude told Him that His mother and brethren were outside and wanted to speak with Him. You would think the mother or brother of someone could gain entry to that person without hindrance. Instead, Jesus answered, "Who is my mother? and who are my brethren?" He continued by explaining that whosoever did the will of His father, the same was His brother, sister, or mother (Matt. 12:48–50). So, the emphasis is dependent not on relationship or presumption of kinship, but on obedience to the Father. God existed in heaven long before He created earth and He spent just as long a time without a relationship with humans. He was not lonely.

God chose to reveal His character when He created man. We are the recipients of that revelation. We must comprehend the blessing of being allowed to receive His revelation. The bottom line is about Him being God and that we have been chosen to see that great truth. Our goal should be to point as many as possible to that realization.

David Jeremiah states in his book *Escape the Coming Night* that "this is what apostasy is all about: forsaking the true meaning of biblical doctrine or choosing which doctrines to believe and which to discard."[9] Jonathan Edwards warned in his book *Religious Affections*, "For us to emphasize something that Scripture minimizes, or for us to minimize something that Scripture stresses, tends to give us a warped idea of religion. It leads us indirectly and gradually away from a healthy realistic view of ourselves and into delusion and hypocrisy."[10] Churches must stop trying to make the gospel more palatable to its listeners. We are leaning to our own understanding and trying to explain too much. The gospel is most effective when it is declared, not explained, because it is addressed to faith and not the intellect.

Chapter 8

MIXTURE: PART 1

But they set their abominations in the house, which is called by my name, to defile it.

—Jeremiah 32:34

I T'S ONE THING to be secular while in the world, but it's a whole different standing to be worldly while in the church. God would rather a person be hot or cold (Rev. 3:15). We are to be committed to the world or completely committed to Him. Worldly Christians are spewed from God's mouth. He hates mixture.

The church is like a boat in the ocean. All is well as long as the ocean stays on the outside of the boat, but when the ocean comes in, the boat sinks. The Bible speaks of the wicked being like the troubled sea (Isa. 57:20). When the wicked bring heresies into the church, tragedy results. The union of good and evil through compromise eventually leads to deception. This deception clouds the eyes of those who refuse to see the fatal mixture.

In a parable, Jesus said that while men slept, enemies came and sowed tares among the wheat field. He explained that the field is the world, the good seeds are the children of the kingdom, and the tares are the children of the wicked one (Matt. 13:25, 38). Good men and evil men can be present in the same place, yet remain distinctly separate.

Wheat and tares look alike to man's eyes, but God knows the difference.

Paul was troubled "with tears" for three years about what he saw would happen in the church when he left. He told the church that grievous wolves would enter in, sparing not the flock. He warned that even men of their own flock would speak perverse things to draw them away (Acts 20:29–31). How can children of the wicked one be inside our churches? Even worse, how can Satan's men be in church leadership? If Satan is truly the great deceiver, and he is, what better way to trick people than to infiltrate from within. Isn't that the goal of many terrorists today?

We are less vigilant with familiarity. As an enemy of a country is more likely to do damage after infiltrating its boundaries, Satan, too, makes himself at home before he grasps his victim in his hand.

We are to "beware of false prophets" that wear sheep's clothing, but inwardly are "ravening wolves" (Matt. 7:15). We should constantly be on guard in our churches and pray for our pastors. We must be vigilant to the enemy's tactics. The Bible mentions more than once the presence of strangers in the sanctuary (Jer. 51:51). Jeremiah's heart was broken because both prophet and priest were profane in God's house (Jer. 23:9, 11). God commands us not to allow the heathen into the congregation (Lam. 1:10). Paul gives a serious warning concerning God's wrath against the "ungodliness and unrighteousness of men, who hold the truth in unrighteousness" (Rom. 1:18).

In the last days, Satan will deceive with "signs and lying wonders with all deceivableness of unrighteousness" (2 Thess. 2:10). The text continues to say that the cause of deception is because people do not love the truth. God, therefore, sends "strong delusion" so that men will even "believe a lie" (2 Thess. 2:11). God doesn't protect those who refuse His truth.

Since the church is not seeking to know God as fervently as we are seeking to know the latest worldly attractions, we are falling away and being deceived. We must stand fast for the truth without compromise!

There is no safety cut-off valve for deception. It continues and multiplies with no end. If only a sinful shepherd could be deceived, then the sheep would be safe. But, bad shepherds lead sheep astray. Many times people even love to be led astray. (See Jeremiah 5:31.) When people are deceived, they do not want to hear truth and the "word of the Lord is unto them a reproach; they have no delight in it" (Jer. 6:10).

We must hearken to God when He warns us about things we have previously been unaware of. We must not be like Judah, who would not receive correction. (See Jeremiah 7:28.) We must not harden our hearts and continue to pollute the Lord's house with worldliness. Pastors must heed the warning of the prophets and be willing to turn from doctrines that are leading their flocks astray. Like one bad apple in a barrel, evil that enters a church can corrupt the fruit of that church. We must reject worldliness and deception and delight only in godliness and the Word of the Lord.

We must realize that we are a generation of Christians who despise God's judgments, walk not in His statutes, and who are polluting His Sabbaths because our hearts are seeking after idols. (See Ezekiel 20:16.) How is it that we are despising God's judgments and are not walking in His statutes? We do it by respecting men's laws over God's laws. While we are adamant about wearing a seatbelt, we are nonchalant about putting on the armor of God. Although God is clear concerning conditions for divorce, it is common among Christians for various reasons because judges allow it. We also feel it is fine to gamble or drink when men's laws permit it. Some Christians even feel abortion is not wrong since man's law has legalized it. These are not God's laws.

Men's laws concerning drinking and gambling allow these activities at certain ages. Does age make a difference with God? It is maturity that makes a difference to God. Maturity prepares a person for His work. Contrary to modern thought, maturity and reaching a certain age does not enable a person to delve into worldliness without effect.

If we believed what God's Word says, we would see that youthful lusts should be resisted. Maturity brings us out of those entanglements. Maturity enables us to flee youthful lusts. (See 2 Timothy 2:22.) Maturity says, "I'm twenty-one now, so I will not drink." We see results of how people who have flirted with drinking, smoking, and drugs in their youth now have matured to see the harmful effects. Other times, we see those experimenters did not mature and have major problems as a result. The regret is that many of them were introduced to their problem by a parent or a law that said they could handle it because they were old enough.

In the verse mentioned earlier, we were told that our hearts are seeking after idols (Ezek. 20:16). How? We are a generation that loves pleasure more than we love God. (See 2 Timothy 3:4.) We mix enticing pleasure such as entertainment into our church sermons, prayer meetings, worship services, children's classes, and life groups. We do not easily recognize idolatry in our churches. We associate idols with fat chunks of stone or wood. But, we should know that idolatry is a hidden matter of the heart rather than an outer, visual matter of stone images. The idolatrous heart assumes that God is what He is not. We assume He does not care that we are making Him into our own pleasure-loving image.

Romans 2:22 cuts to the quick by asking if we that think we abhor idols commit sacrilege? Are we guilty of violating that which is sacred, holy, and set-apart? We must not think we are standing when we are not, especially when entertaining thoughts about God that are unworthy of Him (1 Cor. 10:12).

Ephesians 5 and Colossians 3 outline ungodliness that pollutes God's house. See if you recognize any of these among today's Christians: fornication, uncleanness, covetousness, filthiness, foolish talking, jesting, inordinate (exceeding proper limits) affections, blasphemy, filthy communication, and lying (Eph 5:3–4; Col. 3:5–8). However, many newcomers to church are characterized by these traits. As the church, we should first show love and acceptance and teach godliness later.

But as Christians, how can we stand before the Lord in His house as we wear our scanty clothing and caps that flaunt filthy logos? Why do we show worldly videos with all kinds of uncleanness? Is there laughter at inordinate phrases? How many leaders succumb to foolish jesting by telling beer jokes, off-color jokes, disrespectful jokes, blasphemous jokes? How common is it to hear the language of the world in church? Isaiah 5:20 warns, "Woe unto them that call evil good."

A. W. Tozer noticed how "worldliness is an accepted part of our way of life. We are not producing saints...Our literature is shallow and our hymnody borders on sacrilege and scarcely anyone appears to care."[1] God instructs us not to be partakers with the world and to have "no fellowship with the unfruitful works of darkness, but rather reprove them" (Eph. 5:7, 11). If God tells us to reprove them, why are we accepting them?

What fellowship hath righteousness with unrighteousness and what fellowship hath light with darkness? (See 2 Corinthians 6:14.) God is specific about separation. The profane should not be mixed with holy (Ezek. 22: 26), and the precious should be separated from the vile (Jer. 15:19).

Does a label that reads "church" make everything inside its doors clean? Does a cup of clean water purify a contaminated sewer? No. But a cup of sewer water contaminates a crystal-clear pond. Does our fusion of unholy with holy cause everything in the church to become holy? Do Christians' tattoos become holy because they are Christian symbols? What rubs off, the good or the bad?

The prophet Haggai explains:

> If one bear holy flesh in the skirt of his garment, and with his skirt do touch bread, or pottage, or wine, or oil, or any meat, shall it be holy? The priests answered Haggai and said, No. Then said Haggai, If one that is unclean by a dead body touch any of these, shall it be unclean? Then, the priests answered and said, It shall be unclean. Then answered Haggai, and said, So is this people, and so is this nation before me, saith the LORD; and so is every work of their hands: and that which they offer there is unclean.
>
> —Haggai 2:12–14

So, we see that our association with worldliness affects everything we attempt to do inside the church. Paul cautioned that "a little leaven leaveneth the whole lump" (1 Cor. 5:6). It's our worldliness that affects everything we have contact with, not our godliness.

TAINTED WORSHIP

> Her priests have violated my law, and have
> profaned mine holy things: they have put no
> difference between the holy and profane, neither
> have they shewed difference between the unclean
> and the clean, and have hid their eyes from my
> sabbaths, and I am profaned among them.
>
> —Ezekiel 22:26

"You're crazy!" yells the song leader as the congregation laughs at such an implication. But what's new about that? Christians today are not ashamed to be labeled wild, mad, raving, confused, unbalanced, frenzied, excited, or insane. They even say they are "wasted on Jesus."

A. W. Tozer's words were prophetic for what we see today.

> People have been over-stimulated to the place
> where their nerves are jaded and their tastes
> corrupted. Natural things have been rejected to
> make room for things artificial. The sacred has
> been secularized, the holy vulgarized, and worship
> converted into a form of entertainment.[2]

Children's brochures are printed en masse with the heading "Getting Wild for the Kingdom," which includes "wild worship, wild games, and wild fun." T-shirts are advertised declaring the person is "brainwashed." Others read "rebel with a cause," draped above a picture of Jesus hanging on the cross. Another cleverly states "A bread-crumb & Fish" hoping the viewer will be reminded of Jesus instead of the popular clothing store known for its filthy advertising. Another T-shirt displays Jesus hanging between the two thieves, boasting of a "public display of affection." What filthy mixture. The good message becomes tainted by corruption.

A pastor exclaims, "Hail, almighty choir!" He continues by stating "reverence is appropriate at times, but so is expression!" The song leader yells, "Let's hear it for the band," as colored lights flash and the steel guitar still rings in the congregation's ears. An upcoming singles' event is modeled after a 1930s dinner theater and features music, horse races, and a big band. Yes, I'm still talking about church. Halloween is celebrated with all the costumes, candy, and festivities, except a "clean" label is put on it.

Test the waters. Walk into church and be alert. Do you see inappropriate attire? Do you hear inappropriate language? Don't complacently turn away and say, "Who am I to judge?" Look at it. Would Jesus approve? Is the Holy Spirit present? Compare what you see with fifty years ago. Are we more enlightened because we know the true definition of freedom? Do we see coffee cups and water bottles because people cannot die to the flesh for one hour? Do Christians refuse to treat the sanctuary in God's house as a separate place, or do they treat it the same as the grocery store or their living room? Is God's house common?

> They have cast fire into thy sanctuary, they have defiled by casting down the dwelling place of thy name to the ground.
>
> —Psalm 74:7

Numerous modern Christians think that denying the flesh means only denying extra comforts. Others feel it is a denial of sinful things. They do not usually think that denying necessary, daily needs are a part of the Christian walk. When modern Christians arrogantly say they have denied their flesh by not stopping at Starbucks that morning, I think of tearful imprisoned missionaries living a meek existence for Christ.

Dr. Nick Needham has well said that "there is something slightly sinister about Christians having a self-indulgent spiritual party while the world around them is sliding into the outer darkness, where there is weeping and gnashing of teeth, where the worm never dies and the fire is never quenched." He also points out how "Jonathan Edwards teaches us that we need to confront the soul-destroying idolatry of entertainment and fun that dominates our society, and appears to be hypnotizing and seducing the Church."[3]

When fun is our main focus, we are out of balance. When fun is the daily cry of our flesh, we are out of balance. However, mankind has been blessed with the ability to experience fun, amusement, and entertainment. We can praise the Lord, for we are fearfully and wonderfully made (Ps. 139:14).

God instructs us to set our affection on things above, not on things on the earth (Col. 3:2). Evidence of earthly affection is often revealed in modern worship services. This may hit a sensitive nerve with many, but it is nevertheless true. The glorying of the flesh and the lifting up of unholy hands in the sanctuary is prevalent in many American worship services.

The guilt lies mostly with Charismatic churches. In our bold ridicule of "lesser" churches for being prudish, we've swung the pendulum of error further in the opposite direction toward liberty. In an attempt to correct cold, hard-hearted church services with spiritual ones, we have allowed the world to step in and offer a mixed worship that appeals to our flesh.

In the place of holy, reverent, biblical worship has come a golden calf. Aaron listened to the requests of the people and decided they could worship God their own way by using an eye-pleasing visual that supposedly manifested God's presence. We are guilty of the same idol worship, today. We are doing it our way. We are doing it just like Egypt. We are different from the world only in our calling it godly. The world does not claim to be worshiping God at their rock concerts or at their parties. The world is cold, but we are a lukewarm mixture.

God quickly dealt with Nadab and Abihu for offering "strange fire" to Him. (See Leviticus 10:1–2.) Most churched children today haven't heard this story. They are hearing stories with happier endings. They are being told that freedom in Christ is the ultimate goal. We learn from Nadab and Abihu that it is very serious to offer what is unintended for worship before the great King whose name is dreadful (Mal 1:14). His name is Jealous and He is a consuming fire (Exod. 34:14; Deut. 4:24). Can we really offend God in our worship? Doesn't grace cover mistakes? The fact remains, God is holy.

Evidently, worship is important to God because He gave clear instructions for it. David tried to bring the ark of the covenant back into the Hebrew camp his own way on a new cart. Uzzah died as a result (2 Sam. 6:3–7). God didn't cause His grace nor His mercy to cover that mistake even though Uzzah sincerely thought he was doing the right thing. God still wanted it brought in His way. Today's worship leaders lead the congregation to worship their own way and many others are seeking how to worship God in a new way. David and the Israelites "played before God with all their might, with singing" and with instruments (1 Chron. 13:8). Wouldn't we argue that singing with all our might before God would be pleasing to Him? But, in this story we find the anger of the Lord was kindled nonetheless because they did not sanctify themselves and did not seek God's "due order…according to the word of the Lord" (1 Chron. 15:13, 15). The new cart used by Israel was just what the Philistines had used. Israel followed the world's idea of transporting God's holiness. (See 1 Samuel 6:7.)

Certain things must line up before a person dances with zeal. Having zeal for God is stressed in our churches, but we fail to remember that God commands that the zeal be according to knowledge (Rom. 10:2). We must not be ignorant of God's righteousness and go about establishing our own righteousness (Rom. 10:3).

John Bevere states in his book *Fear of the Lord* that "this lack of knowledge caused the Israelites to mimic the gentile, or world's, way of carrying the presence of the Lord."[4] When the Israelites corrected their mistake, we find that they went back to the way that was written in the law and decided to have only Levites carry the ark. They were told to sanctify themselves before they carried the ark of God upon their shoulders with the staves on "as Moses commanded" according to the word of the Lord. After doing it God's way, then, the Israelites were ready to sing, "lifting up the voice with joy" (1 Chron. 15:2, 12, 15–16, 26).

There is a proper order for worship, whether we are feeling a newfound freedom or not. Bevere, again, puts it well:

> As noted in the Scriptures, music plays a significant, key role in cultivating an atmosphere for the presence of the Lord. It has the ability to open and prepare a person's heart. Consider the contemporary Christian music that is so popular today—it often gets its inspiration from the demonic music of the world. If the world has hard rock, we can too! If it has rap, we'll copy it. If the world has

a certain dance, we'll imitate it. If the world has MTV, we can too. The list goes on. In each case, we try to copy the world. How far will this go? If you want to predict the new music ministry trend, don't pray—just turn on MTV and watch or listen to what the world is doing. So, who is leading whom?[5]

Sometimes, God's people are doing everything they've been told to do, but He still rejects their worship. Why? The condition of their heart is wrong. Worship is very serious. It must be done correctly. Our insides and our outsides must line up. In Amos 5:21–24, God tells His people, "I hate, I despise your feast days, and I will not smell in your solemn assemblies. Though ye offer me burnt offerings and your meat offerings, I will not accept them: neither will I regard the peace offerings of your fat beasts. Take thou away from me the noise of thy songs; for I will not hear the melody of thy viols. But let judgment run down as waters, and righteousness as a mighty stream."

Why would God despise the very things He had established for worshiping Him? It was because His people continued to flirt with the pagan idols, Moloch and Chiun (v. 26). The Israelites would not give up the world's way of worshiping. They clung to false worship. They thought they could have both. They thought they could have a mixture of the world's gods and their God. Their heart was divided (Hosea 10:2).

I had the opportunity to go to Israel in 2001. We had a wonderful tour guide who was very knowledgeable, and I was hard pressed to keep up with him in my note taking. I remember visiting Chorazin. Our tour guide pointed to a toppled pillar with an engraved Medusa and said that it had been a pillar in the temple. What mixture! The tour guide said it was excused and not seen as wrong to the congregation. I thought of how similar we are today. I then understood why Jesus told that city in Matthew 11:21, "Woe unto thee."

In 2002 I visited Washington D.C. When we arrived at the National Cathedral, built in 1888, I was shocked when our guide pointed to the 110 gargoyles lining the roof and commented that Darth Vader had been added to the top! How could this be? Darth Vader? It was very sobering to notice that among our large group of Christian teens, not one seemed shocked. Everyone just commented on the beauty of the church and how "cool" it was. I looked up to see the gargoyles grinning.

Today, our hearts are divided. We want what the world has to offer. We think we can present the gospel in a "new" way to appeal to more young people. It seems so right. But, our hearts are not fully focused on God and His way. We are distracted. There are many distractions. We do not even consider that we are distracted. We do not even consider the possibility of God's refusal to acknowledge our worship. We do not even consider we may be worshiping wrongly. We are presumptuous.

We assume we have a place next to God that we do not really have. When He shows us our error, we must be thankful and immediate in our response to Him. We must correct it and pray daily for mercy to remain pure-hearted before Him. We slip so easily. Satan gently guides us into slipping in the areas we are most confident in.

We can come boldly to the throne only when we fully understand our true standing with God. It is one of dependence. It is a status that is wholly dependent on Jesus. It requires a recognition of His worthiness and not our own. We come boldly, placing our boldness and self-sufficiency at His feet. We can praise and sing and jump and dance by His provision. We are nothing without Jesus' sacrifice. We must realize we were born in sin and we are lost without Him.

There was absolutely nothing we could have done to change the condition of our souls. Can a drowning man swim to shore? He may think he can, but, in truth, he is still drowning. It doesn't matter what we think; it matters what is really true. We are mimicking the world's ways, glorying in our flesh, thinking we are something we are not, and ignorant to the fact that God wants no part in it. The flesh is our downfall. All flesh is a disgrace to God. He came to save us from our flesh and the world, not to give us more access to it.

HUMANISM

For I know that in me (that is, in my flesh,) dwelleth no good thing.

—Romans 7:18

Humanism is basically man's religion. Its main focus is man and his problems or man and his happiness. That is a simple definition and will suffice for what is written here.

Small shifts in our way of thinking are causing worship to slant toward humanism rather than focus on the things of God. We are mixing the image of God with the image of man. Humanism is contaminating the pure gospel. We may have a great song service, but a few of our new songs turn out to be hybrids. We may hear good sermons, but there are some one-line shifts that point to man's goodness. Ninety percent of a Sunday morning service may be scriptural, but ten percent can be focused on man and his importance. Things are being said that preachers of the past would never have said. Recently, it has become common to hear preachers say that man is a creator, not a creation! Beware of this infiltration of humanism. It is so strong, it is deceiving even the elect. Pray for your pastor. His job is very hard. He has the capability of influencing many souls.

Another preacher said that the criminal on the cross was convicted. He explained that his "conviction" was that Jesus was the Son of God and that Jesus was His true brother. He realized his birthright had been stolen at birth, and God was his real Father. The error in that perspective taints the whole purpose behind the cross. Man is not brothers with

Jesus until he is convicted of his sin and repents. Man must be born again to become brothers with Christ. Before that takes place, our birthright is to go to hell. God is not our heavenly Father at our natural birth. We receive Him as our Father only through accepting Christ. Until then, we are of our father, the devil (John 8:44).

One song leader said she wanted to dedicate the next song to the "warrior women" of the group. That was the first time I had been in a worship service where a song was not dedicated to the Lord, but instead to humans. That's not true worship.

How about the flesh-appeasing song that states that Jesus thought of me above all when He was on the cross? The Bible says Jesus was thinking of obeying the will of His Father above anything else. His mind was on the Father, not us. How many of our songs contain I, me, and myself as subjects? Count them. You'll be surprised.

A TV preacher said, "God never intended for us to be the creation. He intended for us to be creators." Creativity is reserved for the true Creator. One of humanism's main tenets is to attribute this trait to mankind. As a result, creativity is being praised more than ever. Remember, "there is no new thing under the sun" (Eccles. 1:9).

Local churches have Web sites explaining their plan for their youth groups declaring, "It is you. It is us. It is God." Are the youth supposed to use deductive reasoning and assume that we and everything else is all God? I know this particular church was not promoting this lie on purpose, but do young people understand?

The trend seems to be for churches to name their youth groups anything whatsoever. The less the name means, the more proudly the kids are to adhere to it and the more the youth pastors boast. Churches are not realizing this message to America's youth is detrimental. Young people now believe Christianity and God, for that matter, can be associated to any thing, any person, or any place. Pantheism is being driven home to them that God can be in anything and, as a result, *is* in everything. The other danger is that youth groups' meaningless names are now linked to godliness. Youth are not being taught that God has everything to do with real meaning and relevance. In truth, God cannot and will not comply or fall under any label man decides to give Him.

It is the exact lie they hear from the world. Notice TV commercials, greeting cards, and catalog ads. Listen to athletes, movie stars, and talk show hosts. They all promote the doctrine of becoming "uniquely you" or expressing your "true self." The doctrine that "everyone is unique" is the gospel of a new day.

The same Web site for this church urged the children to become the "true you." We are all in trouble if we become our "true" depraved, base selves. That should never be encouraged by a church. Other youth pastors teach that every child is "unique with seeds of greatness." Mankind needed a redeemer because of his complete and total lack of greatness. We cannot teach children that they have any capability without Christ. Otherwise, they will depend on that rather than surrendering to their need for Christ.

The new shift of focus to our becoming the unique self God created us to be is heavily implying that we were good in our original state. If a person believes that, he does not believe in the doctrine of original sin. The sound doctrine of man's original sin has been preached for centuries, but recently mainstream Christianity has come against it with their tweaked teachings.

So easily church leaders have turned the focus away from Jesus. During communion one Sunday, the pastor shifted attention toward his congregation when he said, "If you have a need, lift the cup." But, Jesus told us to remember Him, not ourselves, when performing that event. Some preachers smoothly mix in their own personal stories, hobbies, sports news, and movies into their sermons. Then, we leave the service with another meal of humanism.

Some also have special seminars where ladies learn to make Christmas ornaments or decorate their houses. One pamphlet invited "girls only" because it was a "babe seminar." Can you believe that? A church conducting a "babe seminar"? Teen girls were promised to learn expert tips on guys, fashion, makeup and of course, self-image.

The new church mentality promotes godliness as anything perceived as good and that if it is "bad," it's from the devil. Good is defined as something I want and bad is defined as everything I don't want. If I want it, it must be God blessing me; if I don't want it, it must be Satan coming against me. This gives Satan too much credit. There are several scriptures clarifying that on some occasions God comes against His own people and even does "bad" things. (See Amos 3:6; Isaiah 45:7; Lamentations 2:5.) What's the youth's perspective on this new mentality? Does it leave them any room for persecution, such as Paul's prison stay? Does it allow lessons from God through afflictions? The psalmist wrote, "It is good for me that I have been afflicted; that I might learn thy statutes" (Ps. 119:71).

The church has come a long way. Beware of the new humanistic feminism that magnifies women as goddesses. It is sickening, and it's invading the church. It is a rejection of male authority and the traditional family. One TV preacher alleged men should treat women like "the queens they really are." Did God say women are queens? The world is pushing womanhood, and now the church is, too. To claim "girl power" is exercising humanism to the fullest. Those who proudly boast of fighting like a girl should read the Old Testament accounts where those who did were the losers (Isa. 19:16; Nah. 3:13).

Another pastor spoke of making young people the "diamonds they are supposed to be." Flattery and flesh-petting is not advisable in church. One prominent preacher said while referring to young people, "It's not about us, it's about them." When young people are told that they are the center of the church's attention, their pride and arrogance perpetuate. Humility is what is needed in our young people.

One must come to Christ in humility, not under entitlement.

While on a mission trip to Mexico, one student saw me crying and, not realizing that I was crying because of the mixture you're reading about, she asked if she could pray for me. She said, "Ms. Seymour, you're so beautiful. God can't even look at you." Oh how the youth are being deceived with airy lies of human worth. It is perversion that implies God is lacking without us.

TV programs tell us God makes beautiful people with great potential. We continually hear them say "follow your heart," suggesting we have the answers to our problems already within us. Christians seem to believe it is true. It is a shame we are hearing it in our churches, too.

Many times worship services are designed for what people like and for what they desire. People want a fun, light, and happy atmosphere. However, we must not forget that worship was never intended to satisfy those fleshly appetites. Leaders are asking, how can we keep people or attract young people if we don't make it fun? I received a brochure in the mail advertising a Bible-based seminar at a local church. Below the speaker's picture read "with much humor and laughter" in bolder letters than the rest of the print. We justify this fleshly tactic because it lures in more people. But, whether it makes sense to us or not, God did not command us to appeal to people's flesh.

We must have worship services that appeal to the spirit. Humanism must be removed. It will be a completely different service than some Christians are used to. Few may attend, but those who are there will mean business with God. Numbers do not necessarily matter to God. Is it better to own one authentic diamond ring or fifty fake ones? Is it better to own one real automobile or fifty toy cars? Is it better to have one live tree in your yard or fifty plastic ones? What matters to God is the authentic, the real, and that which is alive.

Worship services claim to be an alternative to a worldly program, but it's obvious how much it still resembles that which it is supposedly opposed to. Why do our churches offer supplements for those things Christians have been forbidden? Why do churches not represent a place where we die to ourselves?

When God says to stay away from something, He means we should resist it, shun it, flee it, and even abstain from the appearance of it (1 Thess. 5:22). We must call a snake a snake and stop trying to dress it up to be suitable for God's presence. Since we now think everything is good and lawful, God's people are eating rats and calling them delicious. Just because something is inside the church walls, does not mean God allows it. Our new freedom in Christ does not knock down all our boundaries.

It is prevalent for Christians to come to the house of worship seeking what they can get from God. We go to receive and we call it worship. To receive something from a church service is not wrong, but we shouldn't call that worship. People leave church feeling good about themselves, but in reality, they offered no sacrifice to Him. They did not get serious with God, pray for help to continue to fight temptations of the flesh, or repent of any sin. All was on the receiving end. There was no sacrifice, no cost. We should be offering God a sacrifice by not even considering our hurting souls.

David said that he would not offer to the Lord that which "cost me nothing" (2 Sam. 24:24). We must be careful about what we call worship. Instead of believing He is available for our pleasure, we must realize that we were created for His pleasure. We should get our eyes off ourselves and onto the Lord.

> I beseech you therefore, brethren, by the mercies of God, that ye present your bodies a living sacrifice, holy, acceptable unto God, which is your reasonable service.
>
> —Romans 12:1

Chapter 9

MIXTURE: PART 2

And be not conformed to this world: but be ye transformed by the renewing of your mind, that ye may prove what is that good, and acceptable, and perfect, will of God.

—Romans 12:2

Culture

CONFORMING TO THE world is natural and easy. But, we must strive to be separate. Each Christian must transform his mind because it constantly wants to conform to the world. We must strive to be unlike our natural tendencies. We must realize that our natural magnetism is toward sin, not toward progress.

In the world, a nation's culture is the accumulation of traditions and values that are subject to gradual modification. Eventually, new forms of behavior emerge as acceptable. We can all agree that as new behaviors emerge in America, our culture deteriorates according to God's standard. We are a culture without shame and without natural affection. We condone sin because we fear being labeled intolerant. Our culture is marked by moral corruption and perversion. Dr. D. James Kennedy, author and president of Coral Ridge Ministries, observed, "When you have an immoral society that has blatantly and proudly violated all of the commandments of God, there is one last virtue they insist upon: tolerance for their immorality."[1]

Tolerance for all cultures, including our own backsliding culture, is glorified in the name of love. I have heard pastors say that the church needs to be culturally relevant to reach people for Christ. This is a common perspective among church leaders, but we are deceived into thinking the world is becoming Christian rather than realizing that Christians are becoming worldly. When we bring worldliness into the church, it doesn't sanctify the world; it pollutes the church. At the expense of being culturally relevant, we have become spiritually irrelevant.

Rather than effectively preserving our culture by living a separate life or by remaining steadfast in an ever-changing world, Christians now believe it is necessary for us to change with the new culture in order to impact society. The Lord condemns doing "after the manners of the heathen that are round about" us (Ezek. 11:12). The Bible says, "Come out from among them, and be ye separate and touch not the unclean thing" (2 Cor. 6:17). If we "mingle among the heathen and learn their works, " we will be defiled (Ps. 106:35, 39).

Jesus prayed to the Father saying, "The world hath hated them [disciples], because they are not of the world" (John 17:14). Christians should not seek to be accepted culturally in order to entice participation in the church. I have heard good arguments in favor of cultural adaptation. Someone used as an example the instance where Paul said, "I please all men in all things" (1 Cor. 10:33), yet Paul did not seek his own profit. Instead, he sought the profit of those whom might be saved. To be all things to all men is a humble place, not a glorified, popular place of honor among men. It is not a place of compromise with the world. We should realize our separation from current culture will cause rejection and ridicule, but still, we should not seek favor and popularity with our current culture.

There is also this perspective: Jesus prayed that God would not take the disciples "out of the world," but that He would "keep them from evil" (John 17:15). So, there's a balance. Yes, we must be in the world in order to witness, but it includes a life of separateness. We must not partake of the evil defilement of worldliness, but should be sanctified (set apart) through the truth. (See John 17:19.) Truth is exclusive. There is no getting around that. Jesus endured the hatred of the world because He was different, very different. He was not motivated by selfish gain or fleshly lusts. However, the world's actions, including culture, are always centered around fleshly drives.

God tells us to endure hard circumstances. When our friends despise and forsake us, we should remain steadfast in obedience to God's Word. Jesus told his disciples that they would be betrayed by parents, brethren, kinsfolk, and friends; and some would even be put to death. He told them they would be hated for His name's sake (Luke 21:16–17). Jesus appeared to be a failure until the resurrection. His disciples thought He would be a great and glorious king in the eyes of the world, but His glory was not the glory that appeals to mankind. Jesus was rejected by society. It was the popular crowd that crucified Him. The popular crowd sways with sentiment, yet the church today is imitating the popular crowd and attempting to draw young people to church with popular enticements.

Second Timothy 2:3–4 tells us to be as a soldier who is not entangled with the affairs of this life. A soldier's life consists of bare necessities without fluff. A soldier tries to please the captain of his army with his optimal obedience. We should resist the temptation to please others, which causes us to disregard our "general." If our self-image is hurt in the process, praise the Lord. He must increase, and we must decrease (John 3:30).

Our modern culture is reflected through popularity. The action pursued by society is always, for a fickle amount of time, based on whatever new pattern of behavior that has become desirable. People seek to be popular because the praise and flattery that goes with it appeals to the flesh. However, popularity is very unstable and subject to change. Sometimes, the popularly praised activity is nothing new at all. The fact that it is new and different to the current generation is the satisfying element that fascinates them.

Jesus said, "That which is highly esteemed among men is abomination in the sight of God" (Luke 16:15). God chooses the base things of this world and the things that are despised so that no flesh should glory in His presence. (See 1 Corinthians 1:28–29.) Popularity with the world is not a good thing. It is not a "blessing" from God.

When we bring the popular cultural behavior of the day into the church, we are either seeking to be well liked, avoiding the hatred of the world Jesus talked about, or we are trying to bridge the gap between two opposites. The church and the world are opposites or, at least, should be. We try to narrow the gap thinking God wants it that way, and we fail to realize the necessity of maintaining their inequality. A. W. Tozer speaks of an illicit marriage between the two. The results are illegitimate. Tozer also commented, "There was a day when our religious leaders were made fun of and laughed at and opposed, even put in jail and driven out of town, but nowadays they are riding on the shoulders of the mobs and the multitudes because they are trying to make Christianity as much like the world as possible in order to win the world."[2]

The new strategy of cultural evangelism and becoming a church for the twenty-first century is an indication that Christians believe the gospel is outdated and must be modernized. When asked this question, many would deny it. Yet, they will continue to advocate that it is a new day and a new generation and that we must use new methods in order to adapt to our changing culture. Paul asks, "Where is the wise?…hath not God made foolish the wisdom of this world? For after that in the wisdom of God the world by wisdom knew not God, it pleased God by the foolishness of preaching to save them that believe" (1 Cor. 1:20–21).

A person cannot see in the dark, but he can hear. We live in a day where Christians think preaching is outdated and foolish. We think we must add to such a boring method.

But, God calls our new methods foolish because they are the wisdom of the world. They are the methods that make businesses succeed, but they do not cause the church to succeed.

If Christians would remain steadfast in a shaken, unstable world, the stability would shine like a beacon to attract the lost as God intended. If we would stick to preaching God's Word, the power of it would pierce hearts as God promised it would. Peter was recognized as being a disciple of Christ because he talked differently from the status quo.

When the world sees the fickleness in the church to the same degree that it's in the world, there is no sense of refuge in the church. Kids are seeing adults, and even their own parents, trying to act like teenagers. They have little respect for the shallowness. Once Christians were criticized for talking the talk but not walking the walk. Today, many Christians will not even talk it, let alone walk it.

Tozer noticed this problem in his day. He said that we "simplify the truth for the masses by using the language of the masses instead of the language of the church. It has not succeeded, but has added to, rather than diminished, religious confusion."[3] The simplification of truth that has currently been justified is under the banner that it is God's will in order to reach this generation.

There is no doubt that simplification draws people. Pastors are amused as large, mesmerized crowds draw to their carnal attractions, but in the end, people are not being converted. Just as crowds are drawn to the mall or movie theater, they walk away with only their flesh having being influenced. A true conversion requires a heart turned toward God, not toward crowds, popular activities, entertainment, or any other means of enticement that is being used in modern churches. The job of the church is not to get people to attend but to get people to Jesus.

It is important to understand culture. Missionaries must learn about cultures in order to discern what they are up against, but missionaries do not participate in any worldliness in order to proselytize. Once a convert is made, he is taught to forsake the tattoos, witchcraft, voodoo dolls, unclean practices, and other pagan rituals. In Acts, Paul taught toward the mind-set of the Athenians by preaching against their false beliefs. He did not join them (Acts 17:22–28).

The gospel should never be watered down or made less "offensive" with a motive of appealing to and attracting the lost. Many argue that our only hope for evangelism is by making Christianity more palatable. However, the truth of God's Word is stronger than we credit it. We must combat this mixture of half-truths by remaining steadfast to biblical truth and stop trying to doctor it up.

> No man can say that Jesus is the Lord, but by the Holy Ghost.
>
> —1 Corinthians 12:3

We must trust the Holy Spirit to compel sinners and stop thinking we can work the magic with our new tactics. Just because style, popularity, rock music, and money work in the world doesn't mean we should use them for appeal in the church. We must create an atmosphere for the Holy Spirit.

We actually hinder the Holy Spirit from convicting sinners when we attract sinners into the church and show them there is no difference between the church and the world. It's ineffective for them to see church activities identical to the activities outside the church. Yet many would argue that the whole purpose is to show sinners that we are just like them.

The danger is in the implication that all you have to do is come to church and you'll be called a child of God. A Christian label or a church sign outside your building is not what God's Word requires for salvation. To encourage no real change or separate behavior is not what Jesus preached. We are supposing we have converts when people flock to the altar after Sunday morning's big show. To claim we are winning them is not understanding that many sinners are coming to the altar to seek what they can get out of it, rather than giving their lives to God. Rarely do modern pastors abstain from preaching a "what's in it for you" gospel. Pastors have drifted from their past stand that truth was enough for their hearers.

One pastor said while speaking to middle school and high school students, "The truth alone is no longer enough for the lost." His reasoning was that people must experience truth in order to believe it. He concurred that many people's experience told them there was no God. Yet, the Bible clearly states that faith does not require experience or sight: "Faith is the substance of things hoped for and the evidence of things not seen" (Heb. 11:1). We should not seek evidence in order to believe. Instead, we should seek evidence because we believe. Jesus told those He had healed not to tell anyone. He didn't promote His package with evidence. He didn't seek to become popular through advertisement.

We have become increasingly impatient with invisible, spiritual things and are requiring visible, carnal things to fill our appetites. The church does not profit a person when it does not allow the measure of faith in them to ignite. We must not manipulate it through false signs and flesh-appealing works. True faith is ignited by the Holy Spirit through hearing God's Word. Faith comes by hearing (Rom. 10:17).

This new church appears to be specially designed to accommodate a golden calf or anything else the people desire. Where is a church where the only attraction is God?

The Church of the Twenty-first Century

> Because my people hath forgotten me, they have burned incense to vanity, and they have caused them to stumble in their ways from the ancient paths, to walk in paths, in a way not cast up.
>
> —Jeremiah 18:15

> Moreover thou hast taken thy sons and thy daughters, whom thou hast borne unto me, and these hast thou sacrificed unto them to be devoured. Is this of thy whoredoms a small matter?
>
> —Ezekiel 16:20

There is a precarious delusion in the world today. We hear the media, movie stars, rock stars, and even preachers saying, "It's a new day!" There is strong belief in the world that foundations must be supplanted with new and improved ideas. Preachers pray for creativity, new visions, and new dreams. They strive to outdo the world with fresh innovations for attracting crowds and appealing to the masses. Churches sing songs stating that all God ever does is "change the old for new."

However, God has long ago provided His exact blueprint for His people. It's nothing new. Creative visualization promises to provide an entirely new reality. It parallels the teaching of the mind science religions. It is an invitation for demonic instructors to give visions for developing a completely new religious system.

Before the masses accept major change in a system, however, they must first be persuaded that the old system is bad or has failed. Preachers make fun of hymns from the past and songs from previous generations. One preacher caused much laughter when he sang Psalm 113:3 in a geeky way, claiming it was fine for the past. (Notice the words of the old song were straight out of Scripture, unlike many songs today.) His inference was that today's songs are far above the ones of the past. He went on to explain how this generation understands more about God than any previous group of people.

Satan has a lot to work with in this "new day" with all the pride and arrogance of this generation's claim to be more enlightened than any previous generation. It is an ideal seedbed for his delusion.

Is this generation truly more informed? Do we have more revelation than Jonathan Edwards, Charles Finney, Charles Spurgeon, Andrew Murray, Oswald Chambers, Martin Luther, A. W. Tozer, or Watchman Nee? Are our two-lined ditties more edifying than past songs about the Cross, the blood, and the greatness of God? In reality, we are falling further from the truth. A "falling away" from truth and resulting deception is what Paul warned about in 2 Thessalonians 2:3.

The "new" vision of glorifying man is actually nothing new at all. Since the Garden of Eden, the lie has been the same. The lie is, "Ye shall not surely die...ye shall be as gods, knowing good and evil" (Gen. 3:4–5). Satan often entices with flattery, telling us we have special standing with God. He lures with lies that pride is harmless.

Preachers who align with this mentality stress that we are a people who deserve more. Our enemy is steadily working toward a new day where resistance will be minimal and hordes will flock in approval of the new agenda legislated by the Antichrist.

Approval will readily be given to the Antichrist because anyone who is disapproving or resistant to new ideas is condemned in today's society. They are viewed as intolerant, closed-minded, radical, and unreasonably extreme. In churches, they are classified as the old people.

On television, this rigid mentality is attributed to Christians in general. Christian children are easily persuaded by these media depictions of Christians and believe they are off the wall in their stand for truth. The sad reality is that most Christian characters that are portrayed are not even true Christians, while they over-exaggerate their rigidity and at times stand against something that doesn't even matter. This propaganda is very convincing to weak Christians and their children. All the while children are developing the belief that the former way of thinking is bad.

For answers to our problems, we do not need to look forward but back to the beginning. God did not save new doctrine for this generation. He did not withhold truth from previous generations and the early church. To the contrary, 2 Timothy talks of the last days when men will not endure sound doctrine, but shall turn away from truth (2 Tim. 4:3–4).

Preachers claim that one reason we are special is that we are the generation to see Christ's return. We constantly tell our youth that they are the chosen generation. I would agree that seeing Christ's return is a special and unique situation, but the error is in viewing the people as being special rather than the event.

The truth according to Scripture is that the unique, special quality attributed to the last days is one of falling away from the principles that have been maintained up to that point (2 Thess. 2:3; 1 Tim. 4:1). In the past, when Alexander the Great, Napoleon, and Hitler rose up to attain world dominance, men rose up in opposition. But, the people of this last generation will be guilty of applauding a dominant world ruler without resistance. He will be praised as being the man with all the answers for a new day, just as the Germans applauded Hitler. No group will rise against him. This generation will be guilty of throwing out foundational truths in order to establish the new concept of government and religion. They are the chosen generation, chosen for strong delusion.

This new religion will be a religion of the masses. It is the broad way Jesus talks about in Matthew 7:13. It will encompass all religious doctrines and blend the "truths" that are resident within all cultures. Some preachers claim exclusiveness is wrong and that God hates it, but truth is by its very nature exclusive. Do not be swept away by this cunning current, and remember that narrow is the way to truth and life and few there be that find it (Matt. 7:14).

The inclusive doctrines of a new age put everyone on the same level. All religions contribute their good and Christians are urged to accept pagan rituals that were once condemned. A genderless god will replace Him, and goddess worship will be accepted. Bible versions will refer to God as "the father-mother" instead of "the Father" alone, and Jesus will be a "child" of God instead of "the Son." These changes will not occur over night but have already began their descent toward this very goal.

If we do not maintain the purity of the gospel and continue to taint God's Word with mixture in the name of tolerance and love, we will one day face the fact that we have been completely deceived. I fear the delusion is so strong that we will be shocked at who is left behind standing en masse to receive the mark of the new day. Those standing in line will be laughing with their friends and making new friends oblivious to the cliff ahead. They will be excited that soon they will be able to buy, and to sell, and to trade with the whole world without any barriers. Their hope lies in the fact that the world will be one and exclusiveness will no longer be an issue.

Some preachers appeal to the masses by focusing on the hurting children who "have problems never witnessed before in the history of the world." Our focus has shifted from preaching the fear of the Lord to focusing on the fears of the world. Altar calls for those who are hurting because someone has mistreated them replace calls for accountability. It is producing counterfeit repentance.

The road to the altar is smooth and easy because so many are doing it. It has become popular rather than contrary to the status quo. Sometimes the whole congregation says the Sinner's Prayer in order to camouflage the ones who are really praying the prayer. All embarrassment is avoided. The unsaved are not asked to stand out in their belief in Christ.

Without true repentance and a turning toward Christ, results are false. This smooth path is a lie concerning the cost of true repentance and discipleship.

The stabs of the conscience are suddenly stopped in the belief something was actually done when going forward. A. W. Tozer clearly stated, "The idea that God will pardon a rebel who has not given up his rebellion is contrary both to the Scriptures and to common sense."[4]

I cannot stress the dangers of the pathway these preachers are paving. I've heard an advocate of this new way of preaching say he would present the gospel in the "sweetest, nicest, most attractive package" possible. He is preaching "another Jesus," one who appeals to all men (2 Cor. 11:4). He also claimed that he did not plan to compromise foundational doctrines for this new agenda. How can you do both? Paul did not hesitate "to declare unto the church all of the counsel of God" (Acts 20:27).

The full counsel of God includes offensive doctrines: the sinfulness of sin, judgment, hell, suffering, repentance, the blood of Christ, self-denial instead of entertainment, sacrifice and not humanism, God's culture instead of the world's, dying with Christ and not living with the world, God's worship instead of not man's idea of it, and God's purpose instead of man's dreams. The dilution of the watered-down mixture that is being presented in the name of God is causing Christianity's salt to lose its savor.

While misguided preachers are stressing the importance of change in order to be current and modern, they are preaching a sweet gospel of compromise. As a result, young people of our day are not hearing the foundational truths. They are being conditioned with fervor to readily accept the new and improved way instead of the tried and true. They are readily accepting new doctrines for a new age because they have been indoctrinated with the gospel of change in their own churches. The devil is very clever, and he has his appetite whetted for this generation.

In order to be modern and current, these preachers are forsaking advice from the older men. When warned, they do not heed. Like Rehoboam, who "forsook the counsel of the old men," preachers are claiming it's best to seek after "advice of the young men," and when they awake to their error it will be too late (2 Chron. 10: 13–14).

What a coup for Satan. These preachers were once preaching how we should watch out for end-times delusion, and now, through a weakness they were unaware of, Satan has pulled them away from the true gospel. Modern preachers are claiming we must give the crowd what they want. If they want shorter sermons, do it. If they want more skits, plays, and drama, do it. If they want fun and entertainment, do it. God told Isaiah to tell His people, "Hear ye indeed, but understand not; and see ye indeed, but perceive not. Make the heart of this people fat, and make their ears heavy, and shut their eyes; lest they see with their eyes, and hear with their ears, and understand with their heart, and convert, and be healed" (Isa. 6:9–10). While these leaders are claiming more fervor for the Lord than any generation, they are falling further away into a great apostasy.

The shifts into major deception are occurring swiftly. What was once seen as sin and rebellion in young people is now being viewed as hurt. Where correction was once applied, pity is now offered. What was once labeled regression in youth is now labeled progress. In the church, what was once labeled worldly flesh is now labeled freedom.

Man's sin nature has always justified itself. In reading the Old Testament clear illustrations of the tendency God's own people to justify sin is illustrated as they rebelled in rising up to play before a golden calf, in trying to bring in the presence of God on a "new" man-made cart, and in offering strange fire to Him.

One television preacher asserted that the youth seen dancing on the screen were not putting on a show, they were just being who they are. He continued with saying this generation of kids haven't had a chance to become arrogant yet. He said, "They are real and innocent." He failed to notice the abundance of disrespect, lack of discretion, and yes, arrogance among kids today. To let kids worship how they feel with their own music reflects an ignored rebellion on the pastor's part.

He then justified what was happening by explaining how each generation desired to change their parent's music. Has that been a good thing throughout the years? Has that not been rooted in rebellion from the start? This is the first generation in history where Christians have openly encouraged that rebellion. Never before has that rebellion been labeled godliness until now.

Jesus said in the book of Revelation to the church at Pergamos, "Beware of the doctrine of the Nicolaitanes, which thing I hate" (Rev. 2:15). The Nicolaitanes were a group of people who arose in the apostolic period of the church. Their doctrine was associated with encouraging idolatrous worship. They were guilty of mixing in a false freedom that abused the doctrine of grace. They taught antinomianism (freedom from obligation). They, like many of us, justified their actions by saying we are "delivered to do all these abominations" (Jer. 7:10).

David Jeremiah wrote this about Pergamos:

> True believers, who had been previously perse-cuted, were now lauded by political and civil authorities. Pagan temples became Christian churches and heathen festivals were converted into Christian ones. Idols were named after so-called Christian saints. Christians who had suffered were now welcomed to the imperial palace and they swallowed the bait, sacrificing allegiance to Christ, and becoming locked in fatal union with compromise.[5]

We are focused on the here and now and not eternity with God. Our concentration on establishing a new church for a new day and our obsession with what the next generation holds is not in accord with the fact that the Lord is coming soon. We are stressing a future on earth when our future is in heaven. Let's not continue to depress this generation of children further by giving them no hope for eternal things.

In his passion to change with culture and justify modern worship techniques, one preacher alleged that David "broke all the rules of temple worship" when he brought the ark of the covenant back the second time. This preacher did not read the passage further to see that David did not break the rules but offered sacrifices continually, morning and evening, and did "according to all that is written in the law of the LORD" (1 Chron. 16:40). The rule-breaking occurred the first time David brought the ark back, and the consequences were not pleasant (1 Chron. 13:7–10).

Trying to peddle change in the name of freedom from the law is not hearing from God. One commentary said that the Nicolaitanes' freedom became self-indulgence. They turned the grace of God into lasciviousness forgetting that grace was intended to free us from sin so that we could be servants of righteousness. (See Romans 6:18.)

Church leaders are claiming that new freedoms in the church are not necessarily fleshly. They claim it's what the people want. They want coffee bars, video games, and an atmosphere of fun. They justify it by saying they are things people really like, so what's wrong with it? Isn't it the flesh that does our liking and disliking and, according to Scripture, must die?

If church becomes a fun, entertaining place to hang out, it's not fulfilling its duty. These pastors need to realize they will never get the whole world into the church. If the world is in there, it's not the true church.

A certain TV preacher's dream was to have a night club in every city. Guess what happened then? Cheers from his listeners praised his vision of worldliness. Yes, we must seek to convert as many as we can, but we must realize it will not be the masses and it will not be through worldliness. Quality in the church has been overlooked for quantity. Some preachers would probably be happy to place a giant ichthus over the local mall and claim everyone under its roof to be a new Christian. His congregation would cheer that now they have a popular religion that fits the latest styles and they no longer have to be treated as strangers in a foreign land.

The idea of change is so strongly preached in the name of keeping up with God. Remember, God does not change, people do (Mal. 3:6). Preachers accuse their flock of being legalistic, insecure, or distrusting God if they are withstanding the changes that are trying to be sold to the flock. However, God will return for a remnant who did not change with the world but who remained steadfast and separated unto Him. Jeremiah reminds us that the problems of his day were because people had changed. There was the need for them to return to the "old paths, where is the good way, and...ye shall find rest for your souls" (Jer. 6:16).

If we are seeking answers for the terrible problems of our generation, we must go back to the day when foundations were laid. We must go back to the day when children were taught manners, respect, reverence, obedience, and godliness. We need parents who model it for them. The fact that we have changed is our problem. Changing and seeking new solutions is ignoring God's Word. His answers are there and they were written long ago.

Some preachers claim that the old way didn't work, but they didn't go back far enough. We can't go back one or two generations. We must go further. The best scenario is found back in the first-century church. From that point, the rebellion of each generation can easily be traced. Each generation's flesh has cried out for the new and different, and they have struggled to free themselves from their parents' rules. Look where we have ended up. How can it go further? The world is not evolving; it's devolving.

Some preachers have not dealt with their rebellion against their own parents and are, therefore, extending the problem to the youth in their congregation. Jesus tells us in Revelation when referring to the church at Sardis that we are to be watchful and to strengthen those things that remain and are "ready to die" (Rev. 3:2). It's a shame that church leaders are the ones killing the things God has arranged in the first place. It is interesting to note that Sardis was known for being a church that was alive, yet they were dead. (See Revelation 3:1.)

Jesus corrected the church at Ephesus by telling them that they had "left their first love" and calling for them to remember from whence they had fallen, to repent, and to do the first works. Unless they repented, God warned, He would remove their candlestick (Rev. 2:4–5). Again, A. W.

Tozer puts it well. "There is no new technique; if it is new, it is false. The old, old method, still works."[6]

Teens' mentality and disillusionment with traditional Christianity is fertile ground for prevalent atheist and humanist thinking. New ideas in a day of strong delusion will be deceptive ones. Satan is going to pull the biggest conspiracy in history with his man and the "best" solution. The attempt to abandon tradition and customs of the past and embrace new customs for the modern age is the very tactic he will use. No one will want to be left out of this new move. It will be ultra popular. The new church of the twenty-first century recommends throwing out the old for the new, just as Satan is advocating.

Our new churches advocate a church that is "just like you." I don't know how many advertisements for churches I have seen stating this. They even claim it is a place where you can become someone more like yourselves, advertising different worship services at different times so you can pick the one more suitable to your liking. Recently, a large billboard ad for a local church said, "This is your house." Not too long ago, children were taught that the church was God's house.

Churches boast of pool tables, PlayStation2s, iMacs, iPods, and big screens featuring appealingly normal people. They spend thousands of dollars keeping up with the latest trends and TV fads. Advocates of this approach claim it is working because thousands of worldlings are flocking to the place of fun. We are putting effort into looking good rather than preaching, but it's actually being good that counts.

People out of the world have their guilt appeased and their consciences pacified when they find the very things they were spending time with in the world are stamped with approval in the name of a loving God who wants them to be happy. They are comforted because they feel no accusation against them. They faithfully attend church just as they faithfully attend the movie theater because they are so appealing. They do not hear that fleeing youthful lusts is necessary for their newfound religion.

William Penn observed:

> These pretended innocents, these supposed harmless satisfactions, are more surprising, more destructive; for as they easily gain an admission by the senses, so the more they pretend innocence, the more they secure the minds of people in the common use of them; till they become so insensible of their evil consequences, that with a mighty confidence they can plead for them.[7]

These churches do not want to preach the cost of discipleship, nor do they teach that Christians must reject the world. This new church presents the gospel in the sweet, nice, attractive, flesh-appealing package and tries to make church a place that even the world can't compete with in fun, entertainment, and hi-tech advertising. They do not realize that "an increase in programs and activities breeds a decrease in love for Christ."[8] I fear, as the serpent beguiled Eve through his subtlety, so our minds are being corrupted from the simplicity that is in Christ (2 Cor. 11:3).

We are condoning evil by not mentioning it. We are of the camp that hears no evil, sees no evil, and certainly does not speak of any evil. God corrected Israel by causing them to bear shame and be confounded because they would not mention Sodom with their mouths and were a "comfort unto them" (Ezek. 16:54, 56). God said it was because of pride that they would not mention Sodom. Are we guilty of the same? We refuse to mention the world's sin and resulting judgment. We feel it is best to comfort people. God will require their blood at our hands. God also told Israel that Sodom was "more righteous" than them (Ezek. 16:52). We who know better are doubly guilty. We are guilty of knowing the truth, yet rejecting it.

Our new churches are dream churches filled with fun games, tasty food, casual attire, and common interest groups, ranging from rock 'n roll fans to bowling buddies. The new youth sanctuary is decorated with the world's rock stars and other heroes of the new faith. However, William Penn explained, "Such attire and pastimes do not only show the exceeding worldliness of peoples inclinations, and their very great ignorance of the divine joys, but by imitating these fashions, and frequenting these places and diversions, not only much good is omitted, but a certain door is opened to much evil to be committed."[9] It's a disgrace to note that Penn was referring to the world when he wrote that, but today it is applicable to the church.

Jesus told the Pharisees in Matthew 23:15:

> Woe unto you...hypocrites! For ye compass the sea and land to make one proselyte, and when he is made, ye make him twofold more the child of hell than yourselves.

Youth groups are spending thousands of dollars. They'll do whatever it takes. We compass land and sea for new ideas. We plan parties, design posters, and schedule celebrations. We invite bicycle stunt teams who display skull-and-crossbones tattoos and body piercing as they perform their crafty tricks. Our churches boast that the kids have big smiles, but it's beyond their comprehension that the cause of Christ is rarely or only lightly mentioned during the arrogant exhibitions.

If God is ever referred to at these exciting sporting events, it is to thank Him for giving the talent to minister with. The message portrayed is to say, "Look, the Lord made me famous, and that's my testimony." Is the Christian's goal in life to become well known for an athletic ability? Is that an indication of God's blessing? Where in Scripture did God tell us to revel in our pastime, slap a godly label on it, then call it a ministry?

Over and over the youth are told they can live a life of pleasure as long as they call it good and as long as they claim they are ministering for Christ. A person is less deceived to know he is going to hell than the person who thinks he's going to heaven.

Can a person learn about Christ and His gospel through a bicycle stunt? How about a Santa Claus display? A Hollywood movie? A cockfight? The answer is simple. Not if He's not there. It's like a drunk who says, "I see Jesus at the bottom of every shot." How deceived are we, and how much more deceived are our young people? We are failing our children by not telling them the truth about Jesus and man's sinful nature. We are doing damage by giving the world occasion to mock when these young Christians go about their lives acting like the unsaved world. It is better to lead one to Christ than to entertain thousands under the false disguise of converting them.

The argument in favor of church-sponsored entertainment and show-off demonstrations is that the people who attend them would never otherwise set foot in a church building on Sunday morning. But, if a person would never attend a church building on Sunday morning, then his heart is not drawn to things of the Lord. Our Christian example should be drawing the lost to church.

To say that the person will hear the gospel at these exhibits is to admit an ignorance of what the gospel truly is. People come for the entertainment. They patiently sit through the less-than-five-minute mention of God and Christianity. If the name of Jesus is mentioned, it is easily swallowed up by noise, lights, and other attention-getters. People's hearts come for fleshly reasons, and their flesh leaves satisfied.

There's a difference between Jesus feeding the multitudes and how we are attempting to do it. He fed them after they followed Him all day listening to truth. They would not go away. They needed the food because they had not eaten. We are feeding them what they do not need, and we are doing it so they will follow us. What a difference.

In our attempt to appeal to the masses, Christianity has developed a teen-friendly Bible that looks like a teen magazine. We do not need a church that looks like Hollywood or a Jesus that looks like a movie star. We cannot continue to tell our youth that they can be like the world as long as they put a clean label on it.

Man is born guilty and headed for hell, but when his religion sends him there, too, because it is false, he is "twofold the child of hell" (Matt. 23:15). Another application of this term can be that when a person thinks he is right, he is not likely to repent and admit he is wrong. Again, he is trapped twice, once by his flesh and twice by his beliefs.

Our children must be saved from these lies. We cannot assume that our children are converted because they are in a Christian home and because they are attending church with glee. People who convert only to be the same way they have always been are not truly converted, nor have they repented. How dare we as parents, youth leaders, Christian leaders, and advertisers use worldly slogans, logos, popular styles of dress, and phraseology to continue to indoctrinate our children with the idea that they need not shun the world and its ways.

The church is courting the favor of the world. By using the world's methods, language, and appearance, we are turning our churches into amusement parks that are ignoring the foundations of what Jesus taught. We are blinding our children to the seriousness of true discipleship. We are saying to Jesus, "We will eat our own bread, and wear our own apparel: only let us be called by thy name" (Isa. 4:1). The spiritual application is that the church wants the Christian label to take away their reproach, but its people are not willing to commit to the duties of being a wife. These women were not willing to fight or strive to be the man's wife. They settled for less.

We have the Sermon on the Mount in reverse. We teach, blessed are those with high self-esteem, blessed are those who laugh, blessed are the haughty, blessed are those who hunger and thirst after fleshly comforts, blessed are the selfish, blessed are those who are popular and never persecuted for righteousness sake. Our sanctified frivolity is not what Jesus preached. If our youth groups were really making an impact, our kids would be very unpopular.

What are we winning the world to? True discipleship? Self-denial? Separation from the world? What are we saving them from? Nothing. By teaching our children that the Christian walk is a playground and not a battleground, we are not preparing them for real life. They are growing up depressed and distressed because we are guilty of not providing them with the necessary skills for life.

While Christ calls men to carry a cross, we are calling men to enjoy life in His name. He calls us to forsake worldliness, and we are assuring men that they were destined for greatness in the world. He calls us to suffer, but we are calling men to comfort and stardom. He calls us to die to our wills, while we are calling them to have big dreams and to fulfill their destiny. As He calls us to holiness, we are calling men to "freedom." Oh, how we have betrayed our youth! In the hour when mature Christians are so desperately needed, we are clamoring for baby rattles and seeking excitement from the latest games and toys.

James calls us adulterers when we seek friendship with the world. He states friendship with the world as enmity with God. (See James 4:4.) Charles Spurgeon said, "That very church which the world likes best is sure to be that which God abhors."[10]

Chapter 10

INAPPROPRIATE BEHAVIOR

The words of the LORD are pure words: as silver tried in a furnace of earth, purified seven times.

—Psalm 12:6

INAPPROPRIATE LANGUAGE

CHRISTIANS FEEL THERE are no boundaries for their language. Since the language of television and movies has deteriorated, Christians, too, have allowed theirs to disintegrate. Some are bold enough to talk about certain topics without blushing and are even proud to be unembarrassed by it. Church leaders use base exclamations, expletives, and even the Lord's name in vain. There's no regard for the third commandment. We seem to think, "If it's funny; what does it matter?"

As the temple of the Holy Spirit, we have the duty to keep ourselves from the defilement of indecent language. Someone may ask, where is the line of indecency? Our answer is that it is not so much a line as it is a goal. Jesus is our goal. We measure using His words, which are "purified seven times" (Ps. 12:6).

Today, though, we are not even striving for purity. Instead, we Christians are found endeavoring to be like the world. We cringe if someone notices we are different. To fit in, we throw into our conversations the common language of the day.

When Peter began to "curse and swear," he did not want to be identified as one of Jesus' disciples (Matt. 26:74). Is that why we do it? Are we embarrassed to be associated with prudence? Proverbs 8:12 says that wisdom dwells with prudence. As defined by the dictionary, *prudence* is "foresight…to avoid error or danger."[1] It is the Christian's job to avoid error. Yet, we seem to want to be accepted and are therefore flippant in our disregard for error.

Peter's act was called a denial of Christ. Do we see our words as being a denial of Him every time we use them? The measurement for decency is far below what it used to be. Just because we have become calloused to certain words doesn't mean we are innocent. In fact, our speech and our calloused attitudes toward it adds sin to sin. We preach how each generation accepts more evil, yet we don't seem to think it is happening to us.

Today people experience shock if their child uses the phrase "shut up." It's a bad word by the world's standard because the fear is that it may hurt someone's self-esteem. "Shut up" is not accepted because it does not portray a tolerant attitude. Our reactions are backward. While we wince at "shut up," we are calloused to certain vulgarity and irreverence. We shouldn't be offended if our self-esteem gets put in its place. We should, instead, be offended by filthy and irreverent language.

I have shed many tears while attending youth services where the pastor threw blistering words of filth out over the crowd of children while being oblivious to the fact that the children were becoming more and more calloused to it each week. One teacher started out a chapel service by saying she wanted to give them a secret word. That word will not be mentioned here, but she definitely had their attention and their laughter after saying it.

Youth pastors like to show the children that they cannot be shocked. They reason that a reaction to worldliness seems puritanical or prudish, and they fear this turns children away. Children naturally cross boundaries until they get a reaction from an adult. Adults are afraid that any shock on their part may indicate ignorance, so they remain calm when, in fact, the child is screaming out for a reaction.

If pastors continue to talk the world's talk, they will continue to see corruption in children's actions. It becomes normal behavior to children when that is all they hear. Our children need a place where they are not faced with sinful appetites and behaviors. They need a refuge that is separate from the world. In spite of the warning in 1 Corinthians 15:33 to "be not deceived: evil communications corrupt good manners", we continue with the status quo, wondering why Christian's statistics are no different than the world's statistics. If children could receive a steady diet of God's Word without the garbage, we would notice a change.

Pastors especially should be careful to not let "filthy communication" come out of their mouths (Col. 3:8). As examples of good citizens and people with godly character, we should try to remember to reflect qualities of Jesus rather than traits of the world. We must remember to guide children into thinking on things that are true, honest, just, pure, lovely, and of good report. They should notice a marked difference in our speech.

Have the problems with teenage pregnancy and diseases related to promiscuity become better or worse through the years? That's an easy question. Isn't it strange that in a day where few girls remain pure, sex education materials—most of which amount to little more than how-to books—are being thrust at them? Ephesians 5:12 admonishes us that "it is a shame even to speak of those things which are done of them in secret" (Eph. 5:12). In the day when many remained pure, nobody talked about sex.

A large contributor to our statistical problems has been the language accepted in America today. We have allowed sin to have a voice. We could stop the rampant misbehavior among Christians if we, first, would learn to shut up.

> For out of the abundance of the heart the mouth speaketh.
> —Matthew 12:34

> But every man is tempted, when he is drawn away of his own lust, and enticed. Then when lust hath conceived, it bringeth forth sin: and sin when it is finished, bringeth forth death.
> —James 1:14–15

We are naïve to think our talking about certain things will go no further.

One pastor commonly told the students that they were going to graduate and then go wild. He said, "I guarantee 50 percent of you will go wild." What a discouragement. He went on to beat them down with, "I know it's the end of the year, you're tired, you've been stuffed with the gospel, and it's hard to persevere." But, he did not encourage them with, "Having done all, to stand. Stand" (Eph. 6:13). God encourages us to continue rather than telling us, "You're going to quit," and we should say the same.

There's not much resistance for kids today to go wild after high school. In fact, it is expected. How we present information to children is very important because we can be very persuasive in how we portray our expectations. This pastor also suggested that the kids were tired of hearing God's Word since they were "stuffed" already. This was not even true. I had been with them for several years and had heard minimal references to God's Word during that time. It is very important for youth pastors to present the gospel rightly, and it is vital to pray for the Lord to "set a watch before our mouths and keep the door of our lips" (Ps. 141:3).

Leaders' inappropriate talk in churches has led to sinful actions committed by our teens. It took a few years, but the language allowed in church meetings has taken root. The fruits are beginning to ripen. Some Christians along the way got the bright idea that if Hollywood can talk about sex, so can we, and one preacher went so far as to say that that kind of talk needs to be in the church rather than Hollywood.

What we need is a refuge where we aren't hearing it. If Hollywood is our goal rather than Jesus, how deluded are we?

When Scripture says that "it is a shame even to speak of those things which are done of them in secret," it's meaning is not too hard to figure out (Eph. 5:12). When pastors talk about inappropriate things, especially in mixed company, the Bible calls it a shame. Wake up, Christians. This shameful talk will not be ignored by a holy God. Philippians talks of "enemies of the cross of Christ, whose God is their belly, and whose glory is in their shame, who mind earthly things" (Phil. 3:19).

If a Christian condemns talking about these private matters of marriage, he is said to be condemning one of God's favored deeds. Psychology has been so deeply engrained into American thought that most feel it is imperative we talk about it. There is a time, a place, and an appropriate audience—and it's not the public setting of church. Nor is it in the mixed audience of teens.

It is not rare that perverted preachers are bringing their pollution into the church. Youth pastors love to attract teens' attention while speaking of certain deeds and by getting off-color. They boost their pride by thinking they are an interesting and gifted pastor because young people laugh at their humor. Jude 18 talks of men in the last days who will "walk after their own ungodly lusts."

A typical youth service during the eight years I was involved with teenagers included about five to ten minutes of off-color references. In one instance, the pastor said the church he once attended thought he was a pedophile because he loved kids so much. Inappropriate! Others were so blatant, it was distressing to think it was occurring inside a church. Some entire chapel services for high school youth were nothing but indecent. Mental images, especially for boys, were pouring from the wolf's mouth trying to entice the helpless sheep. They were defenseless because their protectors, the faculty, just laughed along with the kids. Adults and parents blindly thought, "That is what these kids need to be hearing."

Like the world, churches feel that teens must hear about certain things to avoid certain problems. Actually, it only perpetuates problems. Sometimes leaders just plant thoughts into the kids' minds that, otherwise, might not have entered there. Some Christian children may actually be trying to fight temptations in their mind, but they attend a church service and there's the devil to offer nicely painted pictures of perversion. Isn't it ironic that the devil can actually get more done inside a church? More is accomplished because these kids start to believe that, evidently, it is all right to think and talk about certain things because their youth pastor does it.

When we look at history, we see how humans have always had trouble with impurity in this area, but it was less of a problem when it was an off-limits subject. How many churches one hundred years ago had preachers telling jokes that made you cover your children's ears or caused you to take them out of the service? Not many, but it's common today. Too bad parents let their children listen. Why not? They've already heard the same filth from the television the night before. Don't we realize it has more impact when it comes from the "good" guy's mouth? It makes it seem legal.

God has told us to either be in the world or to get out. Mixture is something He hates. He hates for Christians to call evil as though it were good. Christians have followed the lies of psychology that tell us to solve problems of lust by talking about and participating in them more. Real genius, huh? The Bible says to repent and turn away from these problems.

Evidently, the Bible's answers have become outdated. Pure speech, which aids in pure thinking, which leads to pure living, is a thing of the past. I heard a prominent pastor's wife say, "Girls want to know about purity. They just don't want to hear it from someone who is legalistic." Does she mean from a stickler for God's advice? Oh, how we think God's Word is outdated. Oh, how we think modern times call for new solutions. How deceived we are.

If a teenage girl gets into trouble with her boyfriend, we say, "She didn't know enough," but those kids who know enough are often the ones who get into trouble. At least, that was my experience in middle school and high school when I was growing up. The girls who talked about sex in grade school were the very ones who got into trouble in high school. How do we think educating our children on the subject will cause them to abstain? Is it God who is advising us to take this route?

Today, being protected from such information is criticized by Christians because it is criticized by the world. Christians flee from the old school, calling it legalistic and old-fashioned. High praise for psychology and counseling for young girls is the trend for a church trying to keep up with the world and avoid being labeled prudish. We should be ashamed of our unashamed approach to a subject clearly portrayed in the Bible as a problematic area for humans. Christians must seek purity in this area. The answer for purity in our youth is not an impure approach.

I wisdom dwell with prudence.

—Proverbs 8:12

New thought criticizes Jesus. He didn't expand in detail about fleshly lusts. His speeches about the Father, His teachings on how to pray, His warnings of false prophets, His advice on helping neighbors, His recommendation on being the salt of the earth, His lessons on not worrying about tomorrow, His charge to avoid hiding lights under bushels, and His commandment to love our enemies are considered to be too boring for the supposedly enlightened teens of today.

Jesus did use the words *adultery, fornication,* and *lust,* but he went no further. He knew how to talk about the subject without talking about it. He painted no visual pictures. None. Modern adults love to paint pictures and then call it a sermon. God would rather they go to a bar and talk trash than bring it into His sanctuary to defile it.

There have been attempts from the pulpit at depicting visual pictures and going as far as possible with words that it is a wonder we are still experiencing God's longsuffering. How have we come this far? How do pastors excuse themselves to fulfill the lusts of their own flesh? Do we think because a pastor is saying those things, it must be acceptable to the Lord? What does God say? He says, "Be ye holy; for I am holy" (1 Pet. 1:16). He says, "Let no corrupt communication proceed out of your mouth, but that which is good to the use of edifying, that it may minister grace unto the hearers" (Eph. 4:29).

Ephesians 4:30 tells us not to grieve the Holy Spirit. We are definitely grieving the Holy Spirit with our impure speech and crude remarks. We can no longer justify what we know to be wrong. If we do not think it is wrong, then we are deceived. Pastors who boldly conjure up congregational giggles in the name of Jesus must stop.

> Now therefore, what have I here, saith the LORD, that my people is taken away for nought? they that rule over them make them to howl, saith the LORD; and my name continually every day is blasphemed.
>
> —Isaiah 52:5

We are not solving problems of lust and impurity by going into detail about them. The devil is probably still shocked how easily Christians swallowed the pill of perversion. The only hesitation before we washed it down was when we asked, "Are you sure?" Satan winked and nodded his assurance, so we quickly threw back our heads and swallowed.

Pastors once resisted lewdness by preaching against it. Movies were forbidden because of indecency. If you talk to someone older than sixty-five who was raised in the church, they will likely tell you that as a child they thought going to the movie was a sin. Not us new, enlightened Christians; we go freely, and even save a seat beside us for the Holy Spirit.

The worst result of all is that Christians are starting to think it's normal. The children, especially, think off-color references are normal, in mixed company or not. Their next step is acting out those statements. Children, and many adults, do not even blush at such talk. They honestly feel there has been no wrong committed. That is evidence of a seared conscience. According to God's Word, a wrong has indeed been committed. Jeremiah 6:15 asks, "Were they ashamed when they had committed abomination? nay, they were not at all ashamed, neither could they blush: therefore they shall fall among them that fall: at the time that I visit them they shall be cast down, saith the LORD."

Some youth pastors have shown video clips of romantic scenes to muster up attention from lethargic kids. This is becoming more and more common. If our young people aren't seeing enough indecent exposure in the world, they can certainly count on an unhealthy dose of it in their local churches. Distasteful references to all types of bodily functions are not off limits to these pastors, either. We wonder why teens are unresponsive. They can't be shocked. Their consciences have been seared with a hot iron.

As a teacher of history, I have seen a noticeable theme of decadence in the world, but recent years have shown major downfalls and compromise. It is definitely the last of the last days, and these are truly perilous times. (See 2 Timothy 3:2.)

In private, do pastors in America have pure speech? Could you sit your five-year-old daughter next to them in their conversations? Do they think God doesn't notice? I have been shocked while sitting next to the pastor's table at a meal. They didn't even seem to care that girls were nearby. Later, when a girl was corrected during class for using an inappropriate word, she replied, "But, Pastor so-and-so said it in chapel yesterday, so why can't we?"

One of the new ways to joke in the world is to imply a man is interested in another man. Do you think that kind of joking should occur in church services? We ought to be shocked, but aren't. We are embarrassed to give any disapproval. As mentioned earlier in this book, one pastor went so far as to imply Judas' kiss was that kind of kiss. He wanted a laugh, and he got one. How disgraceful to use the moment of Jesus' betrayal as a means to get a laugh. He went on to mock the verse in Isaiah where the prophet cries, "I'm undone." He faked a cry and asked how a person could be undone. He should have read why. Isaiah said, "I am undone, because I am a man of unclean lips" (Isa. 6:5).

May we be like Ezra, who humbly said, "O my God, I am ashamed and blush to lift up my face to thee, my God: for our iniquities are increased over our head, and our trespass is grown up unto the heavens" (Ezek. 9:6). We must be like David, who purposed that his mouth should not transgress. (See Psalm 17:3.)

DISRESPECT TOWARD OLDER PEOPLE

For God commanded, saying, Honour thy father and mother: and, He that curseth father or mother, let him die the death.

—Matthew 15:4

With the ancient is wisdom; and in length of days understanding.

—Job 12:12

Children have had such a heavy diet of disrespectful talk that I doubt there is anything that can be done to regain respect or change the way they think of older people. Many young people believe old people are stupid. The common practice among Americans is to criticize older people and anything associated with the past. Satan is strategic. If he can cause this generation to reject old people, then it will more readily reject old standards and traditions. Then, Christianity is one step closer to extinction and he can set up his earthly rule.

Disrespect's slide toward decadence did not take long. The advice seemed to flip-flop over the last twenty-five years from "respect your elders" to "you don't want to be like an old person." This mentality is driven into young people every week in our churches.

Always wanting giggles and laughs, a certain youth pastor explained his trip to a convalescent home. He joked about how ladies' gowns were not properly in place and implied that he was still reeling from the mental pictures. One pastor joked about women in Malawi having massive arms, "not like my grandmother's, but massive." Another joked about an old woman driving down Hwy 175. The punch line was that she thought that was the speed limit. Youth pastors talk about their childhood from the perspective that their dumb parents were just out of touch and unaware of their deeds. Many feel these are harmless tactics to get a group of young people to listen, but hearing them every week and never hearing respect toward the elderly has had a definite destructive effect.

Children also hear this same dishonor on television. I don't have to give examples here because it is obvious. When I was a child, it was possible but rare for someone to demean the elderly. Mostly I heard indifference toward the elderly, which was a nice stepping stone for Satan to later bring in ridicule. Fifty years ago, respect was taught. Tracing back the timeline, each generation taught respect more than the generation following it. The latest generation has heard nothing but mockery of old age.

Children today see old age as a pitiful, pathetic state. Christians should be teaching them the truth. Yes, the flesh is weakened by old age, but that enables the spirit to grow if the person is a believer. Wisdom can be attained in the later years, which is something youth lacks. While teaching school, I heard how children honestly believed their grandmothers and grandfathers should just die because they had lived long enough. They would attend a family funeral, and I would express my sympathy. But, without one tear streak on their face, they would reply, "It's all right, it was just my grandmother. She was old." One student adamantly said he hoped he died before he got old. There's a nugget of youthful wisdom. They also thought older people should not be driving and that their licenses "should be revoked." They failed to observe their own driving skills were a far cry from safety and highway regulation.

Disrespectful talk about parents being clueless was a daily occurrence when I was a high school teacher. For some reason, parents do not correct this foolish talk because it makes them feel accepted by their teenager. Wake up, parents! When your children are checking you into an old-folks home while counting your money, you'll think differently.

DEFILING THE SANCTUARY

Wherefore, as I live, saith the Lord GOD; Surely, because thou hast defiled my sanctuary with all thy detestable things, and with all thine abominations, therefore will I also diminish thee; neither shall mine eye spare, neither will I have any pity.
—Ezekiel 5:11

Thou hast despised mine holy things, and hast profaned my sabbaths...in the midst of thee they commit lewdness.
—Ezekiel 22:8–9

It is especially inappropriate to bring a flippant attitude into the sanctuary. Some song leaders have preceded their live entertainment with comments that it's time to party or to get drunk in the spirit. When the saints of Acts got "drunk" in the spirit, it was not a sporting amusement, but leaders like to precede their sermon with something humorous. Why? Do we think God's Word is not an attention-grabber? Do these preachers want you to like them? Does laughter feed their ego? Preplanned humor is not usually being led by the Spirit, and it is a waste of time. Watchman Nee stated in his book *Spiritual Authority* that commonness is the opposite of holiness.[2]

As I taught, it became commonplace to start high school chapel services with a short video for the purpose of lightening the mood. As if it wasn't already too light. Even the song leader said, "This year we are going to start with videos. These are by no means spiritual. These are strictly for entertainment, so we can start off with a laugh." At least he saw the difference, but I am asking, why do we not leave fleshly entertainment at the door when we come to meet Him in the sanctuary? Can't we have one hour a week set aside just for God, or do we have to make it enjoyable to our flesh?

Christian youth rarely see any demonstration of how to prepare their hearts to meet a holy God. Many times I saw how the video would demean the elderly or even be a clip from a beer commercial. Immediately after the screen went blank, the leader would bow in prayer. There was no time to prepare their hearts.

I also witnessed evidence of this on a mission trip to Mexico. I quickly found out that one of the students, a high-school athlete and very well-liked, had a very foul mouth. He was disrespectful in the small Mexican church as he slouched over and attempted to go to sleep. However, that night he was full of energy as he walked around the room and had "words from the Lord" for the other students. He had been taught that you can instantaneously dispense a word from God on a whim, but your character or lack of it didn't really matter to God. David asked the Lord, "Who shall ascend into the hill of the Lord? or who shall stand in his holy place?" The answer was, "He that hath clean hands, and a pure heart; who hath not lifted up his soul unto vanity" (Ps. 24:3–4).

Many profess that Christians can enter into worship immediately whenever and wherever they are. Therefore, much inappropriate carnality enters the holy places. Modern thought slants toward a belief that rooms that are set aside for worship and preaching should be just like your living room. Preachers want an inviting atmosphere where you feel like you're in the presence of your friends and family, not a fearsome God. Children are allowed to run and play in that room, wear their caps, wear their short skirts and spaghetti-strap top, flaunt their tattoos and body piercing, and say whatever they please. We do not "know how we ought to behave ourselves in the house of God, which is the church of the living God, the pillar and ground of the truth" (1 Tim. 3:15).

Dressing down in our churches is encouraged. We think God doesn't require anything set aside, purposed, dedicated, or consecrated just for Him. Where did we get that idea? In that old book called the Old Testament? Should we throw that out because it's a new day?

Do we not see the vast difference between man and the one true God? Do we really believe that "all is one and that one is all" under the yin and yang bliss blanketing the whole world as we unite under one leader? Do we believe the myth that everything is connected? Do Christians not see their compromise in the move toward world unity?

I am quite accustomed to huffy reactions when I get on a roll, because many Christians don't want to hear it. But nonetheless, the message is true. If we cannot see that our error will continue to slide downhill and that it will not be content where it is, then we are deceived. God means it when He says He will bring strong delusion. If we are teaching our children the principles of the Antichrist, then they will easily fall for his strong delusion mentioned in scripture. Taking a mark into their skin will be no big deal. They have been taught that if the world does it, so do Christians.

A very unfortunate situation occurred at one particular chapel service I attended. The children were allowed to dress as one of their favorite characters to celebrate home-coming week. (Bible characters were not even considered or mentioned.) Students were dressed as the Karate Kid, Marilyn Monroe with nothing lacking, three nuns, Power Rangers, Miss Piggy, and when the worship leader was asked who he was, he replied, the Beast. That was proof enough for me who was really leading that day. These kids went before the Lord to worship dressed in their worldliness and never realized God spewed it right back at them.

The casual and light attitude seems commonplace among youth services. When youth pastors talk as if they are a Bible character or talk to the Lord, they often use common street language. I've heard, "Yo, God, what's up?" Can you imagine Aaron or one of his sons trying that in the holy of holies? God has not changed. Do we not see how the abomination of desolation will actually take place? We are accepting more and more defilement each year. Countless Christians use their own conscience as their guide. The plumb line is not if we're offended, but if the Holy Spirit is offended. The devil will not stop, but will want inch after inch until there is total defilement of the sanctuary.

Ecclesiastes 5:1–2 warns us to "keep thy foot when thou goest to the house of God, and be more ready to hear, than to give the sacrifice of fools: for they consider not that they do evil. Be not rash with thy mouth, and let not thine heart be hasty to utter any thing before God: for God is in heaven, and thou upon earth: therefore let thy words be few."

Contemporary drama seems to cast a unique light and perspective on the gospel. At a recent drama commemorating a church's twenty-fifth anniversary, a woman was asked to play the part of a prostitute. She felt honored to be asked. When is it ever all right for a Christian to "act" like a prostitute? Evidently in church! Christians honestly feel they will reach people for Christ by playing these parts. Nowhere in Scripture does God say we should represent or even act out sinful behaviors in order to convert people. Christians forget the verse that we are to abstain from the very appearance of evil (1 Thess. 5:22).

Why do we want to mimic the world? There have been youth trips advertised as "hippie trips." Why do we entice children with rebellion? Singles events are modeled after horse races or casinos. I've even seen a church event called the New Year's Hypnosis Comedy Show. Other Christian events try to draw a crowd by advertising the fact they will "have more fun than the law allows." Churches build cozy cafés that are now starting to replace prayer rooms. Should we be taking all this so seriously? It doesn't really matter if we are serious about unimportant things, but we must be afraid if we take with levity things that are truly serious.

> It is a fearful thing to fall into the hands of the living God.
>
> —Hebrews 10:31

Chapter 11

HYPE

For when they speak great swelling words of vanity, they allure through the lusts of the flesh.

—2 Peter 2:18

Woe unto the foolish prophets, that follow their own spirit, and have seen nothing!

—Ezekiel 13:3

YPE IS VERY prominent among Christians today. But God doesn't need it. He cannot be coaxed or persuaded. He is not obligated to our whims. According to the dictionary, *hype* is "intentional excess verging on deception that creates great popular enthusiasm for a person or a product." The word originates from the term "hypodermic needle."[1]

That describes exactly what some of our churches are doing. They are injecting people with fake bliss. There is intentional excess of colorful speech and raised voices. Showmanship is readily agreed upon by church leaders to bait attending members. Because the world uses hype, Christians feel they must use it too.

Pastors are promoting their churches rather than the gospel. Jesus is their main "sponsor." They try to create great enthusiasm for their cause, which is usually to build a more fabulous facility. Popular professionals are sought to attract more people. Christians are deceived into thinking certain churches have something really great, when all they have is a hyped focus on human effort—humanism.

We are fruitful in man-made inventions and techniques for church growth, but barren in the true fruits of the Spirit. Hank Hanegraaff, president and chairman of the board of the Christian Research Institute International, commented in his book *Counterfeit Revival*, "When selling and sensationalism become more tantalizing than truth, the very fabric of our faith is compromised."[2]

In reality, most of these churches are offering a shallow, empty, and trivial version of the gospel. It's a false version. It's not the real thing, so they are hyping it in order to sell it. If they had the real, they wouldn't need hype. As a result, the Holy Spirit has withdrawn Himself, while church leaders try to make up for the loss with optimism and zeal.

Jesus did not promote Himself. What He had spoke for itself. When fame and great multitudes grew, He withdrew Himself into the wilderness and prayed. (See Luke 5:15–16.) Matthew 12:19 records that He did not strive, nor cry; neither did any man hear His voice in the streets." He could have easily persuaded people, but He didn't want them to be impressed by the show of power, rather than the reality of it.

We have accepted the heresy that hype, loud music, size, and activity make us more acceptable to God. Who is able to hear the still, small voice anymore? To follow Him takes faith, not sight. True faith does not have to be supported by evidence. Blessed are those who have not seen, yet they believe (John 20:29).

A large component of the hype agenda is to offer fleshly entertainment and pleasure instead of truth. Janet and Craig Parshall's book *Tough Faith* notes that "if we are looking for the emotional highs of the Christian walk, 'theology' comes across as a real low."[3] Since real study of the Bible is so "boring," churches are offering superficial answers and, as a result, temporary solutions. We are presenting Jesus without the truth of suffering and cost. Entertainment is a refuge for apostate people who do not want to face their sin. How many plays and dramas did Jesus and His disciples create and practice? Was Jesus careful to mix comedy with His parables or to start His sermons with jokes?

To only present Christ as a cure-all for fulfilling human desires is a misrepresentation of Him. To entice people with promises of fulfillment, happiness, and freedom is deceitful. To say He will meet our fleshly desires and dreams is unreal. Modern Christianity is lying to the world about Christ. We lack depth in our presentation of the gospel. It is superficial.

We are not offering the real gospel, which includes a daily cross. Churches are preying upon the fact that man judges by outward appearance. We fail to announce that all our display means nothing because God is looking at our hearts. (See 1 Samuel 16:7.)

Janet and Craig Parshall also remarked in their book:

> Placing too much of an emphasis on getting a "spiritual high" in the Christian walk creates other problems for believers in addition to making us gullible to the lies of the enemy. It also creates a

willingness to respond to the invitation of almost all cults and false religions that promise peace, joy happiness, prosperity, or excitement. Whatever it is that we are craving and feel we are lacking, these false teachers will claim they can provide it....What we need to establish is a Christian walk that will endure through a lifetime of service to the Lord, and not create a spiritual thirst for more gimmicks, bells, and whistles.[4]

THE HIGH COST OF HYPE

Will young people be willing to respond to the invitation of the Antichrist because they've been conditioned by the church? Human nature is naturally led by the lust of the eyes. Our tendency is to be captivated by outward show rather than real value. Hollywood receives large paychecks as they rely on this weakness in man. Should the church also cater to what works in the natural? Shouldn't we be telling people that "the wisdom of this world is foolishness with God" (1 Cor. 3:19). Our gauge must not be what appeals to men because "that which is highly esteemed among men is abomination in the sight of God" (Luke 16:15).

We are guilty of setting stumbling blocks in the way of new Christians by not telling them what really matters to God. They are then sorely disappointed by unfulfilled promises produced with the hype. Modern churches are not innocent. Jesus said, "It is impossible but that offences will come: but woe unto him, through whom they come!" (Luke 17:1).

We cannot continue to tell the world that value is attributed to those things that are perceived through our senses. Our job is to tell them where genuine value is located. Jesus asked the Pharisees if the gift or the altar that sanctifies the gift was greater (Matt. 23:19). We, like the Pharisees, are foolish and blind in our placement of value.

We think value is in looking good as we spend our time and money making sure a fresh coat of white paint glistens on the outside of our churches, but we care not that inside lies the bones of dead men who refuse to preach or hear the true gospel (Matt. 23:27). God tells us to "let nothing be done through...vainglory" (Phil. 2:3). To look appealing should never be our goal. In fact, when we are looking good to the world, we are in danger of error.

While wanting as many in attendance as possible in order to look good, churches advertise their next services by saying, "You don't want to miss it. God will be here and it will be phenomenal!" God will arrive according to His Word, but who can predict how the Holy Spirit will move? (See Matthew 18:20.) James, the brother of Jesus, said, "Whereas ye know not what shall be on the morrow....For...ye ought to say, If the Lord will, we shall live, and do this, or that. But now we rejoice in our boastings: all such rejoicing is evil" (James 4:14–16).

Churches exaggerate for effect and attention. We raise our voices at the wrong times. We constantly hear from leaders what we can expect from God but rarely hear what

He expects of us. Churches are like businesses that sell their product based on what the people want. Surveys and statistics are now top priority to church leaders. But, to follow statistics is to follow change and, therefore, follow rebellion. We have been living by comparisons not standards, but we are accountable to God, not man.

Built on Sand

It is very popular for Christians to say that "we are going to the next level." Are we, indeed, going to the next level with God? Is saying something all that matters? I bet that was the popular phrase at the Tower of Babel, too. It's the same tactic used by the world's advertising scene. They tempt us with the latest new and improved product. It is a farce. It is also the tactic of public schools to press students toward higher-level thinking. The world calls higher-level thinking that which is willing to compromise and that which is open to change.

This new shift in thinking is not based on principle. Foundations in public schools, such as rote learning and other factual techniques, are quickly being supplanted with "creative" methods. Our churches, too, are throwing out foundational Bible principles, assuming they are too boring or erroneously thinking that the hearers "already know it." Many pastors are heard saying, "I don't want to bore you with details because you've heard this a hundred times." But, Christians today have not heard it.

When a foundation is not laid, how can a person go to the next level? Why do we not realize that each level with God requires hours and hours of growth because He is so vast and beyond our comprehension? How can we keep climbing when the level we are at has not even been secured? How can we be sure that the levels we are climbing are godly ones? Why do churches never call for repentance because they have slipped back a level?

The main detriment is to children. They are a generation without foundational principles. They are the ones who will quickly succumb to the lies of false teachers. They are the ones who will not hesitate to follow a world leader who will lead with hype and impressive promises. They are the ones being prepared to associate with the large crowd following on the heels of the popular new commander in chief.

Many mega churches hype a crowd mentality. A child growing up in this atmosphere will most likely feel very uncomfortable as part of a small remnant that is separate from the world and may suffer persecution. Mega churches encourage crowd-following. This encouragement may not be intentional, but God is not concerned with quantity if quality has been left outside the door. David "numbered the people" in 2 Samuel 24 and was judged as a result. We are guilty of the same when we set our focus on numbers and then claim our huge membership indicates we are changing the world for Christ. I do not see how preachers get around this clear illustration of how God is displeased with our obsession with numbers.

Competitive growth to prove God is God is unnecessary. Christianity is not in a contest with other religions. More numbers do not prove God's authenticity. God would still be true if every man on earth denied Him. We seem to justify hype since it causes more people to walk in the church door. But, flies can easily be drawn to garbage.

People are attracted to fleshly things. Americans are effortlessly drawn to the hype of reality TV. More and more programs are putting the camera in an "unrehearsed" position. Christians and non-Christians all over America find these programs appealing and enticing. We watch and wonder what will happen next. How will the characters react? What if something goes wrong? Knowing how television works and how competition for ratings is of supreme importance to producers, we know that these programs do actually rehearse and even reinvent certain scenes. Yet, the fascination overrides our will and we are allured into watching them. We know it's not real, but we like to think it is.

Hype Is Unreal

Our flesh likes make-believe. Stories and fairy tales quickly fly off store shelves. The more time we spend in a fantasy world and less time in the real world, the more we become unaffected by reality. Real doesn't impress people anymore. We want exaggeration. We want misrepresentation. How many movies get our money because of exaggeration? Some Christians spend so much time in a make-believe dream that they do not even know how to discern and detect truth. This is a danger for each Christian who spends time in fantasy-land.

Video games only add to this problem. Already children are bored if something isn't "extreme." Many are not attracted to church unless it is hyped and extravagant. Many church leaders justify hype for that reason. Churches should declare only truth. The Holy Spirit can handle the rest. It is God who gives the increase, not us. (See 1 Corinthians 3:6–7.) Young people might find it refreshing if they found a place that was real. If the youth will only be attracted by hype, we may have already lost them. Christian parents should beware of all the irresistible, mesmeric games they buy their children.

While teaching economics to high school students, I was shocked at their resistance to the fact that certain items held intrinsic value. Many students saw no difference between gold and paper money. If there was a difference, they argued, the paper was better since it produced faster results in our economic society. They felt gold only had worth because certain men of the past concurred it was valuable. The fact that God used it to pave streets in heaven did not attribute enough worth to convince them. The fact He commanded it to be used to overlay the ark of the covenant didn't turn on any light bulbs. Its inability to be destroyed did not persuade them. Its beauty meant nothing. Only man's word seemed to be their guide to truth.

The foundational learning of good and bad has been removed. In a world of tolerance and no wrong answers, our children assume that everything is the same. If they were taught foundational value lessons, they could then be prepared for subsequent lessons. After learning the value of gold, they could understand that God is even better. "For whether is greater, the gold, or the temple that sanctifieth the gold?" (Matt. 23:17). Humans add to their learning, and it builds on foundations. God gives us mini value lessons so we can comprehend His bigger ones. It will take an eternity to learn of all His manifold worthiness, but until a person learns the basics, he'll never mature further.

A recent sermon on television was a four-part lesson on why we worship God. Not one of the four reasons mentioned was that God is worthy of worship. It seems even some adults have lost sight of true value. If our children do not see real value for what it is worth, they will have a hard time understanding God. He is all about value and worth. I suppose Satan wouldn't argue against this new understanding of value.

Christians are promised crowns of gold. Yet, if we cannot be impressed with this reality, we cannot be drawn to His promises based on truth. If we seek to draw people through hype and not truth, we will only have a church of pew-fillers and not of converts. The church has, like society, taken away the significant difference between what is priceless and what is cheap. The intrinsic value scales have flipped. Good things are viewed as bad and bad things are now viewed with praise, but Isaiah 5:20 warns, "Woe unto them that call evil good, and good evil; that put darkness for light, and light for darkness; that put bitter for sweet, and sweet for bitter!"

Many immigrants came to America with the dream that even a peasant could become rich. That ability has recently been accessible without the cost of hard work. Children, today, take for granted that there is nothing unattainable to them. Hype in the world tells them they can achieve whatever they can dream. They are often told, even in church, that they can be president or someone famous. They are not told, however, of the rarity or the uncommon likelihood of it. As a result, young Christians are beginning to think everything, including God, is easily accessible. They are not willing to humble themselves to pay a price. They do not realize God is far above their perception of Him and too expensive for anybody to attain without Christ's blood.

CONTINUED ACCEPTANCE OF FALSEHOOD

With all the danger of not seeing value as God sees it, Christians still feel safe in believing they are not among those who cannot detect true value. We are all inclined to this ignorance. We have gone so far as to let falsehood enter the church. Therefore, we are open to deception. It's one thing to fantasize while sitting in a movie theater or while resting, but it is much worse to let fantasy enter the church. In fact, it has entered as a result of Christians spending so much time with counterfeit scenarios outside the church. It was only a matter of time before it came with us to church.

The world is dying and going to hell. We don't have time for invaluable, sugarcoated fantasy. God is real, and He only deals in reality. The church is supposed to be a refreshing refuge from the world in that we offer truth and reality. People desire a safe harbor where falsehood cannot trick them. They find it in His arms of safety, not in hype.

Yet, churches still try to entice. If we continue to appeal to people in partial truth in order to win more, we will have a church full of weak Christians. We are not doing God a favor. We should not think He wants us to add to truth in order to win souls. We shouldn't think He is proud just because we have gathered a crowd. The Holy Spirit doesn't enter through the senses. He draws people through faith, which only comes through truth.

A Christian's struggle has always been with sticking to truth. Various doctrines have entered the church throughout the centuries that have veered to either side of truth. Our weakness has been compromise. J. C. Ryle, a minister in England in the late 1800s, saw the inability of weak saints to stand for truth. He wrote:

> The tendency of modern thought is to reject dogmas, creeds, and every kind of bounds in religion. It is thought grand and wise to condemn no opinion whatsoever, and to pronounce all earnest and clever teachers to be trustworthy, however heterogeneous and mutually destructive their opinions may be. Everything, forsooth, is true and nothing is false! Everybody is right and nobody is wrong! Everybody is likely to be saved and nobody is to be lost![5]

Are we compromising truth in church because that is what the world teaches us? Does tolerance reign supreme? Is there truth everywhere and in every religion or does Christ stand alone? Can salvation be by any other name? Is church attendance all that matters and nobody need bother with laws, creeds, or vows to be true to His name? Have we followed worldly doctrines so far as to really believe everyone will go to heaven in the end?

Assurance of victory, secured happiness, great results, miracles, certain wealth, and unfailing conversions have all been promised by teachings in our churches. Humility is rare. There is assumption of God's presence when, in fact, He may be elsewhere.

If the truth were stated without exaggeration, people could come to church for veritable reasons rather than fleshly ones. In other words, it could be real and count for something. Yet, there is continued appeal to the emotions and not the spirit man. We must pray for discernment for what constitutes godliness and what constitutes hype. Hype is very persuasive because people naturally follow a charismatic leader. When the majority falls for something, it's hard to resist falling, too.

People naturally settle for the artificial. They would rather have myth than truth. We settle for what looks good rather than what truly is good. We use adjectives like *incredible* when something is not really incredible or phenomenal or even awesome. Today, it is enough to just suppose something is good. We think we can eat mud and pretend it is chocolate and even believe it is chocolate. But, in reality, it is not chocolate.

Hype and fervency often spring from supposition and high opinions of self. False emotion would instantly die if we could honestly see ourselves as we are. Churches are glamorizing their building programs, youth groups, decorating committees, and other groups with *colossal* descriptions of *phenomenal* and *unprecedented* importance. Everything and everyone is bragged upon for being absolutely *amazing*. Yet, Jesus corrected a certain ruler when he addressed Him as Good Master. Jesus asked, "Why callest thou me good? none is good, save one, that is, God" (Luke 18:19). That should put our hype into perspective. The word *good* is reserved for God, but we use *great* for ourselves. We should remember that we will give account for every idle word on the day of judgment. (See Matthew 12:36.)

Children receive praise for doing what they should have done in the first place. They receive unmerited praise for doing nothing. The world says that if children are made to feel good about themselves, it doesn't really matter if they do well. Our children's actions are not receiving realistic appraisal. Therefore, true results and accomplishment are not happening.

Whatever our children are doing, we are accepting as grand. Sometimes, we tell them they will receive a certain reward if they produce a certain behavior. When they do not achieve it, we give them the reward for at least trying. The adults will receive a much different reward for trying so hard to produce a generation of lazy, socialistic dependents.

A high school in Texas was having problems with student attendance. To avoid correcting students by providing consequences, the staff decided to give laptop computers to seniors with perfect attendance. Some students were even given cars! Here again, big awards were given to kids who did their reasonable duty. They were highly praised for doing only what was expected. This reward system conveys to students that they are performing above normal expectations when, in fact, they are not.

Today, children are learning that everything is acceptable. They believe they can do whatever is right in their own eyes. They have become their own judges. This is more dangerous at its root than it appears on the surface. It does not seem wrong to praise a kid for doing a job halfway. We think maybe next time he will do better in order to receive that desired pat on the back, but humans do not work that way. If we can get a pat on the back for doing it halfway, then we'll do it halfway. The sad thing is that most children are receiving pats on the back for doing nothing. They are told, "At least you didn't do something bad, so here's a reward." How fake. How unreal. Are we Christians content with this unreal approval when we could be teaching our children real worthiness and accountability?

When a generation is raised without accountability, there is no easy reversal for the damage. They become so accustomed to falsity that they come to believe there is no truth. Therefore, they are not easily convinced by it. Truth becomes irrelevant when you've learned to live without it. It's odd how something so sweet and nice as praise and rewards creates a generation without a conscience toward right and wrong. How clever and deceiving Satan can be. No wonder he is called the father of lies.

Our technique of praising all behavior has actually already backfired. Kids are so accustomed to it, it means absolutely nothing. They learn quickly in today's culture that everything is good and acceptable. What a danger for Christian children to think that way. We should be teaching them the things that are unacceptable to God. We've come a long way from basic Bible teaching.

Instead of receiving praise only when it is merited, our children are being taught entitlement. They are not being taught how to work for achievement. They are not taught accountability and consequences. They will likely expect the same type of oversight from their job, spouse, and government.

Since an appearance of doing good seems to be what matters, children have learned that appearing to be sorry for their actions is all that is necessary. With parents, a hasty "sorry" is all it takes to get their children off the hook. Like the world, we work hard to hear that word rather than working to see a change in behavior. Kids learn quickly that "sorry" is successful, and therefore use it readily, but it means absolutely nothing when their hearts have not changed. People can act humble, but God is concerned with real humility. Second Corinthians 7:10 says, "For godly sorrow worketh repentance to salvation not to be repented of: but the sorrow of the world worketh death."

Many young adults already have a hard time facing reality. When they face an employer who fires them for laziness, they become depressed. They become disgruntled when they do not receive a raise for showing up each day. They are shocked if "sorry" doesn't acquit them. Depression is widespread among Christians for many reasons, but one reason is because we magnify unreal achievement.

We are also guilty of overly praising people who are in the spotlight but not people who are really doing the work. Churches put their pastors up as idols while nursery workers, teachers, maintenance people, and others are overlooked. The appearance of things seems more important than the results.

In the world we see the same glorification of the shallow. To raise money for the families affected by disaster, a fireman bleached his hair for one thousand dollars. He was praised and spotlighted one morning on TV, and nobody mentioned those who had contributed the money. Is it really worthy of praise to bleach your hair? It sure gets attention. Our children are being drilled that whatever gets attention is what really counts, but they don't understand that it doesn't count with God.

Christian youth have been praised and given standing ovations for being "phenomenal young people" when there is no difference between their actions and the world's. Is flattery supposed to be used to produce good results? Does it help to overstate and brag on children? Will they act better if they hear that they are God's "chosen generation"? In truth, every Christian since the book of Acts is considered to be the chosen generation. Will it really make better kids if they hear how good they are? Can we live off pretense until the Lord returns?

An end of the year Christian school newspaper announced an "incredible year" with "unprecedented growth." It was stated that the biggest blessing of the year was the spiritual growth of the student body. Exaggeration claimed that you could walk into the high school and sense the presence of the Lord over the students. Students were said to be learning to use the gifting God had given them. It was recorded that chapel days were met with great anticipation.

All of these hyperbolic statements seemed to represent a school that was just bubbling with Christlikeness. Was it really? Was God pleased with the students' zeal for Him? Did it just matter that parents could read the paper and beam with pride in spite of the artificial front that was portrayed? Were the students once more taught that falsity was more important than truth? Why was it not mentioned that many of the students were actually hiding their secret sins from parents and teachers while pretending to be innocent? That would indeed ruin the make-believe myth parents and staff wanted to believe.

Is something really good if it feels good? Sounds good? Looks good? Some things are, in reality, good when they do not even feel or look good. We should not be so gullible to the devil's tactics. Believing something is good means nothing unless it is founded in truth. Believing truth is what counts with God. The Bible tells us that we can believe a lie and be damned (2 Thess. 2:11–12). To believe something does not make it true. We Christians had better weigh what is real and what is not and start believing truth and rejecting myths.

False Prophets

The prophets in Jeremiah's day were telling God's people, "No evil shall come upon you" (Jer. 23:17). They didn't want to scare off any potential customers. They preached a feel-good gospel, but God says they were preaching "lies and deceit of their own heart" (v. 26). God's Word is "like a fire," and it burns some people right out of the congregation (v. 29). We must not be guilty of perverting the words of the living God (v. 36). To hype is to deceive, and God warns, "Cursed be he that doeth the work of the LORD deceitfully" (Jer. 48:10).

Our children are not spiritually affected for good by glamorized church events. Children's services do not produce results just by their flamboyant wording. The church is using exaggeration just like the world. Hype does not work for spiritual matters. Hype with a supposedly revolutionary edge only lures the flesh. We should never use it for spiritual means. We are not influencing people rightly. We are, in fact, influencing our youth toward error by using exaggeration in our churches. We are saying the church is no different from the world. We tell them that no true value merit system is required from the world and none is required at church.

They learn that God loves everyone and everything just as the world teaches them in its tolerance teachings. We would be better off teaching nothing than to teach the pumped-up lies of the world to this generation. Seeking radical transformation and transition in our churches is nothing but a steppingstone to major deception because it will condition children to think it is God's will to radically change what has been established in His Word.

Our boasting does not impress God. It only impresses people. We cannot claim our influence with the world is a good thing when, in fact, it is not. If we boast, it must be in truth, not pretense. We should not boast by using another man's line of measurement. Instead, "He that glorieth, let him glory in the Lord" (2 Cor. 10:16–17).

NO AUTHENTIC RESULTS

What is said and what is actually accomplished rarely share a positive correlation in our churches. If a group of people held a class on carpentry and then sat around drinking coffee and eating donuts while nobody actually picked up a hammer, nail, brick, or board, it would be ridiculous to clap and cheer that a beautiful house was being built. Yet, we are doing just that in our churches. We are applauding phenomenal conversions and results for God's kingdom while, in truth, we casually sat around and socialize.

Hyped programs supplant actual preaching, and we are cheering while few bring their Bibles and even fewer open them. If a person is bold enough to question the results, this enquirer is made to feel out of touch because he does not believe results are there. How has mystical superstition entered our churches? Why do we cheer invisible results? How do we let it continue to occur without questioning it? Jesus talked about belief, but it was neither mystical nor superstitious. It was real. Results happened.

We are also fake in our Bible studies. We brag that we spent a whole year with a Bible study that only required us to divide our life into sections and then review our childhood. We are asked by the study guide to contemplate on those years. Did we actually study the Bible? No, we studied ourselves. That's exactly like saying we're going to study to become an oceanographer, and when asked what classes we are taking, we reply, "Knitting, cross-stitch, and quilting." We are then patted on the back and told, "Oh, how delightful; you'll be the best oceanographer ever!" The bottom line is that Bible studies should be a study of the Bible.

With all the pretense in today's churches, we are in danger of falling for anything. If it enters the church with an enticing label, we are likely to buy into it. Many church members are so hungry for a move of God, miracles, a touch, or a revival that they are ripe to snatch at anything that looks like them. We are in a perilous situation since God said in the last days those who do not stand for truth will fall for the Antichrist's lying signs and wonders (2 Thess. 2:9–10). We are guilty of thinking that the truth is not enough.

Mystical superstition has easily slipped into our midst. Leaders flatter their spectators with, "Everybody here is full of miracles. You're full of God. Get close to each other to get it!" One preacher commanded his audience to "stop waiting for someone to tell you that you can" and for them to "release" themselves to "hear from God and have dreams." He then was bold enough to say that God has to "back up" everything Christians say. Does God obey us unconditionally?

Christians are quickly and easily adding humanism to their thinking. They should know that miracles do not come from their neighbor. Christians are not noticing the shift of focus toward people and not God. We think anyone at anytime can give us God's word of instruction without seeking it from His Word. Friends become an easy-come easy-go dispenser of flattery and praise. We assume it comes from God. Does it? An emphasis on having special words of wisdom for others is not focused on results, but on impression. Weight is given to hearing God rather than obeying Him.

Have you noticed when guest speakers with a prophetic gift for giving words are invited to speak, the crowd becomes much larger than usual? Modern Christians love the excitement used to introduce these men and women. There are some truly gifted prophets who are able to give words of wisdom, but we have made a spectator sport of it. It's a shame.

Preachers read statistics to see what affects the average person. To follow statistics is to follow change. They bribe people to return to their church by saying, "Come ready to receive." It's not popular to state the demands of Christianity and ask people to come ready to sacrifice. Self-denial turns people away. I have heard a pastor say while trying to attract numbers by overstating importance, "You hear world-class teaching and preaching" at our church. Others say they have a "state-of-the-art youth facility." Many flatter their congregations with, "You're the most generous and faith-filled saints in the world."

Some services begin with promotional videos. Star-status members enthusiastically call for participants in some new program. The services include hyper-suggestibility, peer pressure, and high expectations. When people leave the service and nothing actually happened, they do not seem to question it. We just prove our gullibility and say, "What a phenomenal service!"

Our feelings and emotions are affected, so we assume our spirit is. Dave Hunt stated, "There is nothing wrong with emotion that accompanies reality, but we must be careful not to encourage a commitment to Christ that is founded upon emotion and not upon an understanding of and commitment to the truth of who He really is, why He came, and what He demands of us."[6] It is true that our emotions can be moved deeply by Christ, but emotions can be superficial. False emotions more readily come to the surface than true ones. The clearest proof of real affectation is not the outward show, but the results produced in that person's life. Emotions that accompany reality are those affected by the realization that our sin nature is offensive to a holy God. There are times, too, when we should be ashamed that our emotions are not affected more than they are. It is what truly affects us that is key.

REALITY

We assume God has been very pleased with our attendance and worship. We do not validate what has happened in our church services. We do not want to "try the spirits whether they are of God;" we would rather ignore the fact that "many false prophets are gone out into the world" (1 John 4:1). Impunity and exemption are our drugs of choice, and accountability is suppressed as nothing but a false assumption.

We have no fear of God's judgment on our falsity because our fear is "taught by the precept of men" (Isa. 29:13). We are taught it is wrong to fear God's anger. While we continue to draw near to the Lord with our mouths, honoring Him with our lips, our hearts are far from Him (Mark 7:6–7).

Gullibility causes us to be first to jump in line for a hot spot where we suspect God is located. We get tingly from the mysticism and superstition of the age and do not stop to question our flesh. We cheer when leaders yell, "You'll never be the same," or "Something special is about to happen." We do not realize that we are being molded for false miracles from the Antichrist. Only those with discernment will not be tricked. Discernment knows that the Holy Spirit points to Jesus and does not point to people leading a show.

We are guilty of desiring the hyperbole of our day. We want our churches to match the hi-tech magnificence of the movie theater. A prominent Christian women's speaker asked, "Why can't we look as good as the people of the world?" Does the Bible associate "good" with people of the world? We'd rather look good than to take the time for repentance or fighting evil, but those aren't rewarding to our flesh. Yet, if we continue to refuse to teach the whole counsel of God, we will not experience a real move of God.

God is a God of miracles, but they do not occur in an atmosphere of boastful hype. Also, we cannot have a genuine move of God without cost. The price of denying ourselves, fasting, prayer, and humility is not being preached in the majority of our churches. In reality, though, walking with God is not cheap. The Word says that "deep calleth unto deep" (Ps. 42:7), and His ways are above our ways.

Overuse of excitement causes some churches to find silence suspect. It implies the church is dead, so we replace silence with futile sound and ignore instruction to "be still and know that I am God" (Ps. 46:10). He speaks in a still, small voice, and it is unlikely we will hear Him if we are filling the air with noise. There are times to shout and rejoice, but there are also times to be silent.

Sadly, hype is so common that it is getting harder to recognize. Pastors say one-liners that have no biblical backing, but because they are said with such confidence, we accept them. This is a tactic used in liberal universities. When nice-looking, clean-cut, well-dressed men say anything with confidence, people believe it. Lawyers have the same ability. But, their words are hollow when not based on truth. Beware of those who are able to misrepresent with sureness. Question it when your eternity depends on it.

Promises of great change and worldwide conversions are filling our ears. We are told that our miracle offering could change the history of a nation. Who wouldn't buy into that?

The popular belief is that the church is rising up out of slumber to reap a great harvest of souls. We hear preachers say that Hollywood has no idea what's going to hit them when God takes over the entertainment industry. Is the fact that only eight were saved in Noah's day ever mentioned? Is the harvest of judgment or the separation of the wheat from the tares ever referred to? Are the fields that are white unto harvest not being harvested because "the laborers are few" (Luke 10:2)? Do we question this new talk of phenomenal and unprecedented revival? Will it actually be an ingathering of supporters for a new world religion? Didn't God say that "many are called, but few are chosen" (Matt. 22:14)? We should be humbled by our speculation and begin laboring in prayer for each soul that, in reality, is lost.

The topic of religion is at the forefront in the world today, and an explosion of questions about God is even in the media. The atmosphere is saturated with spiritual matters. God is moving, but so is Satan. Be careful not to be swept away with the wrong "revival" or the wrong leader who promises every dream to be fulfilled. Don't be tricked by lying signs and wonders.

TRUE WORSHIP

Modern worship is excessively focused on what happens to the worshiper rather than focusing attention on the One who is worshiped. If we continue to hype worship with artificial lights, action, and other pageantry while trying to affect emotions, genuine worship will die. Trying to affect worship with a technique is deceptive. True worship cannot be engineered.

Superficial words do not count for true worship. How serious is it to tell God, "I bow" or "I give You my all," when we do not really mean it? Are we guilty of honoring Him with our mouths when our hearts are far from Him (Matt. 15:8)? Worship takes place in the heart of a person, and we cannot fool God with hollow words.

True worship can indeed be very loud, but there is a difference between worship and human-induced noise. It is likely that few young people are exerting true worship. They love to be loud, but they do not have much knowledge and understanding behind it. Yet, in our move toward hype and worldly methods, we set up the young to lead. We are guilty of wanting to be like the world. As Tozer said, "The Christlike, the self-forgetting, the other-worldly are jostled aside to make room for the latest converted playboy who is usually not too well converted and still very much a playboy."[7]

Nebuchadnezzar made an image of gold for people to worship. If they didn't worship, they were put to death. (See Daniel 3.) He can be seen as a type of the Antichrist since he, too, will set up an image for all to worship and promises to kill anyone who does not worship it. (See Revelation 13:15.) Daniel tells us that "when all the people heard the sound of [music]…all the people, the nations, and the languages, fell down and worshipped the golden image that Nebuchadnezzar had set up" (Dan. 3:7).

These Bible stories are vital in our learning and should be used as examples for us today. As years go by, I can see more clearly how easily people react to persuasive, noisy crowds. Also, in a world where it is intolerant to boldly stand for truth, I can see how many will bow to avoid being killed. In Daniel's day, only three did not succumb to the delusion. Few were saved from the deception.

Some mega church preachers proclaim that many shall go up "to the mountain of the Lord, to the house of the God of Jacob," but that will occur during the Millennium (Isa. 2:3). Chapter 1 of Isaiah is the story that is representative of the time preceding the Millennium. We are told that God will judge His people prior to the second coming of Christ. He will judge by "purely purging away the dross and taking away all the tin" (Isa. 1:25). The judgment is because they have "provoked the Holy One of Israel unto anger" because they had "gone away backward" (Isa. 1:4). Their only hope was a "very small remnant" (Isa. 1:9).

The Lord rejected their empty worship, saying, "And when ye spread forth your hands, I will hide mine eyes from you: yea, when ye make many prayers, I will not hear: your hands are full of blood" (Isa. 1:15). It is more likely, according to Scripture, that most will go into captivity because of lack of knowledge rather than going to the mountain of the Lord (Isa. 5:13). When false prophets rise up, they deceive many, even the elect (Matt. 24:24).

All our surface hype ignores real Christian obligation and duty. We must be vigilant and alert. Good preaching is necessary, yet it tends to get banned. Paul was rejected in Asia when they "turned away" from him (2 Tim. 1:15). George Whitefield, a well-known evangelist from America's first Great Awakening, was expelled from pulpits when he refused to preach to the fleshly desires of a crowd in order to keep attendees loyal.

GOD REQUIRES TRUE ACTION

If a preacher today requires works from their congregation, he is looked at with critical frowns. Preachers must not back down from these frowns. They must preach the requirements of Christianity and stop living in a shallow realm. Jesus' parable of the faithful steward is a lesson to us. Jesus said, "That servant, which knew his lord's will, and prepared not himself, neither did according to his will, shall be beaten with many stripes" (Luke 12:47). We are risking much by not preparing for the Lord's return.

It is worse to say we are obeying Him when we are not than to just blatantly disobey Him. Consider Jesus' parable of a man with two sons. (See Matthew 21:28–31.) One claimed he would go work in the father's vineyard, but didn't. The other said he wouldn't, but repented and did. Which one actually did the will of his father? Overstatements do not count with God. Actions do.

To survive in these perilous times, we must know more about the Bible than we know about happiness and satisfaction. We must know the Holy Spirit more than we know how to get people's attention. Distinction must be made between action and mere talk, between quality and quantity, between moral acts and surface activity. We cannot continue giving the appearance of progress when nothing really is being produced. Time-consuming activities that provide fellowship but no life-changing answers are not what the starving world needs. We should stop judging works of God by outward appearances. If we support a work for being spectacular yet unbiblical, we will face unpleasant consequences. Our efforts to smooth the way to heaven by taking away guilt and embarrassment is dangerous to the souls of men.

Children must not continue to be deceived by surface quality in churches. We must combat the mentality of the school system, which emphasizes process over product. True progress is lost in the hype of process. Gilded labels and empty promises from modern curriculum are found wanting. Christians must remain focused on what truly matters and concentrate on true results. The race does have importance, but it's the end of it that counts.

Are we listening to lies? Are people promising things that will not happen? "Whoso boasteth himself of a false gift is like clouds and wind without rain" (Prov. 25:14). The Bible warns us of last-days men who use "great swelling words of vanity [and] allure through the lusts of the flesh. While they promise liberty, they themselves are the servants of corruption" (2 Pet. 2:18–19). Fervent and earnest words are just words if, in the end, they amount to nothing. When leaders offer solutions to church problems that are opposed to Scripture, we must reject them. If we do not continue to "grow...in the knowledge of our Lord," we are set up for deception. Peter also warned that we should "beware lest ye also, be led away with the error of the wicked, fall from [our] own steadfastness" (2 Pet. 3:17–18). When we agree with falsehood by inviting those who do not preach the true gospel into our midst, we are then "partakers of their evil deeds." God warns us not to receive them, nor bid them God speed (2 John 10–11).

A. W. Tozer explains, "The directionless Christian is the one who supports the new and spectacular, regardless of whether or not it is in accord with Scriptures and the revealed will of God."[8] There is a danger in these last days of new revelation that is likely to contradict God's Word. I have heard preachers say that God is putting out the lamp of the old system and is going to do a new thing that has no reference to the past.

When God does a new thing in us, it is His salvation, which brings us life rather than the death we had previously been under. We are new creatures in Christ at salvation, and "old things are passed away" (2 Cor. 5:17). Israel will experience a new thing when God will "make a way in the wilderness" for them as their nation is restored and they experience conversion in Christ (Isa. 43:18–19). But, this does not mean that God continues to give us new revelation while destroying the old revelation.

Still, we are intrigued by whatever is new, and we have contempt for the ordinary. Accepting every new idea primes us for deception. We must not swallow anything that is contrary to God's Word. Let us constantly beware of things portrayed as a new move or a new wave of God.

It is not wrong to receive new revelations of certain scriptures, but to believe completely unprecedented revelation that is radical and aside from God's Word is where we are in peril. Even when preachers say what they are doing is written in God's Word, we must check it out. God is serious when He says that the End Times will be perilous. People are on the brink of major deception and damnation, and they don't even see it. As a result, they are like people carelessly walking on the edge of a cliff. The greatest peril is in the fact that Christians do not recognize that they should be careful, watchful, and vigilant.

Teach Us to Number Our Days, o Lord

We must know God's Word in order to be protected from delusion. Bible truths have been supplanted with ideas that appear to be true. But, most Christians don't realize that there is a lot more to His Word than is being preached. We cannot be satisfied with only knowing God is love, that He sent His Son, and we are His children.

The Dark Ages was a period of time lacking in biblical knowledge. Can we even imagine an environment like the Dark Ages? Widespread distortion of the Bible and the ruling church imprisoned men's souls with humanistic corruption and vain religious practices. Are we strong enough to stand against this same onslaught that has invaded our churches today? Are we able to be like Martin Luther, John Wycliffe, or even John Huss, who gave his life for the cause of Christ? Will we stand for truth, proclaim an untainted gospel, and not waver in spite of the cost? Will we stand and give our lives regardless of being unpopular with the world?

Chapter 12

HOPE

Thy faithfulness is unto all generations.
—Psalm 119:90

GOD HAS NOT forsaken His people. He remains faithful. There is still hope for this generation, but despite atheistic influences on modern thinking, God does require certain conditions to be met before He blesses His children.

REPENTANCE

> If my people, which are called by my name, shall humble themselves, and pray, and seek my face, and turn from their wicked ways; then will I hear from heaven, and will forgive their sin, and will heal their land.
>
> —2 Chronicles 7:14

If we, who are called by His name and no other name, reject self-esteem and humble ourselves; if we pray and seek His face; if we turn from wickedness rather than tolerating it; then He will hear us, forgive us, and heal our land. God is "ready to forgive; and plenteous in mercy unto all them that call upon" Him (Ps. 86:5). He is "full of compassion, and gracious, longsuffering, and plenteous in mercy and truth" (Ps. 86:15). There is always hope for God's people. It is written, "The gates of hell shall not prevail" against us (Matt. 16:18).

What can remedy the plight of our sinful nation? Nothing but a sincere inward examination. Each person must consider the condition of his own soul and its attitude toward Christ. Each must be suspicious of his own spirituality. Paul warned the Corinthians, "Examine yourselves, whether ye be in the faith; prove your own selves" (2 Cor. 13:5).

Sin must appear to be sin. We must consider our own participation in loving darkness rather than light because our deeds are evil (John 3:19). The holy light of Scripture must be allowed to expose our pride and arrogance. We must deny our flesh and pursue purity. For it is written, "Blessed are the pure in heart: for they shall see God" (Matt 5:8). If we truly love God's Word, His commandments, and the doctrines of the Bible, we will be willing to forfeit our own will and lay down our lives for the cause of Christ.

The church of the past thirty years has allowed more sin and worldliness than ever before. We have perverted our way, and have forgotten the Lord our God. He pleads, "Return, ye backsliding children, and I will heal your backslidings" (Jer. 3:21–22).

A return to God is our hope. He told His own people in the Old Testament, "O Israel, thou hast destroyed thyself; but in me is thine help" (Hosea 13:9). He has provided the way out of our backslidings. He has shown us what is good and what He requires of us. We are "to do justly, and to love mercy, and to walk humbly with our God" (Mic. 6:8). We are under tremendous obligation to know these truths and to obey them.

The church cannot continue to delight in the forbidden pleasures of the flesh. We must no longer be captivated by worldly satisfactions and popularity. We cannot persist in seeking to solve problems with secular resources. We must not rely on reason and rationale.

Many assume that they are right with God and do not question their standing because they have been told these worldly methods are correct forms of worship. But, we cannot continue to be crowd-followers. We must be like Christ, who "for the joy that was set before him endured the cross, despising the shame" (Heb. 12:2).

Are we willing to abstain from comfort and our spoiled desires for the cause of Christ? Are we offended by the Cross and the rejection it brings from the world? Jesus did not seek reputation. (See Philippians 2:7.) For the love of the One who shed His blood on our behalf, we must humble ourselves and be content to live without reputation. We must flee carnality and truly walk with our blessed Redeemer.

Joel the prophet warned God's people of the solemn importance of repentance. They, too, probably thought they were innocent, until he pointed out their plight. Joel warned:

> Gird yourselves, and lament, ye priests: howl, ye ministers of the altar: come, lie all night in sackcloth, ye ministers of my God: for the meat offering and the drink offering is withholden from the house of your God. Sanctify ye a fast, call a solemn assembly, gather the elders and all the inhabitants of the land into the house of the LORD your God, and cry unto the Lord.
>
> —Joel 1:13–14

We cannot right our wrongs except through repentance. We cannot correct our errors by implementing better systems or new programs that make us forget past mistakes. Good programs do not nullify bad ones. We must turn around and reject our error, not go forward in it. We must start over and go back to the basics of the Bible. Our only solution is an acknowledgment of wrongdoing and then a replacement of right doing.

The natural tendency of our flesh is to accept the world's mentality that the conscience can be appeased by implementing good deeds in order to erase bad ones, but Christians should know better. Many churches fail to see the importance of repentance and overlook bad choices by simply making new choices. But, correction of error comes through repentance. Only then are we given a clean slate. If a solemn assembly has to be called, then so be it. Leaders must be willing to face humiliation in order to set things straight with God.

The modern church is starving for a work in its soul. We need evidence of authentic salvation that turns people away from the broad way and into the narrow way. We need a testimony for the world that portrays a people who has turned from fleshly desires into godly duty, from sin into holiness, from Satan to God. We must abhor ourselves and look away from the tempter and toward the Preserver. We must resist humanistic teachings that "trusteth in man, and maketh flesh his arm, and whose heart departeth from the LORD" (Jer. 17:5).

We must not get distracted by life's circumstances. We cannot continue to focus our attention on our problems and hurts rather than on the Lord. We should shun churches that only entertain and share amusing stories of personal experience. We must avoid ungodliness and bad company. We must realize we are pilgrims in this world. We must not be moved by persuasive worldly enticements. We must be like men of old who sought out the knowledge of the holy.

We are compelled to be immovable in our stand for truth. If we don't, the cost will be high, especially in the souls of our children. They are a deceived generation because of the apostasy we have allowed and so easily succumbed to.

The truth is available, and we must seek it. God will not turn from us if we seek Him. Humility after repentance will cause us to see God from a different perspective. Rather than claiming that we are special and chosen, we can say, as Isaiah said, "O Lord, I will praise thee: though thou wast angry with me, thine anger is turned away, and thou comfortedst me. Behold, God is my salvation; I will trust, and not be afraid: for the Lord Jehovah is my strength and my song; he also is become my salvation" (Isa. 12:1–2).

Humility will direct us to honestly see that salvation is only in the name of Christ. By setting our sights on Christ, we will no longer believe in our own human potential. Human worth, power, and uniqueness will pale in comparison. We will no longer boast of ourselves as individuals who are destined for greatness. We will shift the context of our sentences toward focusing on the Lord rather than on man and his capabilities.

We must pray for the pastors who seek to fulfill only physical needs. We must pray for their eyes to be opened to discern spiritual needs. Christians must stop desiring that their physical needs be met. They must end their tendency to be so easily offended and hurt. If we say with our mouth that it is not about us, then let's live that way. Let's sing praises to Him and stop praising ourselves for being the people of God who are destined to be history makers.

Let's shift the focus away from our satisfaction in Christ to His satisfaction with us. The prominent atmosphere of churches should no longer be one of enticement offering people a "what's in it for them" gospel. The Holy Spirit must be allowed to do the work of drawing people to Him. Paul told the church at Corinth that he and Timothy would preach "not ourselves, but Christ Jesus the Lord" (2 Cor. 4:5). Jesus must be the focal point of each sermon, instead of a how-to message on making life more pleasant. The doctrine of humanism must be refused.

Rather than incorporating worldly doctrines into our churches, we must resist them. Rather than saying God made us unique and that He only desires us to increase, we must realize that He wants us to crucify our "unique" self. We must abandon all our ambitions and be a living sacrifice for Christ. Watchman Nee, servant of the Lord until his death in a communist prison in 1972, observed, "God sets us free from the dominion of sin, not by strengthening our old man, but by crucifying him; not by helping him to do anything, but by entirely removing him from the scene of action."[1] He also stated, "There is an old world and a new world, and between the two there is the tomb."[2]

While the world continues to promote becoming who we really are, the church must return to the understanding that the real "me" must die. The world will always seek to coax the true you, also called the authentic self, out of its shy, little shell. But, this idea is in direct opposition to God's Word.

If we genuinely spend time seeking God, we will have less time for movies, shopping, and other pleasures. Fleshly desires only perpetuate a stronger appetite for them, until the flesh feels it cannot be satisfied. However, "the eye is not satisfied with seeing, nor the ear filled with hearing" (Eccles. 1:8). If we spend time with Him, we won't even want to do those things. They will pale in comparison. If we would stop mingling with the world, we could save time, money, and especially our health. We cannot say we are a living sacrifice until we are truly living a life of sacrifice.

Here's a test to analyze our fleshly desires. Ask yourself the following questions.

What do I want most?
What do I think about most?
How do I use my money?
How do I spend my spare time?
What company do I enjoy?
Whom and what do I admire?
What do I laugh at?

A true analysis should reveal the true you. That true self must come under submission to God. Honest Christians will find they must daily crucify their true motives and must ignore their impatient desires.

When Christians are separate in their practices from the rest of society, they will stand out like a sore thumb. Persecution will surely come when the church is in right standing with God. Denial of self and a defense of principle flies in the face of the tolerant, ecumenical world.

Christians who stand for truth will be accused of pushing their agenda, but the unsaved world does not realize what is good for it. If a nurse pushes loving care or a teacher pushes learning, they are not criticized. They are just doing their job. Nobody questions them. Nevertheless, Satan is active in the world, and there will always be resistance to the healthy agenda of Christianity. We must be convinced of its life-giving health and push it with all our might.

The church must have an active faith in these End Times. We cannot be passive. We must focus on Jesus, not the wind and the waves. We must have a face set like flint in determination to do right in an evil world. We must be doers of the Word no matter what criticism we face. We must "stand fast in one spirit, with one mind striving together for the faith of the gospel" (Phil. 1:27).

If we are truly repentant, our lives will evidence a change in behavior. We cannot just wear the Christian label; we must live it and be separate from the world. There is a conscious side to our sanctification. We must choose to walk according the Spirit. We must be found reading the Word and praying.

It is possible to truly live the life of Christ in a fallen world. Janet and Craig Parshall wrote, "When we live lives that reflect the holiness and power of Christ, we will present the most articulate and persuasive argument for the truth of Christ. When our lives are lived in complete contradiction to the custom and experience of the world, there is no limit to the territory that can be won for the Savior."[3] We must be willing to sacrifice anything that stands in the way of truth, whether it be relationship or reputation. Regardless of the cost to our comfort, we must be adamant about God's Word.

The helpless position of our current culture is a direct result of people who have fallen from truth and righteousness. Who would argue that American morality has not fallen? Still yet, there is genuine hope in God for this hopeless generation faced with living a life in a fallen world. We must become the salt preservative to this generation and refuse to yield to the spirit of the age. We must be willing to deal with our own sin first, then we must spread the gospel to our hungry nation and world.

God promises to heal our land if we turn to Him in humility and repentance. He says, "Return, ye backsliding children, and I will heal your backslidings" (Jer. 3:22). There is hope for renewal. It hinges on our humility and repentance.

We can retrieve ground that has been lost, but not without a vigorous fight. We must concentrate an unyielding line of offense against Satan's tactics. The line must consist of immovable, stubborn, obstinate, rigid, uncompromising soldiers who are determined to reestablish what we have so carelessly abdicated to the enemy. We must not flinch. We must be convincing and set our faces like flint in resolution to gain lost ground. We must have a zero tolerance attitude against sin. We must have the battle cry, "Return to righteousness!" If there is no resolution and no determination, we will cave in.

We must repent of our complacency and contend for the faith. Society is hard after a nullification of real truth and an implementation our own truth. The belief that all roads lead to the same place (heaven) or that nobody goes to hell is poison to this generation. Jude exhorts us to "earnestly contend for the faith which was once delivered unto the saints" (Jude 3). We must defend the purity of the faith from any dilution or pollution. We should fight with zeal and deep sincerity because we know the truth is rooted in a God "with whom is no variableness, neither shadow of turning" (James 1:17).

We must be convinced of God's Word. Like David against Goliath, we should say of false teachers, "Who is this uncircumcised Philistine, that he should defy the armies of the living God?" (1 Sam. 17:26). We must have a righteous anger like David, who was angry as he fought opposition against God (not opposition against himself).

We are to contest false teachings that pervert and lead away from foundational truth. Contending for the faith is mentioned in the book of Jude. We cannot be silent. We are in a rivalry against the father of lies. We are to assert ourselves, and yes, push our agenda to convert the world.

Contrary to modern church thought, the world is not crying out to be saved. The opposite is true; they are running from God. Their flesh is at odds with God. A battle is won each time a person surrenders his life to God.

It is necessary for us to impose our authority in opposition to the enemy. Are we convinced we have the truth or just a better version of it? If we are convinced we are right and other religions are wrong, we will not be silent. We will strive and not lie down in defeat. We can and must stand unashamedly strong. We must say, like Paul, "I know whom I have believed, and am persuaded that he is able to keep that which I have committed unto him against that day" (2 Tim. 1:12). Are you persuaded?

Of necessity, we have to be vigilant. We must be defensive rather than have an "all is clear" attitude. Many who have this mentality are refusing to see any battle. They would rather believe that goodness is the basic drive of mankind and that any visible trouble will dissolve in the light of goodness. They believe truth will prevail without a fight. But, truth and goodness do not prevail without a fight. They do not evolve. Chaos is the result of things being left to themselves. We have to contend for truth. The enemy is persistent, so we must react defensively against him. Any other reaction to him is compromise.

False teachers must be detected. We cannot evade our responsibility of seeking them out when the detection of their error is made difficult because of its mixture with truth. We cannot continue to compromise with questionable teaching and, as a result, fall further away from truth (2 Pet. 3:17). These teachers can no longer creep in unawares. The main defense against falling prey to good-sounding lies is to know God's Word. "Study to show thyself approved unto God," declared Paul (2 Tim. 2:15).

If, in complacency, we think we already know the Bible, we are like a child who thinks he knows more than he really does. He doesn't even realize that there is a vast amount of knowledge unknown to him. People who really know the most are those who realize they cannot know everything because there is too much to learn. The church today stands in pride. We are forgetting the verse that warns us to "let him that thinketh he standeth take heed lest he fall" (1 Cor. 10:12).

We allow Satan to get the upper hand when we demonstrate to the world no difference between a Christian and a worldly unbeliever. Today, the church is struggling with divorce, pornography, child abuse, alcohol abuse, and other problems to the same extent as the world. But we must choose to be separate. As A. W. Tozer aptly put it, "The holy man is not one who cannot sin. A holy man is one who will not sin."[4]

Even after we are knocked down, we should struggle and fight continually. We must repent of letting the enemy bring into our churches human-sensitive teachings. His strategy has dominated the church for the last few decades, preventing salvations and causing Christians to stumble. Satan knows salvation is made sure in Christ. Yet, being the father of lies and the accuser of the brethren, he has gained much ground in causing Christians to be motivated by "I have to" rather than "I want to." Many today are not told Christianity can truly change their hearts and motives. There is a widespread belief that the flesh continues to desire the world and, with grace, a person can actually have it. We have to reject this major shift from past preaching. The Bible promises that we can be more than conquerors through Christ. We are able, with His help, to combat and even destroy the desires of our flesh, which continually rage against God.

We must repent of our lack of love for the truth. We have swallowed the idea that man is worthy of God's love. We have replaced esteem in Christ with esteem for self. But, as Jonathan Edwards put it, "We are not truly humble unless we have a sense of our own nothingness as compared with God."[5] We must shift back the focus of sermons to God and away from man. Sermons must return to the use of illustrations from the Bible and away from the movie theater, fables, and personal experience.

We must repent of our desire to seek out new and improved ways to worship. God has already established the way in His Word. It is not clever or wise for us to say, "Today we must present the same gospel in a new way." Howard A. Snyder wrote, "One of the clearest lessons from twenty centuries of experience is that the church has always been most faithful when it has gotten back to its biblical, spiritual roots."[6] Isaiah warned God's people with, "Awake, awake, put on strength, O arm of the LORD; awake, as in the ancient days, in the generations of old" (Isa. 51:9). New ideas are profitable and efficient when introduced in business. However, new ideas are dangerous when introduced to Christianity. Let's not look at Christianity like we look at a business.

When pastors repent, the results will be effective. When they again bring the message of repentance and of righteous judgment to their preaching, the effects will be reassuring, encouraging, and comforting. We think of judgment as bad, but Jeremiah wrote, "Thus saith the LORD; Execute ye judgment and righteousness, and deliver the spoiled out of the hand of the oppressor" (Jer. 22:3). New converts under this kind of preaching will not have to fake their Christianity because it will be authentic. Once the Holy Spirit is invited back into our midst to convict of sin, we will see lives that are really changed. No longer will lawlessness and lack of restraint be dominant in the church.

We cannot continue to be bold in our sin and claim forgiveness and grace where it was never intended.

> For if we sin willfully after that we have received the knowledge of the truth, there remaineth no more sacrifice for sins, But a certain fearful looking for of judgment and fiery indignation, which shall devour the adversaries.
>
> —Hebrews 10:26–27

We cannot shut our ears to the warnings. God is warning His people. We cannot say we are without sin when we are not separate from the world and there is no visible difference between Christians and non-Christians. Pastors can no longer be more interested in numbers than in righteousness. Quality must override quantity.

God knows where there are churches in America who are pleasing to Him. They are the ones preaching God's Word without mixture. They are the ones striving to obey and keep the faith. So few of these churches are left. The new move of mixture and compromise is too enticing for most churches. Thousands are attending mega churches to participate in the so-called new move of God. Their claim is to be doing the work of the Lord. However, words are cheap when there is no fruit. True, inward conversions will be measured on judgment day. Our sober prayer must be that those we have supposedly converted to Christ will not hear Him say, "I never knew you: depart from me, ye that work iniquity" (Matt. 7:23).

We must not resist the Holy Spirit as He convicts us in these last days. Why not? First Peter 4:17 says, "For the time is come that judgment must begin at the house of God." We must welcome the stirrings in our soul urging us to draw nearer to Him. We must seek His discipline and stop our passivity and complacency. Pastors must restore their preaching by feeding their flocks with real nourishment and not sugar-coated humanism. Our behavior must begin to align with the behavior of Christ. We must submissively repent of our hype. God is not flattered by our exaggerations.

Christians represent the church. Whatever we are doing is what the church is doing. For the church to move forward, individuals must move forward. Is it possible for us to bring back the departed glory? The answer is yes. Our answer is that we must acquaint ourselves with God. We must see Him as the Bible portrays Him. He is not a passive Santa Claus waiting to give abundantly to our flesh, nor is He so tolerant that He loves everything that is occurring in the world. He is not an accepted, popular God. He isn't the God of worldly success and dreams.

He is, however, the Almighty, the Creator of heaven and earth, and the only wise God. He "sitteth upon the circle of the earth…[and] stretcheth out the heavens as a curtain" (Isa. 40:22). He sees that "man is like to vanity: his days are as a shadow that passeth away" (Ps. 144:4). He is so far above the earthly realm. He "hath measured the waters in the hollow of his hand" (Isa. 40:12), and "all nations before him are as nothing; and they are counted to Him less than nothing, and vanity" (Isa. 40:17). He puts no confidence in kings or counselors. Psychology is foolishness to Him. When we truly see Him for who He is, we will abhor ourselves in dust and ashes. We will lay our hands on our mouths and be silent.

According to Tozer, the knowledge of God is "at once the easiest and the most difficult thing in the world. It is easy because the knowledge is not won by hard mental toil, but is something freely given. It is difficult because there are conditions to be met and the obstinate nature of fallen man does not take kindly to them."[7]

Those conditions to be met consist of:

- forsaking our sins
- purposing to obey in all things by keeping His commandments
- carrying our cross
- reckoning ourselves dead unto sin and alive unto God in Christ Jesus
- trampling underfoot the lusts of the flesh
- refusing the values of the world
- becoming detached from things unbelievers set their hearts on
- meditating on God and His majesty; fleeing the doctrine of the age, which puts man in a high place; and reversing the trend of building self esteem by a deliberate act of our will
- protesting the frivolous character of what passes as Christianity today by standing firm for truth
- praying for heaven to be more real to us than earth, praying for God to open our eyes to the spiritual, and avoiding distraction from the visible
- becoming familiar with His voice by shutting out clutter and by being still and quiet
- rejecting worldliness, turning from wickedness, and shunning the very appearance of evil

- seeking truth in the Bible only and stop teaching men's books in our churches

Repentance is an automatic defeat of Satan, but when self is continually given higher regard than what is credible, it avoids repentance. Self-esteem only causes our children to be blind to their need for repentance. It is our duty to proclaim the untainted gospel to a generation who is in the firm grasp of Satan. We must speak, lest our silence offend these little ones and they fall in with the great scheme of the Antichrist. We must pray for God to raise up prophets who will magnify His name and restore the people of God to the knowledge of the holy. Jesus is seated on the right hand of the Father representing us there. Let us faithfully represent Him here. He is faithful to us; we can be faithful to Him.

> Now unto Him that is able to keep you from falling, and to present you faultless before the presence of His glory with exceeding joy, To the only wise God our Savior, be glory and majesty, dominion and power, both now and ever. Amen.
>
> —Jude 24–25

LIFT HIM UP

And I, if I be lifted up from the earth, will draw all men unto me.

—John 12:32

Our man-made methods of bringing souls to Christ must stop. What appears to be working is just that, an appearance. Our direction for spreading the gospel is clearly given in God's Word. If we lift up the name of the Lord, the Holy Spirit will handle the rest. We are wrong to put "confidence in the flesh" (Phil. 3:3). Our minds rationalize that what helps in the world must help in the church. We think we can make more money and get more "customers" if we only try this new technique or invite this or that cutting-edge speaker. But, our job is to lift up the name of Jesus.

We think today's problems call for bigger projects and new solutions, but we are wrong. We must repent of all our showy hype intended to bring in the lost sheep. We must repent of our fun-based entertainment designed to bring in hurting children. We must repent of our borrowing ideas from the world. We must repent of persuading young people to just "be themselves" when God tells them to die to themselves. We must repent of telling children they can worship God their own way when God has a definite pattern of how He should be worshiped. We have abdicated our job of teaching children about God. Instead of pointing them to Christ, we have decided to let them find Him for themselves.

Children must be told they have three enemies according to God's Word. They must be taught vigilance against the world, their flesh, and the devil (world: 1 John 2:15–16; James 4:4; flesh: 1 Pet. 2:11; Gal. 5:17; Rom 8:7; devil: Eph. 6:12; 2 Cor. 4:4). The world wants them to believe their parents and other authority figures are their enemy because they are the ones who "hinder" their dreams or their manifestations of true individuality. It must be made clear to this generation that Satan is God's enemy and, therefore, their enemy too.

This generation must hear how they will be affected by the course they pursue. They must know how their conduct will come home to them. They must understand that delay of consequences is not approval of sin. They must see that broken bones make travel harder. They must be told sin is alluring but dangerous.

Like a mountain road that winds downward to avoid a fast decent, the trip seems harmless and filled with beautiful ponds and evergreens. But, the downward decent eventually ends up at the bottom. Satan will get our children down the mountain if he can first get them on the road. We must warn them of the danger of the "small" sins that lead to that downhill decent.

Professing Christianity is not enough. Judas was a professor of Christ, a minister of the gospel, and an apostle. But, in the end, it was revealed that he was the son of perdition. His true self was manifested. Living a lie does not pay. The truth is what counts. The lies of today tell us that our true identity will eventually win if only we can change our circumstances. We are told problems result from society's mistreatment, not from our sin natures. It is a lie. Our answer is not in circumstantial change, but in the realization of our sin nature and acceptance of Christ's sacrifice for our sins. To receive this, we must repent.

Just as Sodom and Gomorrah were helpless to change their actions immediately before judgment fell upon them, so it will be too late for the church to repent of apostasy when

God's unannounced moment of judgment falls. In the words of S. Maxwell Coder:

> Darkness is ahead for some; light is ahead for others. Everlasting bonds and everlasting fire are set over against everlasting liberty and everlasting glory. Trembling and fear is the portion of the ungodly who await judgment; joy unspeakable and full of glory is even now the experience of all who love and obey the Word of God. God is no respecter of persons. He did not respect the person of angels who once sang His praises. He will not respect men who heed not the message He has given through His servant Jude.[8]

There is still hope because it is not too late. Today, a change can be made.

Glory be to God on high. We praise thee, we bless thee, we worship thee, for thy great glory. Lord, I uttered that I understood not; things too wonderful for me which I knew not. I heard of thee by the hearing of the ear, but now mine eye seeth thee and I abhor myself in dust and ashes. O Lord, I will lay my hand upon my mouth. Once have I spoken, yea, twice, but I will proceed no further. But while I was musing the fire burned. Lord, I must speak of thee, lest by my silence I offend against the generation of thy children. Behold, thou has chosen the foolish things of the world to confound the wise, and the weak things of the world to confound the mighty. O Lord, forsake me not. Let me show forth thy strength unto this generation and thy power to everyone that is to come. Raise up prophets and seers in thy church who shall magnify thy glory and through thine almighty Spirit restore to thy people the knowledge of the holy. Amen.

—A. W. Tozer[9]

BIBLIOGRAPHY

Bevere, John. *The Fear of the Lord*. Lake Mary, FL: Creation House, 1997.

Cumbey, Constance E. *A Planned Deception: The Staging of a New Age "Messiah"*. East Detroit, MI: Pointe Publishers, Inc., 1985.

_____. *The Hidden Dangers of the Rainbow*. Shreveport, LA: Huntington House, Inc., 1983.

Edwards, Jonathan. *Religious Affections*. Uhrichsville, OH: Barbour Publishing, 1999.

_____. *Sinners in the Hands of an Angry God*. New Kensington, PA: Whitaker House, 1997.

Hanegraaff, Hank. *Counterfeit Revival*. Nashville, TN: Word Publishing, 2001.

Hunt, Dave. *America: The Sorcerer's New Apprentice*. Eugene, OR: Harvest House, 1988.

_____. *Beyond Seduction: A Return to Biblical Christianity*. Eugene, OR: Harvest House, 1987.

_____. *Global Peace and the Rise of Antichrist*. Eugene, OR: Harvest House, 1990.

Jeremiah, David. *Escape the Coming Night*. Nashville, TN: Word Publishing, 1997.

Lapin, Rabbi Daniel. *America's Real War*. Sisters, OR: Multnomah Publishers, 1999.

Lawson, Steven J. *The Final Call*. Wheaton, IL: Crossway Books, 1994.

MacArthur, John. *The Vanishing Conscience*. Dallas, TX: Word Publishing, 1995.

Martin, Walter. *The Kingdom of the Cults.* Minneapolis, MN: Bethany House Publishers, 1997.

Parshall, Janet and Craig. *Tough Faith.* Eugene, OR: Harvest House Publishers, 1999.

Penn, William. *No Cross No Crown.* Shippensburg, PA: Destiny Image Publishers, Inc., 2001.

Rowe, Dr. Ed. *New Age Globalism.* Herndon, VA: Growth Publishing, 1985.

Spurgeon, C. H. *Spurgeon's Sermons.* 10 vols. Grand Rapids, MI: Baker Books, 1999.

Tozer, A. W. *The Knowledge of the Holy.* San Francisco, CA: Harper Collins Publishers, 1961.

————. *The Quotable Tozer, I.* Camp Hill, PA: Christian Publications, 1984.

————. *Tozer on Worship and Entertainment.* Camp Hill, PA: Christian Publications, 1997.

Winker, Eldon K. *The New Age is Lying to You.* St. Louis, MO: Concordia Publishing, 1994.

NOTES

INTRODUCTION

1. George Barna, *Real Teens* (Ventura, CA: Regal, 2001), 91.

2. George Gallup Jr., *The Next American Spirituality* (Colorado Springs, CO: Cook Communications, 2000), 144.

3. Brandi Dean, "What Easter Really Means," *Amarillo Globe-News*, March 26, 2005.

1—PASSIVITY OF LEADERSHIP

1. David Alsobrook, *Keep Yourself from Idols* (Paducah, KY: David Alsobrook Ministries, 1986), 71.

2. Quote by Edmund Burke may be found at Laura Moncur's Motivational Quotations, http://www.quotationspage.com/quote/2298.html (accessed May 8, 2008).

3. Jonathan Edwards, *Religious Affections* (Uhrichsville, OH: Barbour Publishing, 1999), 29.

4. *The New England Primer* (Aledo, TX: Wall Builder Press, 1991).

5. Charles Spurgeon, *Spurgeon's Sermons, Vol. 2* (Grand Rapids, MI: Baker Books, 1999), 349.

6. James Strong, ed., *Strong's Exhaustive Concordance of the Bible* (Nashville, TN: Thomas Nelson, 1990), s.v. "pure" and "holy."

7. William Penn, *No Cross No Crown* (Shippensburg, PA: Destiny Image, 2001), 84.

8. Spurgeon, *Spurgeon's Sermons, Vol. 2* (Grand Rapids, MI: Baker Books, 1999), 351.

2—FAMINE OF HEARING

1. Open Bible, Expanded Edition (New York: Thomas Nelson, 1985), 1310–1322.

2. Gallup, 59.

3. Gallup, 59–60.

4. Penn, 157.

5. Ibid., 159.

6. A. W. Tozer, *The Quotable Tozer, I* (Camp Hill, PA: Christian Publications, 1984), 57–58.

7. A. W. Tozer, *Tozer on Worship and Entertainment* (Camp Hill, PA: Christian Publications, 1997), 178.

8. John F. MacArthur Jr., *The Vanishing Conscience* (Dallas, TX: Word Publishing, 1995), 75.

3—Psychology

1. Penn, 3.

2. *Webster's Dictionary of the English Language*, s.v. "Koran."

3. Charles Spurgeon, "For the Sick and Afflicted," *The Suffering of Man and the Sovereignty of God* (Oswego, IL: Fox River Press, 2001), 296.

4. Vergilius Ferm, *A Dictionary of Pastoral Psychology* (New York City: Philosophical Library, 1955), 173–174.

5. Peter S. Jensen, MD, David Mrazek, MD, Penelope K. Knapp, MD, Laurence Steinberg, PhD, Dynthia Pfeffer, MD, John Schowalter, MD, and Theodore Shapiro, MD, "Evolution and Revolution in Child Psychology," *Journal of American Child & Adolescent Psychiatry*, December, 1997.

4—Complacency

1. David Jeremiah, *Escape the Coming Night* (Dallas, TX: Word Publishing, 1997), 50.

2. Penn, 179.

3. Hank Hanegraaff, *Counterfeit Revival* (Nashville, TN: W Publishing Group, 2001), back cover.

4. "Abortion Facts," The Center for Bio-Ethical Reform, http://www.abortionno.org/Resources/fastfacts.html (accessed July 8, 2008).

5. Penn, 170.

6. Vernon McLellan, ed., *Thoughts That Shaped the Church* (Wheaton, IL: Tyndale House, 2000), 211.

7. Joe Chapman, "Group Studies Classic Movies for Life's Lessons," *Amarillo Globe-News*, August 7, 2004, Faith Section.

8. Alexander Pope, *An Essay on Man, Epistle II,* The EServer Poetry Collection, http://poetry.eserver.org/essay-on-man/epistle-ii.txt (accessed July 14, 2008).

9. A. W. Tozer, *The Root of the Righteous* (Camp Hill, PA: Christian Publications, 1986), 32.

10. Richard Winter, *In Touch*, March 2004.

11. Betty Wein, *Stranger in the House* (New York: Morality in Media, Inc., 2000), 7.

12. Tozer, *The Quotable Tozer, I*, 187.

5—A Seared Conscience

1. MacArthur, 50.

2. "Memorable Quotes for *The Five People You Meet in Heaven*," The Internet Movie Database, http://www.imdb.com/title/tt0400435/quotes (accessed July 8, 2008).

6—Unbalanced Teaching: Part 1

1. Tozer, *The Quotable Tozer, I*, 104.

2. A. W. Tozer, *The Knowledge of the Holy* (San Francisco, CA: Harper Collins, 1961, 1992), 152.

3. Brandi Dean, "Churches See Spurt of Growth on Easter," *Amarillo Globe-News*, March 26, 2005.

4. Jonathan Edwards, *Religious Affections* (Uhrichsville, OH: Barbour Publishing, 1999), 275.

5. Tozer, *The Knowledge of the Holy*, 147.

6. *Webster's Dictionary of the English Language* (New York, NY: Lexicon Publications Inc., 1989), s.v. "piety."

7. McLellan, 209.

8. Penn, *No Cross No Crown*, 18.

9. "Northwest Ordinance, July 13, 1787," The Avalon Project at Yale Law School, http://www.yale.edu/lawweb/avalon/nworder.htm (accessed July 8, 2008).

10. Tozer, *The Knowledge of the Holy*, 141.

11. *Webster's Dictionary of the English Language*, s.v. "fable."

12. Ibid., s.v. "parable."

13. Ibid., s.v. "legalism."

14. Jeremiah, 71.

15. Edwards, *Religious Affections*, 317.

7—Unbalanced Teaching: Part 2

1. McLellan, 101.

2. Tozer, *The Quotable Tozer, I*, 71.

3. Hannah Arendt, *The Origins of Totalitarianism* (New York: Harcourt, Brace and Company, 1951), 435.

4. Jeremiah, 253.

5. Tozer, *The Quotable Tozer, I*, 134.

6. Ibid., 26.

7. A. W. Tozer, *Tozer on Worship and Entertainment* (Camp Hill, PA: Christian Publications, 1997), 36–37.

8. Tozer, *The Quotable Tozer, I*, 78.

9. Jeremiah, 189–190.

10. Edwards, 305.

8—Mixture: Part 1

1. Tozer, *Tozer on Worship and Entertainment*, 171–172.

2. Tozer, *The Quotable Tozer, I*, 59.

3. Hanegraaff, 100–101.

4. John Bevere, *The Fear of the Lord* (Lake Mary, FL: Creation House, 1997), 120.

5. Ibid., 121.

9—Mixture: Part 2

1. Dr. D. James Kennedy, "The New Tolerance," *The Salt and Light Solution* (Fort Lauderdale, FL: Coral Ridge Ministries, 1999), 154.

2. Tozer, *Tozer on Worship and Entertainment,* 179–180.

3. Ibid., 127.

4. Tozer, *The Quotable Tozer, I*, 71.

5. Jeremiah, 64–65.

6. Tozer, *The Quotable Tozer, I*, 63.

7. Penn, 160.

8. Steven J. Lawson, *The Final Call* (Wheaton, IL: Crossway Books, 1994), 88.

9. Penn, 157.

10. Charles Spurgeon, *Spurgeon's Sermons, Vol. 6* (Grand Rapids, MI: Baker Books, 1999), 134.

10—Inappropriate Behavior

1. *Webster's Dictionary of the English Language*, s.v. "prudence."

2. Watchman Nee, *Spiritual Authority* (New York, NY: Christian Fellowship Publishers Inc., 1972), 182.

11—Hype

1. *Webster's Dictionary of the English Language*, s.v. "hype."

2. Hanegraaff, 14.

3. Janet and Craig Parshall, *Tough Faith* (Eugene, OR: Harvest House, 1999), 83.

4. Ibid., 86–87.

5. J. C. Ryle, *Holiness* (Durham, England: Evangelical Press, 1979), 16.

6. Dave Hunt, *Beyond Seduction* (Eugene, OR: Harvest House, 1987), 257.

7. Tozer, *Tozer on Worship and Entertainment*, 165.

8. Ibid., 164.

12—Hope

1. Watchman Nee, *Secrets to Spiritual Power* (New Kensington, PA: Whitaker House, 1998), 22.

2. Ibid., 23.

3. Janet and Craig Parshall, 226.

4. Tozer, *The Quotable Tozer, I*, 170.

5. Jonathan Edwards, "Christian Love," eds. Clyde E. Fant Jr. and William M. Pinson Jr., *A Treasury of Great Preaching, Vol. 3* (Dallas, TX: Word Publishing, 1995), 93.

6. Howard A. Snyder, *The Radical Wesley* (Downers, Grove, IL: InterVarsity Press, 1980), 165.

7. Tozer, *The Knowledge of the Holy*, 180–181.

8. S. Maxwell Coder, *Jude: The Acts of the Apostates* (Chicago, IL: Moody Bible Institute, 1986), 49.

9. Tozer, *The Knowledge of the Holy*, 161.

TO CONTACT THE AUTHOR

Susan65@netzero.net